THE SOMME CHRONICLES

THE SOMME CHRONICLES

South Africans on the Western Front

CHRIS SCHOEMAN

Published by Zebra Press
an imprint of Random House Struik (Pty) Ltd
Reg. No. 1966/003153/07
Wembley Square, First Floor, Solan Road, Gardens, Cape Town, 8001
PO Box 1144, Cape Town, 8000, South Africa

www.zebrapress.co.za

First published 2014

1 3 5 7 9 10 8 6 4 2

Publication © Zebra Press 2014
Text © Chris Schoeman 2014

Cover photograph: courtesy of Colonel Piet Schoeman

All rights reserved. No part of this publication may be reproduced,
stored in a retrieval system or transmitted, in any form or by any means,
electronic, mechanical, photocopying, recording or otherwise,
without the prior written permission of the copyright owners.

PUBLISHER: Marlene Fryer
MANAGING EDITOR: Robert Plummer
EDITOR: Bronwen Leak
PROOFREADER: Mark Ronan
COVER AND TEXT DESIGNER: Jacques Kaiser
TYPESETTER: Jacques Kaiser
INDEXER: Sanet le Roux

Set in 11 pt on 15.5 pt Adobe Caslon

Printed and bound by Paarl Media, Jan van Riebeeck Drive, Paarl, South Africa

ISBN 978 1 77022 676 0 (print)
ISBN 978 1 77022 677 7 (ePub)
ISBN 978 1 77022 678 4 (PDF)

Contents

Preface ... vii
Maps ... ix

Introduction ... 1
1. The birth of the South African brigade ... 5
2. Bernafay and Trônes woods ... 18
3. Longueval ... 37
4. Delville Wood ... 46
5. Life in the trenches ... 75
6. The Butte de Warlencourt ... 93
7. The Battle of Arras ... 107
8. The final push ... 120

Appendices:
I   Heavy artillery ... 139
II South African Signal Company (Royal Engineers) ... 149
III South African Medical Corps ... 158
IV Railways and miscellaneous trades companies ... 165
V Victoria Crosses won by South Africans during the Great War ... 171
VI Roll of Honour of the South African Infantry Brigade: Operations on the Somme, July 1916 ... 178
VII A note on the role of black South Africans ... 209

Notes ... 213
Bibliography ... 227
Index ... 231

Preface

Y EARS AGO I had the privilege of listening to the World War I tales of William Thorne, then an old man and one of the few South African survivors of the famous Battle of Delville Wood, when only some 750 of the 3 153 men who had entered the wood mustered when the brigade was finally relieved. He told me about the South Africans' traumatic campaigns in Flanders and on the Somme, of the hell of Delville Wood – when he was a lad of just nineteen – and of how his brother was shot dead next to him at Gouzeaucourt. Tears flowed down his cheeks as he spoke, as he relived the horror of that time like it were yesterday.

William Thorne is just one of many South African soldiers – or Springboks, as they were called – who fought on the Somme. *The Somme Chronicles* is an attempt to tell their story, in their own words, using the letters they sent to family back home and the memoirs they later recorded. It is a story of long days in cold muddy trenches, of hunger and thirst, of misery and suffering, of utter exhaustion and of death. But it is also a story of survival against heavy odds, of tremendous bravery, of wilful sacrifice and of unparalleled camaraderie. It is a story of truly courageous South Africans.

Some of these soldiers appear in the cover photograph of this book. It shows them shortly before they went into Delville Wood – when there was still a wood. A special word of thanks to Colonel Piet Schoeman of Waterval-Boven for his kind permission to use it (as well as others in the photo section). The photograph originally belonged to his great-step uncle, Private Philippus P.J. Grobler (born 21 June 1895), one of the men in the group. Grobler was wounded during the battle, and in the chaos and confusion was left for dead. He was reported as missing in action, but was found by a relieving force and sent to England to recuperate. Sadly, Grobler died while returning to South Africa when the ship he was sailing on was torpedoed and sank on 12 September 1918.

A word of thanks also to the staffs of the Cape Archives, the SA Library, the Special Collections J.S. Gericke Library (Stellenbosch University), the SA Centre for the Netherlands and Flanders (SASNEV) and the Oudtshoorn Museum, and others who assisted me during my research.

This year, 2014, marks the 100th anniversary of the outbreak of that dreadful war, that only ended with the armistice on 11 November 1918. During those years, hundreds of thousands of soldiers on both sides suffered unspeakable trauma, agony and hardship. This book is dedicated to them.

CHRIS SCHOEMAN
APRIL 2014

The Somme in July 1916

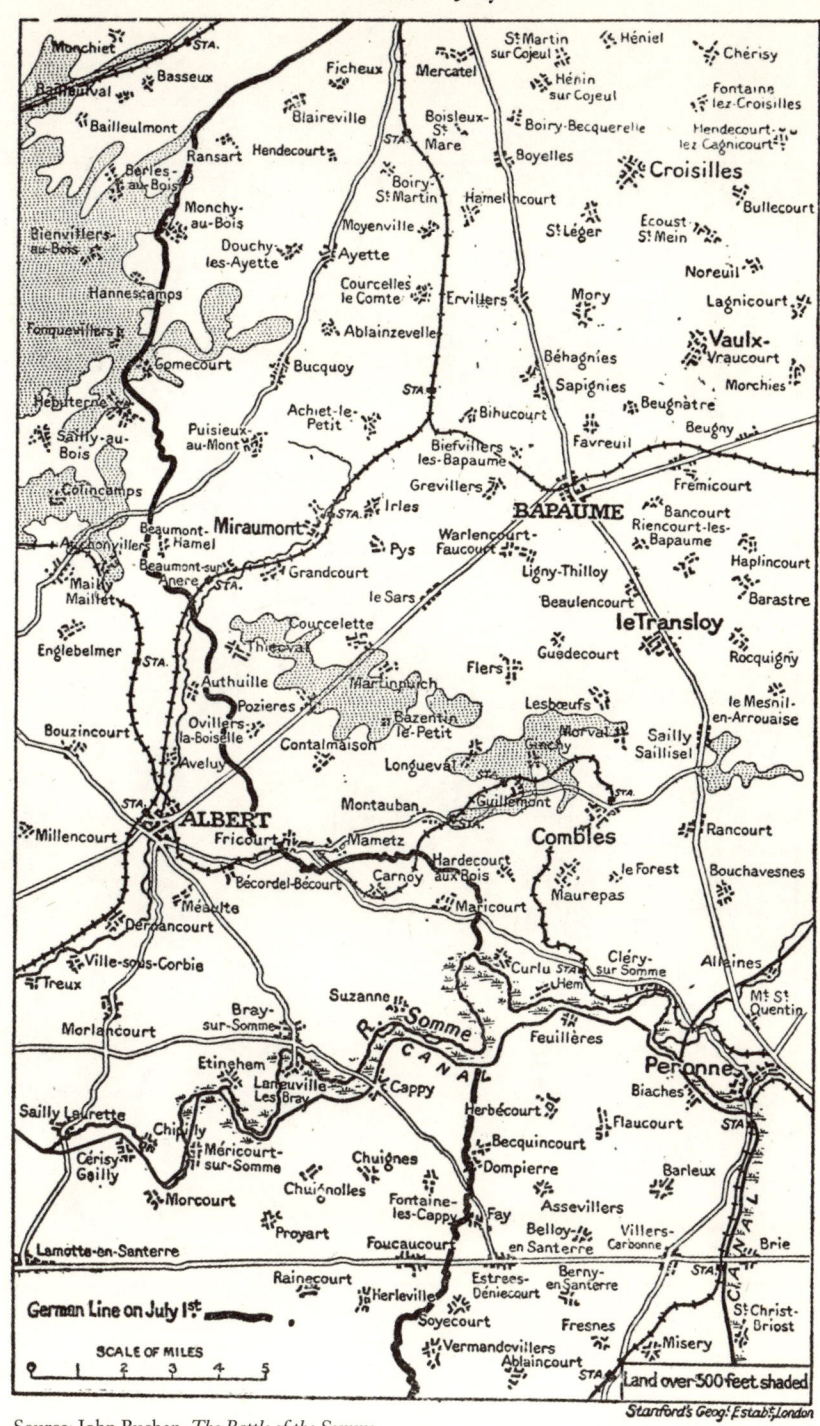

Source: John Buchan, *The Battle of the Somme*

Longueval and Delville Wood

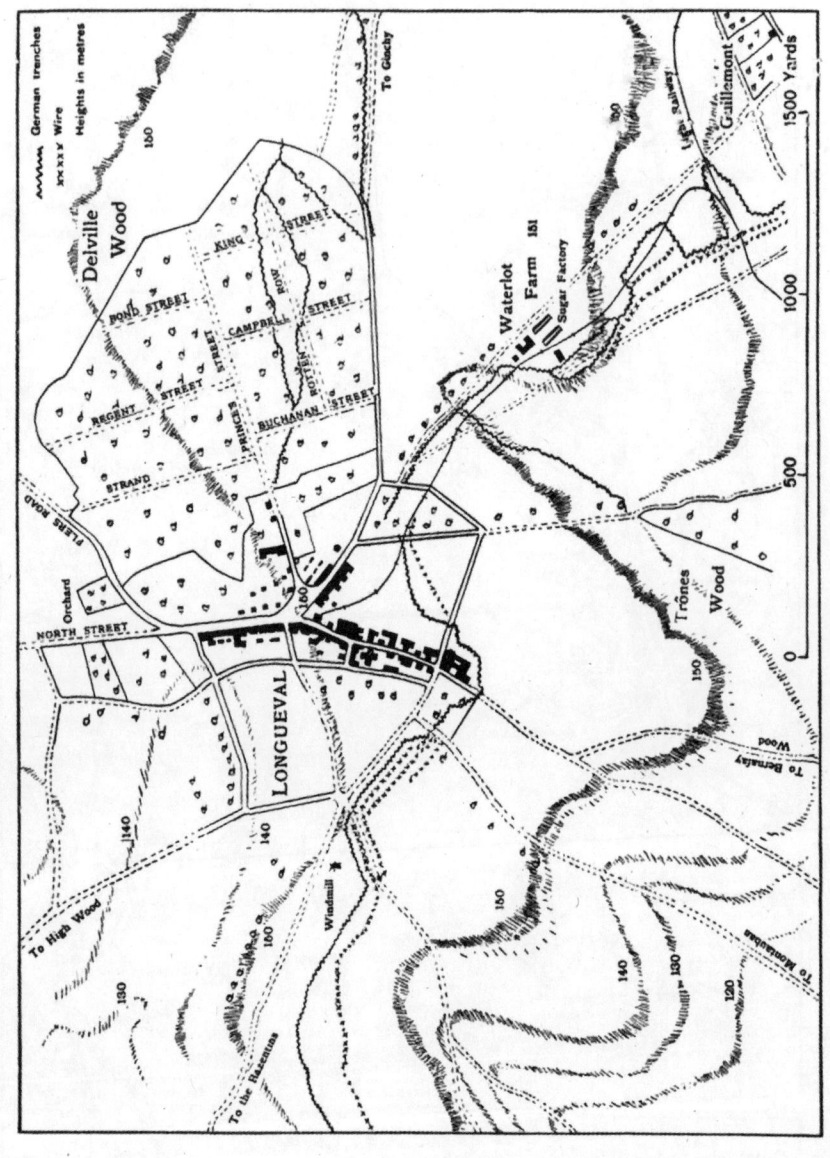

Source: John Buchan, *The History of the South African Forces in France*

The Butte de Warlencourt

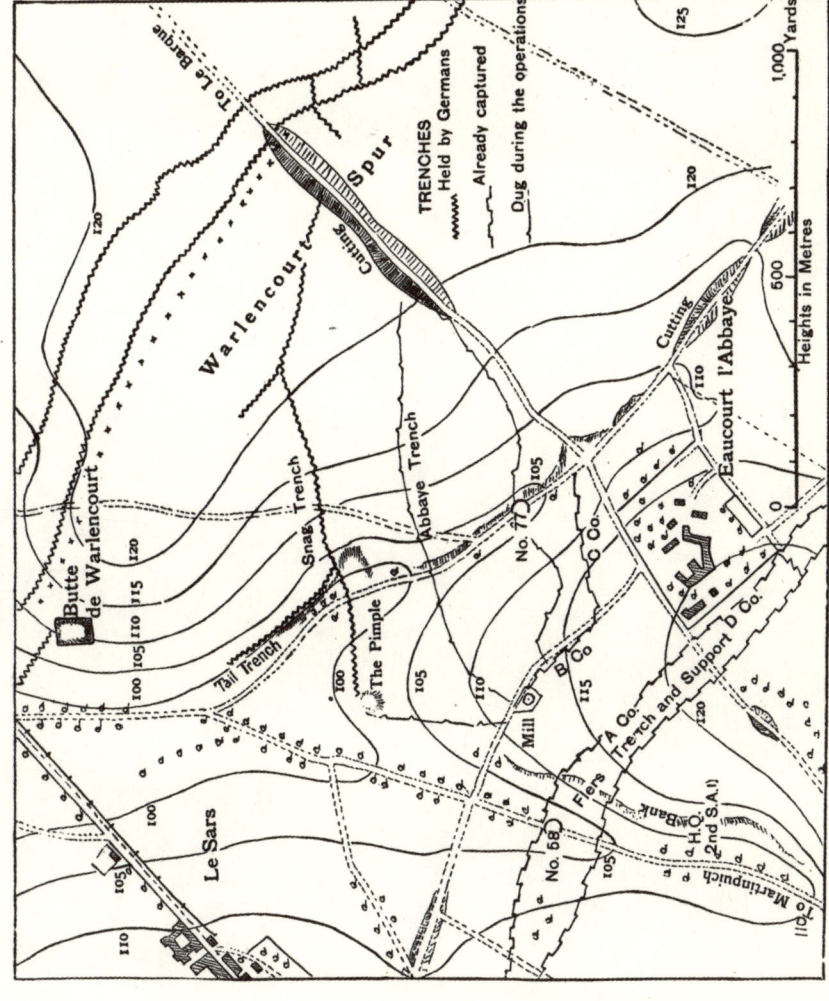

Source: John Buchan, *The History of the South African Forces in France*

The Battle of Arras

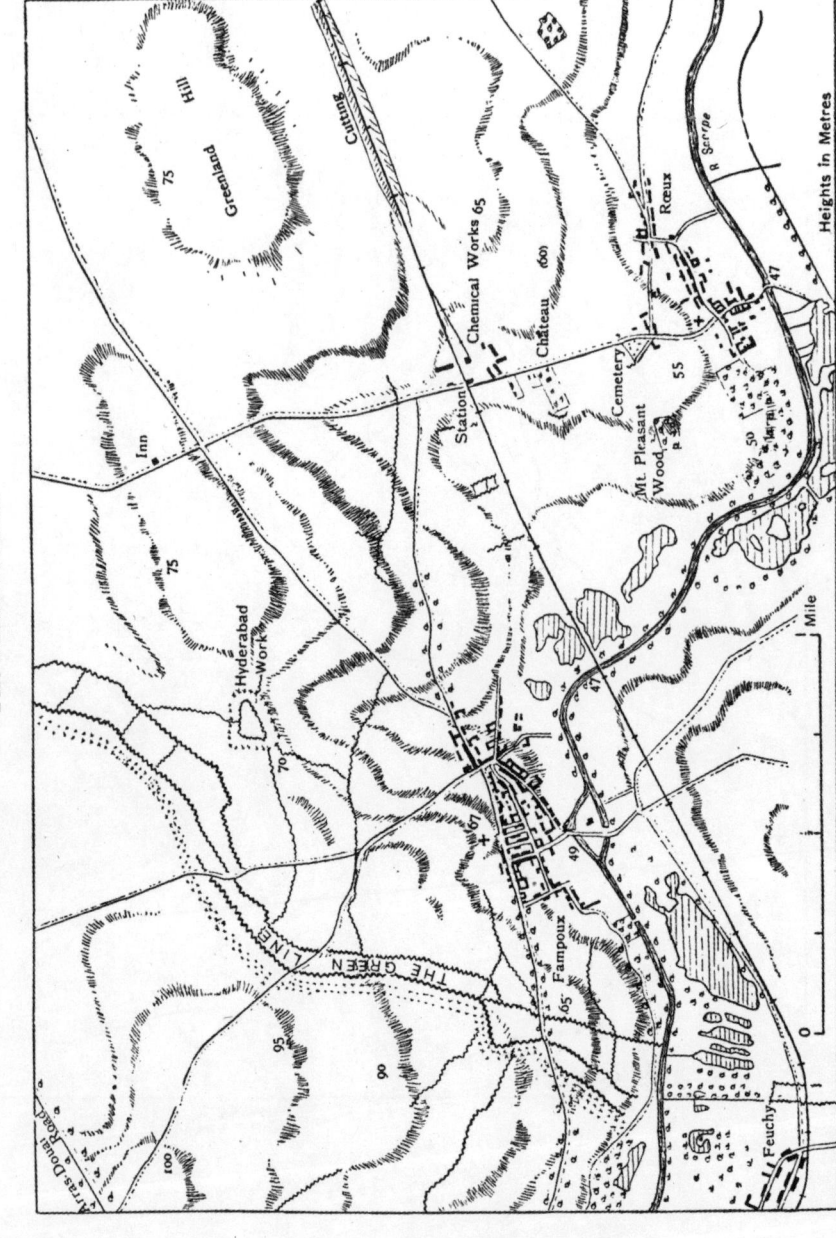

Source: John Buchan, *The History of the South African Forces in France*

The Third Battle of Ypres

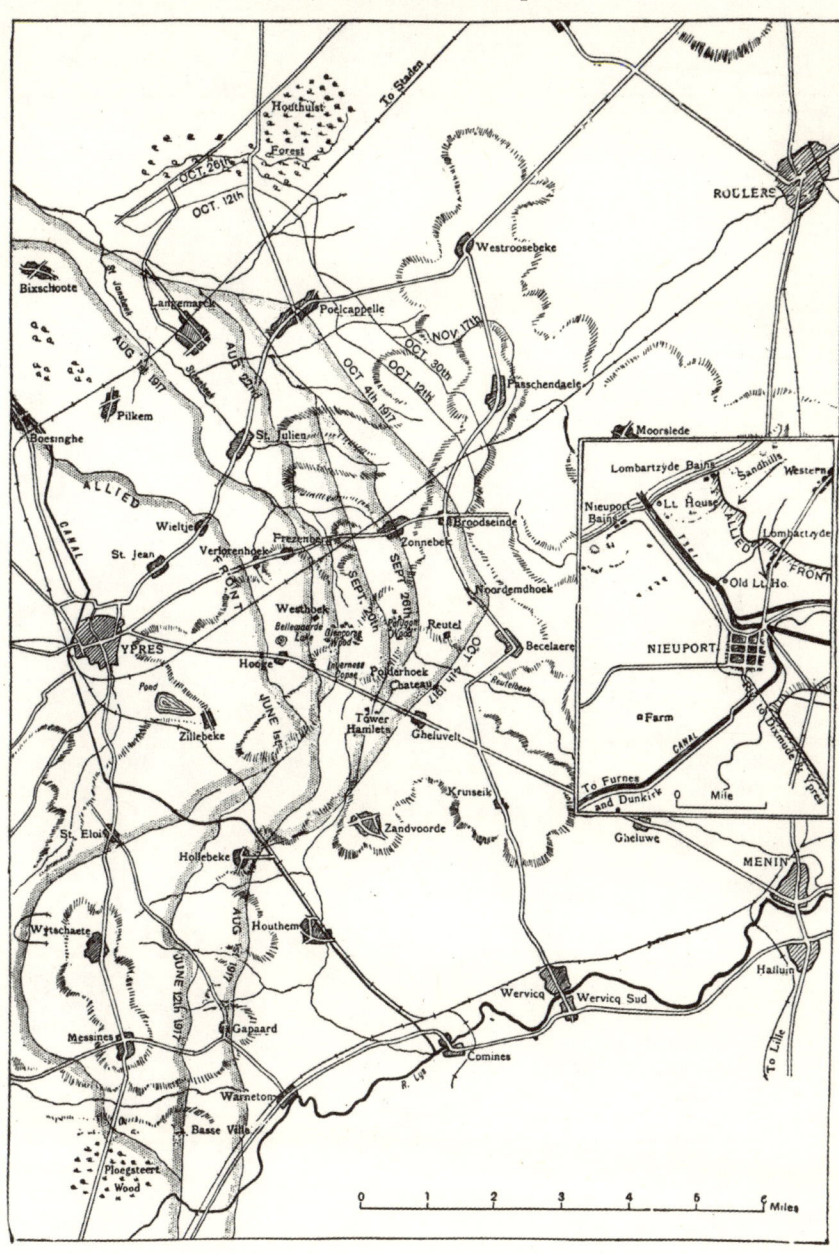

Source: John Buchan, *The History of the South African Forces in France*

Marrières Wood

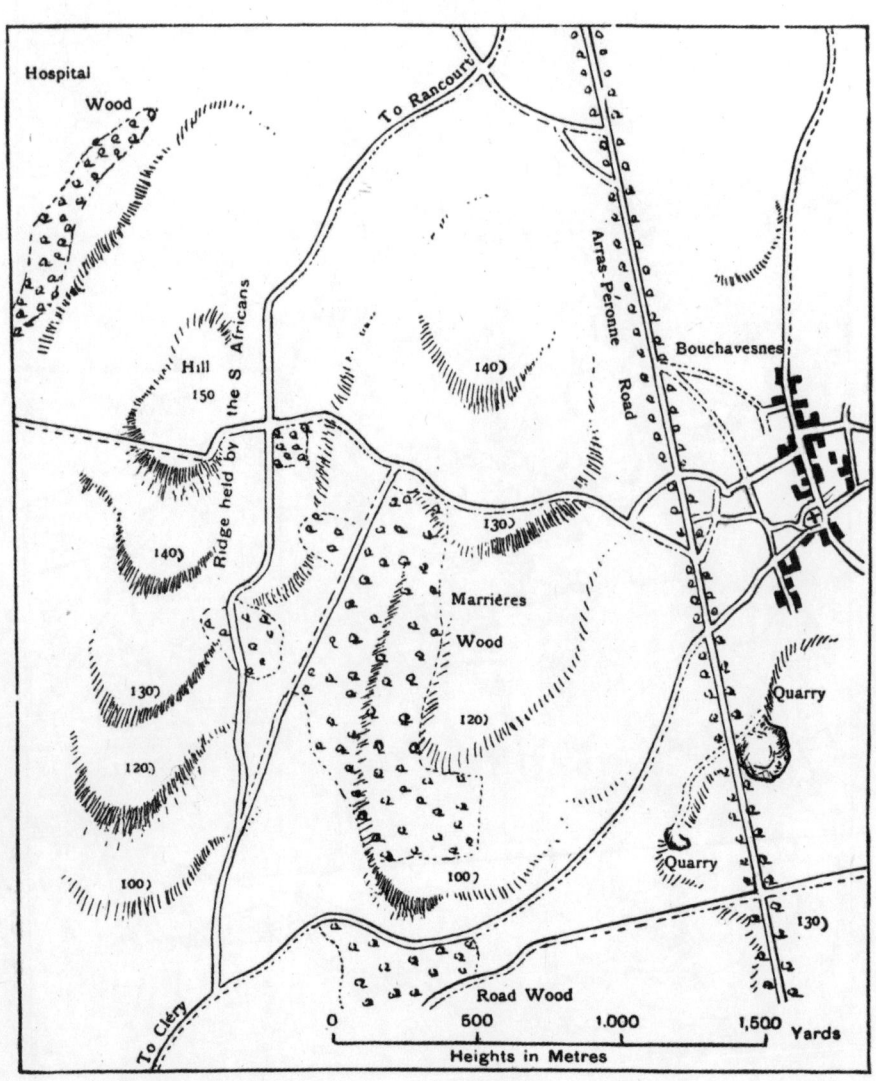

Source: John Buchan, *The History of the South African Forces in France*

Messines Ridge

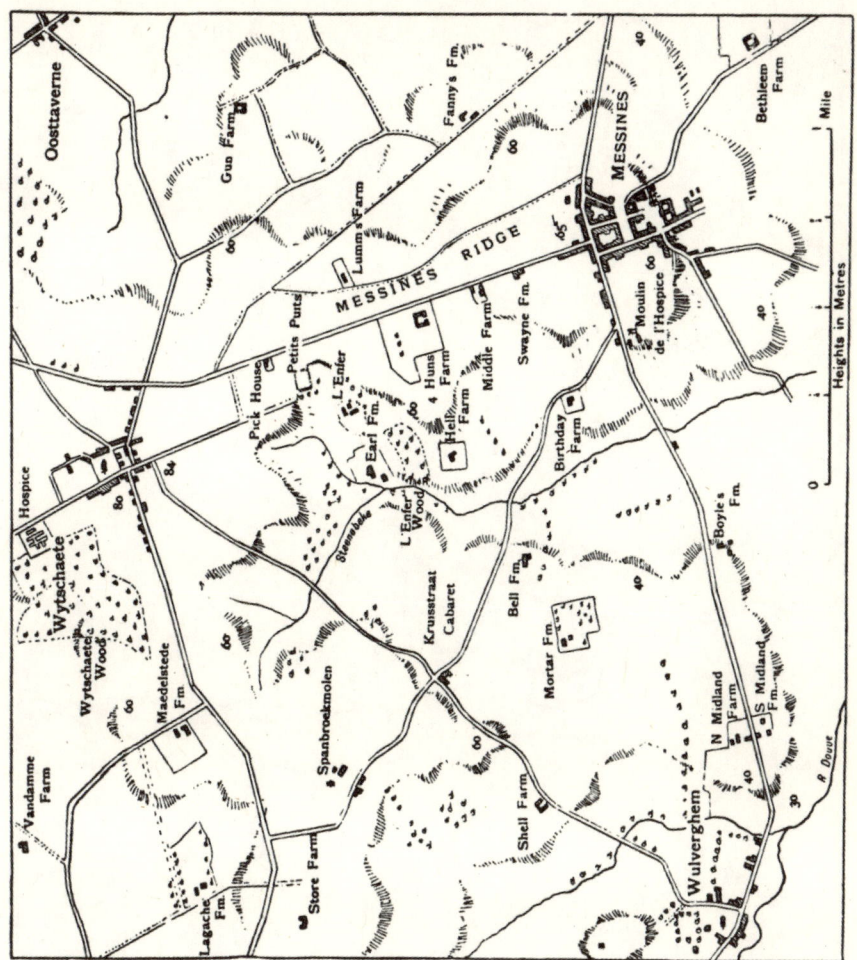

Source: John Buchan, *The History of the South African Forces in France*

Mount Kemmel

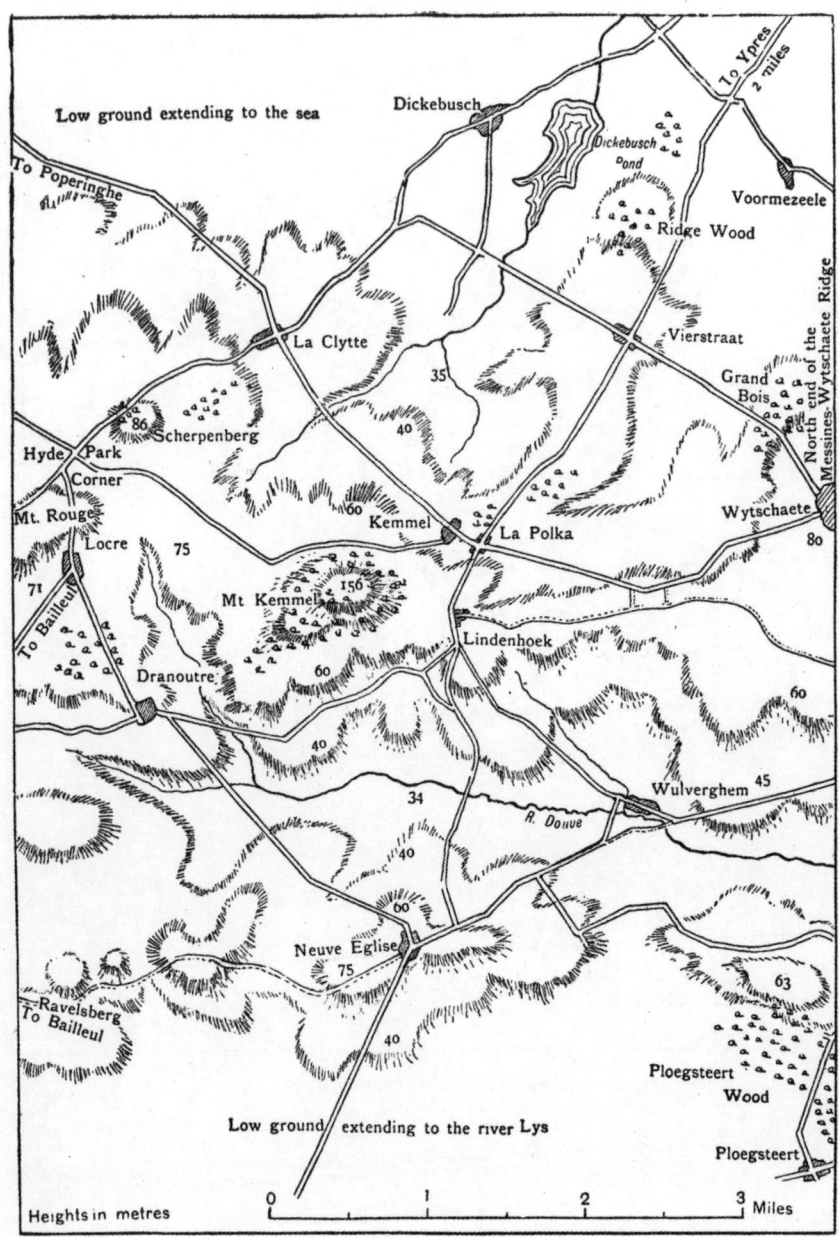

Source: John Buchan, *The History of the South African Forces in France*

Introduction

In the european summer of 1916, a few thousand South African men found themselves in muddy trenches along the Somme River in France. They were there out of choice, having volunteered to sail across the sea to fight in the Great War with the British Expeditionary Force on the Western Front of Europe. Fired with patriotism, at first they could not wait to get there, but before long they must have wondered what they had got themselves into, as their world shrank to mud and filth, hunger, thirst and exhaustion. The continual crack of bursting shells was a stark reminder that death was their constant companion.

It was a truly dramatic and devastating chapter in twentieth-century history. From Longueval to Cape Town, the war touched the lives and homes of millions of people around the globe, and would never be forgotten by those who lived through its horrors.

The global conflict centred in Europe and commonly known as the Great War broke out on 28 July 1914 and lasted for more than four years, until 11 November 1918. On opposing sides were the Allied Powers, based on the Triple Entente of the United Kingdom, France and Russia, and the Central Powers of Germany and Austria–Hungary. These alliances were expanded as more nations entered the fray, with Italy, Japan and the United States joining the Allies, and the Ottoman Empire and Bulgaria joining the Central Powers.

By the end of the First World War, the Allies had mobilised almost 43 million people, while the Central Powers had mobilised just over 25 million. A staggering figure of nearly 10 million combatants were killed.

Underlying the causes of the war was a resurgence of imperialism, but one immediate trigger was the assassination of the heir to the Austro-Hungarian throne, Archduke Franz Ferdinand of Austria, on 28 June

1914 in the Bosnian capital of Sarajevo. He and his wife, Sophie, Duchess of Hohenberg, were shot dead in their motorcade by Bosnian Serb Gavrilo Princip, one of a group of six assassins that included five Serbs and one Bosnian Muslim. During the month that followed, the Allied and Central powers were involved in desperate diplomatic negotiations. Austria-Hungary firmly believed that Serbian military officers of the so-called Black Hand were involved in the plot, and served Serbia with the July Ultimatum consisting of ten demands, intentionally made unacceptable in the hope of provoking war with Serbia. When Serbia agreed to only eight, Austria–Hungary declared war on 28 July. The Russian Empire rallied behind Serbia and started partial mobilisation the very next day.

In response, Germany mobilised on 30 July and, after a tense stand-off, declared war on Russia on 1 August, putting into action its Schlieffen Plan, which involved a 'wheeling arc' invasion through Belgium and France, designed to capture Paris before Russia on the Eastern Front could mobilise its forces and before Britain could effectively intervene in France. On 2 August, Germany invaded Luxembourg, and the following day it declared war on France. On 4 August, after Belgium had refused to permit German troops to cross its borders into France, Germany declared war on Belgium. That same day, when Germany failed to give a firm assurance that Belgium would be kept neutral, Britain declared war on Germany. As a dominion of the British Empire, South Africa was now involved in the conflict.

The war was fought on two fronts, a Western Front and an Eastern Front. The latter stretched from the Baltic Sea in the north to the Black Sea in the south, encompassing most of eastern Europe and stretching deep into central Europe. The Western Front extended from the North Sea to the frontiers of Switzerland, and embraced France and Belgium. Across this area, the British Commonwealth and French armies (including the South African forces) faced the German and Austro-Hungarian armies. Their lines were fixed by miles of heavily defended trenches, decorated with barbed wire and machine guns, where soldiers lived and died like rats in their holes.

INTRODUCTION

Futile campaigns to break through these almost impenetrable defences with infantry wielding rifles and bayonets, such as those at the Somme, Ypres and Passchendaele, were reminiscent of medieval armies laying siege to their enemies' fortresses and, predictably, resulted in massive loss of life.

World War I commanders such as Douglas Haig, John French and Ian Hamilton were Imperial soldiers schooled in the relatively archaic theatres of smaller wars like those in the Sudan and South Africa in the late nineteenth century. The industrial–scientific world of the twentieth century placed new weapons at the disposal of military commanders. The machine gun, for example, dominated Western Front battlefields and established a superiority of defence over offence and, along with heavy artillery bombardments and gas, shaped the suffering of both the Allied and German soldier. The massive artillery bombardments that preceded every offensive ploughed up the landscape and destroyed centuries-old drainage systems, creating a no-man's-land of mud flats and shell-holes that obstructed infantry attacks. The soldiers cowered helplessly in their trenches, waiting for death as shells rained down upon them, before being ordered over the top with fixed bayonets to cross the stretch of no-man's-land in the face of enemy machine-gun and artillery fire.

Terrible casualties characterised every futile offensive. On the first day of the Somme Offensive alone (1 July 1916), 19 240 British soldiers were killed and more than 36 000 were wounded. In the entire five-month battle, more than 300 000 Allied and German soldiers were killed and double that number were wounded.[1] In the 1918 Second Battle of the Somme – the Allied response to the German Spring Offensive launched in March 1918 – the Allies suffered 250 000 casualties and the Germans 240 000. The Battle of Passchendaele, from 31 July to 6 November 1917, claimed over 200 000 Allied casualties and an equivalent number of Germans.

Over 146 000 men served in South African units on three principal fronts. An expeditionary force of 67 000 men was deployed to capture German South-West Africa. An infantry brigade and various other units

3

were sent to France, where they were described by the commander of the British Expeditionary Force, General Douglas Haig, as 'as fine a unit as there is in the Army'.[2] And others were involved in the conflict in East Africa. In addition, about 3 000 South Africans joined and served in the Royal Flying Corps.

The South African soldiers are, however, mainly associated with the Battle of the Somme, which took place between 1 July and 18 November 1916 on either side of the River Somme in France. The battle saw the British Expeditionary Force and the French Army mount a joint offensive against the German Army, which had occupied a large part of the north of France since its invasion of that country in August 1914. The plan for the Somme Offensive resulted from Allied discussions at Chantilly, in northern France, in December 1915, where it was agreed that the French, British, Italian and Russian armies would mount a concerted offensive against the Central Powers. The Somme was to be the Anglo-French contribution to this general offensive, intended to create a gap in the German line that could be exploited with a decisive blow. But with Germany's attack on Verdun in February 1916, the Allies were forced to adapt their plans.

By the end of the Somme campaign in mid-November, British and French forces had penetrated ten kilometres into German occupied territory, but were still five kilometres from their major objective, Bapaume. Over the winter of 1916–17, the German Army maintained much of its front line before withdrawing from the Somme to the fortified Hindenburg Line in February and March 1917.

During the campaign, the South African brigade had been involved in major engagements at places with pleasant-sounding names, such as Bernafay Wood, Longueval, Butte de Warlencourt, Arras and Ypres. But there was nothing pleasant about the horrific and costly battles fought there. By the time the armistice came, the South Africans had suffered some 15 000 casualties in France, including some 5 000 deaths. Total South African casualties during the war amounted to 18 600, of whom more than 6 600 lost their lives.

I

The birth of the South African brigade

When the great war broke out, South Africa found itself doing battle within its borders as well as without. The South African prime minister, General Louis Botha, and his government not only had to contend with the German enemy just across the border in South-West Africa and further north in German East Africa, but with an internal rebellion as well.

When Britain declared war on Germany on 4 August 1914, former Boer War commanders of prominent rank in the Union Defence Force revolted and refused to follow orders to invade South-West Africa. Around 10 000 soldiers, mostly from the Orange Free State and Transvaal, joined the rebellion, which was led by Generals Christiaan de Wet and Christiaan Beyers, among others. Lieutenant-Colonel Manie Maritz was put in charge of the invasion forces, based in the north-eastern part of the Cape Province. But when he resigned his commission and crossed the border to join the German forces, taking with him many of his men, Botha's troops curtailed the rebellion before the end of 1914. Botha treated the rebels leniently, all except Jopie Fourie, who refused to resign his commission and was executed by firing squad following a court martial.[1]

During the rebellion, in an attempt to stem the flow of former Union Defence Force soldiers to the German side, Botha had announced that only volunteers would be used for the campaign. Among the first ten Cape Town recruits to sign up for service was Harold Lewis Silberbauer of Kenilworth, who would serve as a private in the Duke of Edinburgh's Own Volunteer Rifles during the German South-West Africa campaign and later as an officer with the Leicestershire Regiment on the Somme. He would later recall:

It is quite impossible to describe the excitement in Cape Town when war was declared ... General Botha called for volunteers in September 1914, as the Union of South Africa had been invaded near the Orange River. A very motley crowd turned up at the Drill Hall ... a sprinkling of [veterans] from the Boer War days ... clerks, students, advocates, judges. We were all marched out from Cape Town to Oude Molen at Mowbray and spent some uncomfortable days under canvas, without equipment, army clothing or blankets. Our ardour cooled off somewhat!

We were to be called 'Botha's Army', but the response was poor and they marched us off to Wynberg Camp one morning, where, to our indignation, we were told that we were to form 'B', 'E' and 'F' companies of the Duke of Edinburgh's Own Volunteer Rifles, as that regiment was under strength. That was how we became part and parcel of the Duke's and very soon were proud of that fact. Wynberg training was peculiar by modern standards. Parade ground drill, marching and PT [physical training] were the only things that mattered. Discipline was not bad, but on New Year's Day 1915, only fifty men turned out on parade and some had to support others. Amongst our riflemen were the ex-Chief Justice Centlivres, Sir Murray Bisset and ex-Judge President Jackie de Villiers.

I was really pleased with myself when I became an unpaid lance-corporal, then corporal, and then a sergeant. None of the non-commissioned officers knew anything at all about Drill, Arms, Field Work or, in fact, anything at all about anything they should have known. The same applied to most of the officers.[2]

Early in 1915, General Botha, with General Jan Smuts as his second in command, started his drive against the Germans in South-West Africa. Men who had fought side by side during the Anglo-Boer War a decade earlier were now on opposing sides and former enemies on the same side. The Union Defence Force rolled on, reaching the capital, Windhoek, on 12 May 1915 and forcing the surrender of the German troops on 9 July.

Of their arrival in Swakopmund before the final push for Windhoek, Silberbauer wrote:

> Heat, dust, flies and general confusion were our enemies. The Germans seemed to have disappeared into the sand dunes four miles away and there were light skirmishes in that direction. Now that we were on active service, we did our best to train and become efficient, but it was fortunate for us that the enemy did not attack.[3]

Later, Silberbauer and seven others were sent to guard a blockhouse in Walvis Bay along the railway line to Swakopmund. They could buy food in Walvis Bay and were close enough to the sea to bathe and spear fish.

> Life, for the eight of us, was not thrilling. The sandbags, out of which the blockhouse was made, were old sugar bags and attracted flies and we all suffered from diarrhoea ... We practised Morse and semaphore, but it was difficult to pass the time and no-one was sorry when we moved on to Swakopmund after 'keeping the enemy at bay' for six weeks.[4]

The company's commander, Captain P.J. Jowett, later went missing at Delville Wood in France.

More engagements followed at Swakopmund, and then Karibib, before the Germans finally surrendered. 'The regiment could not say that it had been in action, but the chaps had toughened up well, were very fit, and the discipline and morale were fine,' Silberbauer concluded.[5]

During the campaign, the Germans had been taken by surprise by the South Africans' ability to deal with the harsh conditions. 'Discipline the burghers have no idea of,' wrote Captain Trevitt of the South African Engineers, 'but the capacity for getting through desperate places, seems for them almost limitless.'[6]

With the immediate threat dealt with, Botha now looked abroad. As the ultimate patriot, he believed that the fortunes of his country were tied up with those of the British Commonwealth and therefore he supported South Africa's participation in the war effort over in Europe. And so, in April 1915, the South African government proposed sending over a South African contingent. In July the Imperial government accepted their offer.

It was agreed that the contingent would be equipped from the Union's stores in hand and paid by the Union up to the date of their embarkation for Europe. Thereafter, they would be paid at the rate of British regular troops and carry the status of the new service battalions of the British Army.

Compared to the powers of Europe, South Africa's (white) population was small and it was accepted that the most the country would be able to raise was a brigade of infantry. The political situation was still unsettled following the 1914 Afrikaner rebellion, and so when it became obvious that South Africa would be required to support the East African campaign, the government realised that it would not be wise to send permanent-force members. Therefore, it was decided that the infantry brigade would consist only of volunteers.

In Europe, considering the rate of casualties, the estimated rate of reinforcements required per month stood at 15 per cent. In Britain, the recruitment drive was gathering momentum. Private F.B. Vaughan, later with the 12th Battalion, Yorks and Lancashires, recalled:

> It was not just a sudden decision that I made to join the Army. My pals were going, chaps I had kicked about with in the street, kicking tin cans or a football, and chaps I knew very well in the city. And then if you looked in the newspapers we saw that Canadians were coming, Australians were coming, South Africans were coming – they were catching the first available boat to England to get there before the war was over ... The whole thing was exciting ... I don't know whether patriotism entered into it or not, possibly so. We were stirred, I know, by the atrocities, or the alleged atrocities, when the Germans invaded Belgium and France. The other great factor was that the womenfolk, fifty percent of the population, were very keen on the war ... the whole effect was cumulative, but we were not pressed, we made our own decisions.[7]

But not all women were keen on the war, especially those who were married and feared the prospect of their husbands going off to the front.

Kitty Eckersley, a mill worker from Clayton, West Yorkshire, was very happily married. But, one evening, at an unexpected recruitment exercise at a concert, her husband decided to join the British Army. 'When we got home that night I was terribly upset,' she said. 'I told him I didn't want him to go and be a soldier – I didn't want to lose him. I didn't want him to go at all. But he said. "We have to go. There has to be men to go."'[8] His sentiments were echoed by many South African men: there had to be men to go.

It was eventually decided that a South African brigade of four regiments (also sometimes referred to as battalions by the men) would be sent to Europe, as well as five batteries of heavy artillery, a general hospital, a field ambulance and a signal company to be attached to the Royal Engineers. Sir Charles Preston Crewe, a man of considerable experience, was appointed director of recruitment for this South African Overseas Expeditionary Force.[9] Volunteers were encouraged to join the regiment of their choice, and, in the end, the four regiments were made up as follows: the 1st South African Infantry Regiment (Cape of Good Hope Regiment), consisting of men predominantly from the old Cape Colony; the 2nd South African Infantry Regiment (Natal and Orange Free State Regiment); the 3rd South African Infantry Regiment (Transvaal and Rhodesia Regiment); and the 4th South African Infantry Regiment (South African Scottish Regiment), recruited from the Scottish regiments existing in the Union, the 1st and 2nd Transvaal Scottish and the Cape Town Highlanders, and from the various Caledonian societies.

The brigade was based at Potchefstroom, where the facilities for mobilisation were already in place, and numbered 1 282 of all ranks. Of these, 595 were South African, 337 Scottish, 258 English, 30 Irish, 13 Welsh and 49 of other origin. There were 292 men younger than 20, and 196 between the ages of 35 and 40. They came from various occupations, including business, government service, agriculture and mining. Most notable, though, were the Afrikaans-speaking personnel in the brigade. As John Buchan, author of *The South African Forces in France*, commented: 'The large Boer contingent, many of whom had fought against us in the South African War, gave it a special romance.'[10]

Each regiment had an honorary colonel. Crewe was appointed honorary colonel of the 1st Regiment, General Louis Botha of the 2nd, General Jan Smuts of the 3rd and Colonel W. Dalrymple of the 4th.

Brigadier-General Henry Timson Lukin, the inspector-general of the Union forces, was appointed commander of the brigade. Lukin was the ideal man for the job, considering his long and distinguished record in South African military campaigns. He had fought in the Zulu War (1879), Basutoland (1881), the Langeberg Campaign (1896–97) and the Anglo-Boer War (1899–1902), when he commanded the artillery during the siege of Wepener and after that the 1st Colonial Division in the Cape Colony. In 1914 he had been appointed commander of the Union forces in German South-West Africa. Lukin was the quintessential soldier and turned out to be the perfect man for the campaign in Europe.

The regiments' commanding officers were all permanent members of the Union Defence Force. For the 1st regiment, there was Lieutenant-Colonel Frederick Stuart Dawson, commander of the 4th South African Mounted Rifles; for the 2nd, Lieutenant-Colonel William Ernest Collins Tanner, district staff officer, Pietermaritzburg; for the 3rd, Lieutenant-Colonel Edward Talbot Thackeray, district staff officer, Kimberley; and for the 4th, Lieutenant-Colonel Frank Aubrey Jones, district staff officer, Johannesburg.[11]

Then there was a signal company and five batteries of heavy artillery. A heavy artillery brigade had served in the German South-West Africa campaign, with personnel drawn from non-commissioned officers (NCOs) of the Royal Marine Artillery and from the various South African artillery regiments, but was disbanded in June 1915. The following month a regiment of heavy artillery was recruited for Europe largely from this former brigade. The five batteries represented the Western Cape, the Eastern Cape, the Transvaal, Kimberley and the Diamond Fields, and Natal, and were affiliated to the Royal Garrison Artillery.

A most important section of the South African Overseas Expeditionary Force was the medical staff. Lieutenant-Colonel P.G. Stock, the appointed senior medical officer, arranged for the mobilisation of a field ambulance and a general hospital. The 1st South African Field

Ambulance was to provide staff for the South African Military Hospital at Richmond, near London, and for the No. 1 South African General Hospital in France.

In addition, a medical unit with South African personnel was formed in the autumn of 1914 by the Société Française du Cap. In early 1915 this unit was established at the Hotel Beau-Rivage in Cannes as a hospital for treating sick and wounded French soldiers.

There was another component to the South African force overseas – the crucial railways and trades companies. In 1916 all the railways, roads, canals and docks in the British zone in France were placed under the control of the transportation department commanded by Sir Eric Geddes, a British businessman who later served as First Lord of the Admiralty between 1917 and 1919 and then as the first minister of transport between 1919 and 1921.

At Potchefstroom, where the South African brigade was based before its departure, the August winds were blowing, raising clouds of dust. The scene was one of stark contrast to what awaited the men in the beautiful green fields and woods of Belgium and France.

Training was tough, but the men were enthusiastic. Dudley Meredith, a new recruit, wrote:

> The transformation of the motley crowd of civilians into soldiers now began to move apace: uniforms and rifles were issued, and exercises and drills assisted in the organisation of what was without doubt a fine body of men. All types were represented: miners, farmers, tradesmen, old soldiers who had seen service in South-West Africa, and raw recruits such as ourselves.
>
> At first the rough life was strange and we did not take kindly to army cooking, to sleeping on the floors without mattresses, and to the mixing with men from all strata of society, but the very evident spirit of comradeship and good humour and the prospect of an almost immediate trip to England, followed by a period of training there, soon resulted in our feeling at ease and very much interested in our new life.[12]

Between 28 August and 17 October 1915, the whole South African contingent gathered in Cape Town ready to sail for England. The infantry brigade numbered 160 officers and 5 648 men of other ranks; the heavy artillery, 34 officers and 636 men of other ranks; and the signal company, 6 officers and 198 men of other ranks. Meredith recalled that when they left Cape Town, 'the mountains were clothed in mist ... but the delicious freshness of the green grass and cool atmosphere, were most refreshing after the journey through the Karroo, and it was with light hearts that we filed on board the *Dunvegan Castle*'.[13]

By the beginning of November 1915 all units were established in England, with the infantry based at Bordon, the field ambulance at Fleet and the heavy artillery at Bexhill. For the next two months they were kept busy training. They were honoured with inspections by General Sir Archibald Hunter, the general officer commanding of the Aldershot Command, and the Duke of Atholl, as well as Queen Mary. On 21 November the senior officers went to France for three days' duty with the British Army.

The South Africans' arrival coincided with a critical moment in the Great War. The Russian retreat had come to an end, but German field marshal August von Mackensen[14] had overrun Serbia and driven the Allies back to Salonika, and Gallipoli was about to be evacuated. Everyone now realised that the war was going to take longer and would be more grim than had been foreseen.

The South African 1st Infantry Brigade was initially attached to the 16th (Irish) Division, and it was expected that by mid-December it would be operating in France. Plans, however, were altered on 7 December when it was decided that the brigade would retrace its course and return to the African continent. And so, on 30 December 1915, the four South African regiments embarked at Devonport for Alexandria, Egypt.

The campaign in western Egypt
By the end of 1914, the main British force in North Africa was concerned with the defence of the vital Suez Canal, which was under threat from the Turks based in Syria. But in April 1915, a new inland threat

emerged when Gaafer Pasha, a former Turkish Army officer in charge of a force of Arab regulars stirred up by agents from Germany and Turkey, arrived from Constantinople with large supplies of money and arms to mobilise the Arab and Berber tribes of the Libyan plateau for an attack on Egypt from the west.

In that region Turkey relied on the support of the Senussi brotherhood, a Muslim political-religious Sufi order and tribe with its headquarters in the oases of the northern Libyan Desert. At the outbreak of war, the Senussi leader, Ahmed Sharif as-Senussi, had given assurance of friendship to the Anglo-Egyptian authorities, but the scheming of Gaafer proved too much for the tribesmen of the Senussi and the Grand Senussi himself.

Although the possibility of trouble had initially been detected in May 1915, it was not until August that the first hostilities took place, when Arabs fired on two British submarines that were sheltering from bad weather off Tripoli. Then, in the first week of November, HMS *Tara* and HMT *Moorina* were torpedoed by German submarines, and their crews were taken captive and delivered to the Senussi in Cyrenaica, Libya. In that same week, the Egyptian port of Sollum was shelled by U-boats and an Egyptian coastguard cruiser was sunk. To the British, it was clearly war.[15]

On 9 December Major-General A. Wallace, in command of the Western Frontier Force, advanced from Mersa Matruh and drove the enemy from Wadi Senaab. On 13 December his force defeated some 1 200 Arabs near Beit Hussein and on Christmas Day marched against an enemy force of 5 000 under Gaafer Pasha, 12.8 kilometres southwest of Mersa Matruh. Gaafer suffered heavy losses, but in early January 1916 he reappeared some 40 kilometres south-west of Mersa Matruh with another force. To safeguard the frontier, Gaafer had to be driven westward out of Egypt and into the desert, but Wallace lacked the troops for such an operation.

It was around this time that the South African 1st Infantry Brigade arrived in Alexandria aboard the RMS *Saxonia* (arrived 10 January) and the SS *Corsican* (arrived 13 January). The brigade settled at Mex

Camp, ten kilometres west of Alexandria, where they spent a few days in training and enhancing local defences.

Orders came on 19 January for part of the brigade to reinforce Wallace's attack on the Senussi near Mersa Matruh. The 2nd South African Infantry Regiment was chosen for this operation, with two companies departing that day and the remainder of the regiment the day after. By the evening of 21 January, the 2nd South Africans under Lieutenant-Colonel Tanner were gathered at Mersa Matruh. The whole force moved out the next day to Bir Shola, 29 kilometres away. On the morning of 23 January, Wallace deployed his troops in two columns, with the South Africans, the 1st Battalion New Zealand Rifle Brigade and a squadron of the Duke of Lancaster's Yeomanry marching under Lieutenant-Colonel J.L.R. Gordon and his 15th Sikhs.[16]

The 15th Sikhs led the attack, and together the column forced the Senussi back from their forward positions, finally breaking into the main position at Halazin and putting the enemy to flight. Heavy rain and muddy conditions compelled the Allied troops to move to Bir Shola before returning to Mersa Matruh on 25 January.

In their baptism by fire, the South Africans lost one officer (Captain J.D. Walsh) and seven other ranks in action, while one officer (Lieutenant W.G. Strannock) and two other ranks later died of wounds. Four officers and 102 other ranks were wounded.

Due to health problems, Wallace was now replaced by Major-General W.E. Peyton,[17] while the Sikhs and the New Zealanders were replaced by more of the South African brigade (by this time the entire brigade had arrived at Mersa Matruh). In early February the main Senussi forces were near the port town of Sidi Barrani, with a smaller body at Sollum. On 20 February a column under Brigadier-General Lukin, which included the 3rd South African Infantry Regiment, moved out from Mersa Matruh with orders to occupy Sidi Barrani on their way to Sollum. Their route lay north of the Khedival Highway, practically along the line of an old Roman road dotted with Roman wells. The scorching sun and strong winds made it a gruelling march, but at least the men could take dips in the ocean, as the route ran along the coast. At

Unjeila, 51 kilometres from Mersa Matruh, the 1st South Africans joined the column.

By now the Senussi forces were at Agagia, 22.5 kilometres southeast of Sidi Barrani. On the morning of 26 February, Lukin moved out his whole force with the 3rd South Africans, under Lieutenant-Colonel Thackeray, in the centre, and Yeomanry and armoured cars on either flank. The 1st South Africans formed the general reserve. It didn't take long to conquer the Senussi and capture Gaafer, a move that deprived the rebels of their principal general. Two days later Lukin's men occupied Sidi Barrani without a blow. They were now able to bring in supplies by sea and establish a new advanced base there.

The Battle of Agagia resulted in some losses to Lukin's force, chiefly among the mounted troops. Infantry casualties, almost all incurred by the 3rd South Africans, included one officer (Lieutenant Bliss) and 13 other ranks killed, and five officers and 98 other ranks wounded.[18]

A 19-year-old private, Henry Sherman from Port Elizabeth (1st Regiment, B Company), wrote to his father that the fight had lasted all day and that they had covered between 16 and 20 kilometres of enemy territory. The next day search parties were sent to look for the fallen and clear the field:

> The only man in our platoon to get hit was an old Walmer [Port Elizabeth] postman, in fact he used to live at 9th Avenue for a while. He was with our General Staff, and a stray bullet got him in the stomach. He has gone to hospital marked 'Severe Case'.
>
> One of the 3rds who was wounded in the lungs, was gasping for breath when I came across him. I could see he was far gone, I gave him my water and called for an ambulance cart. I came across several men dead and wounded on both sides, but it is not much of a subject to write on.
>
> The general [Lukin] was well pleased with our work and thanked us all. Compliments came in from all over the country. I was surprised to see how calmly and fearlessly our boys went into the fire. We just duck our heads when we hear the bullets and shells whizz by.[19]

Dudley Fynn of the 3rd Regiment, C Company, who was wounded in the fight, recorded: 'The enemy gave us a very hot time of it and it was wonderful that so many of us came out alive.'[20]

Following their action at Halazin, the 2nd South Africans had been employed in providing escorts for convoys between Mersa Matruh and Unjeila. With this task now completed, the 2nd and 4th regiments joined Lukin at Sidi Barrani, together with the rest of the 2nd South Western Mounted Brigade.

After their defeat at Agagia, the Senussi had retreated west towards Sollum, headquarters of the Grand Senussi before the campaign had begun. Peyton decided to strike again without delay and clear Egypt up to the frontier. On 9 March a column under Lukin left Sidi Barrani for Sollum, some 80 kilometres off, to secure the plateau by way of the Nagb Medean Pass. His troops consisted of the whole South African brigade, a squadron of the Dorset Yeomanry, the Hong Kong and Singapore Mountain Battery, and a camel supply column and train. They were to be joined later by the Armoured Car Battery and a company of the Australian Camel Corps.

One of the biggest challenges for Lukin and his men was securing an adequate supply of water. By the time the 1st and 4th South Africans had secured the Nagb Medean Pass on 12 March, and were joined by the armoured cars, there was not enough water for the entire column to continue on its original line.

Lukin was therefore ordered to push along the top of the escarpment with the 1st and 4th South Africans, the armoured cars, the Hong Kong and Singapore Mountain Battery, and a company of the Australian Camel Corps, while the rest of the infantry and the mounted troops were directed to proceed from Suàni el-Augerín along the coast to the foot of the Halfaya Pass. They set off on 13 March and by midnight Lukin was six kilometres from the Halfaya Pass. The rest of the infantry was at Alim Tejdid, and the cavalry at Ragbag. On 14 March the armoured cars occupied the Halfaya Pass without opposition, as the enemy had evacuated Sollum the previous evening and retreated south-west. On 15 March, Peyton entered Sollum, thus ending the threat from the Senussi.[21]

At the end of the campaign it was accepted that the men would be going to France, to the Western Front. But it transpired that negotiations had been taking place for the South African brigade to be sent to East Africa as part of the Union Defence Force campaign to counter the German threat in that part of the world. After Lukin had discussed the matter with Army Headquarters in Cairo, however, it was decided that they would be joining the 9th (Scottish) Division at Armentières instead.[22]

The South African 1st Infantry Brigade began their return journey by sea from Sollum to Alexandria on 28 March. On their arrival in Alexandria, they were joined by a draft of eight officers and 400 other ranks under the command of Captain L.W. Tomlinson. The next day the brigade received orders to embark for Marseille.[23]

The men had spent three months in North Africa, where they had experienced their first taste of war. They had endured severe hardships – scorching heat, freezing cold, dry desert winds, hunger, thirst, and long and tiring marches – and emerged stronger, both physically and mentally. They couldn't have asked for better preparation for what lay ahead on the fields of Flanders.

2

Bernafay and Trônes woods

HAROLD SILBERBAUER WAS one of several South Africans who had gone through the South-West Africa campaign and were given temporary commissions in the Imperial Army. They were to arrive in England a few months before the South African brigade.

Silberbauer and some 40 men sailed on the SS *Walmer Castle* in January 1916 and 'arrived at Devonport on a real winter's day'. There they took the train to London to receive orders from the War Office. 'All these folk in England had suffered the loss of sons and relatives, but they never said a word and made us feel at home,' he said.[1]

At the War Office, the famous English cricketer Pelham 'Plum' Warner pulled a few strings on Silberbauer's behalf and the South African received orders to join the 10th (Reserve) Battalion of the Leicestershire Regiment at the training camp at Cannock Chase. Years later he would recall:

> This was my first experience of mud. Everything was mud. It had been churned up by men and animals in such a way that it was always there. However, the living quarters were comfortable – the usual army hut, but with a coal stove. Our training followed the usual style of the First World War and did not fit one for much. There was a dearth of trained NCOs and it took time to get to know the men ... English, Scots, Irish, South Africans and Canadians. On the whole, they were a fine lot, mostly just out of school and full of life ... Life in spring and early summer was passable at Cannock Chase. The training went well and I cannot say that I was itching to go to France. However, orders came early in June and I found myself on a Channel steamer at Felixstowe. As we climbed aboard, we heard the news of Kitchener's death.[2]

In the meantime, attacks on the Germans at Loos and other places had resulted in terrible casualties. Silberbauer despaired:

> I still cannot understand why the High Command would send men into battle, fully equipped, tired after a long march, and up against barbed wire and machine guns. And they sent them in en masse! The Staff learn slowly and the slaughter was terrible. The casualty lists filled many pages and a subaltern's life was reckoned to be about five days.
>
> We were a tired and hungry lot when we disembarked at Dieppe and eventually arrived at a training camp near Boulogne. The man in charge believed in hard training and, if we were not sticking bayonets into sandbags with bloody oaths, we were forming groups of four, or listening to lectures and having pep-talks.[3]

Between 13 and 15 April 1916, the South African 1st Infantry Brigade left Alexandria aboard the *Megantic*, *Oriana*, *Scotian* and *Tintoretto*, bound for Europe, where they were to become part of the Allied campaign in Flanders. They reached the Mediterranean port of Marseille on the night of 19 April. Because of a case of contagious disease on board the *Oriana*, the 4th Regiment and part of the 1st had to remain under quarantine, while the remainder of the brigade boarded trains at once for Flanders.

The troops reached Steenwerck, in northern France, not far from Lille, on 23 April. The 2nd and 3rd regiments marched to their billeting position along roads that were flooded, and established their headquarters at Bailleul. They were later joined by the 4ths and the rest of the 1sts, whose term in quarantine at Marseille was up.

The South African brigade was attached to the 9th (Scottish) Division under Major-General William T. Furse. This division formed part of the XIII Corps under the command of Lieutenant-General Sir Walter Congreve[4] of the Fourth Army. The South Africans would later move to the 9th Division's battle headquarters on the Somme at Grove Town.[5] Earlier the 9th Division had distinguished itself at Loos, where it had captured the Hohenzollern Redoubt and the Fosse 8, holding the latter until it was utterly outflanked. It had also spent the winter in the Ypres Salient as part of the Second Army.

The 9th was now composed of the 26th Brigade (comprising the 8th Black Watch, the 7th Seaforth Highlanders, the 5th Queen's Own Cameron Highlanders, and the 10th Argyll and Sutherland Highlanders), the 27th Brigade (comprising the 11th Royal Scots, the 12th Royal Scots, the 6th King's Own Scottish Borderers and the 9th Scottish Rifles) and four regiments of the 1st South African Infantry Brigade. 'It was a proof of the respect in which the South African Brigade was held by the British Command that it should be made part of so notable a division,' commented historian John Buchan, 'and it was not less fortunate for the 9th Division that it received a brigade so competent to sustain its record.'[6]

The South African brigade had arrived at a critical time in the Western campaign. On 9 April 1916 the first and deadliest stage of the German attack on Verdun[7] had ended in defeat for the aggressors. The French lines had held, Verdun was still occupied and both sides had suffered big losses. Part of the French strategy was, in fact, to wait until the Germans had lost their strength and then deploy the forces of both France and Britain in a great movement against their weakened enemy. The South Africans therefore just had to wait. 'It was a difficult time, for there was no great objective to quicken the spirit, and those indeterminate months imposed a heavy strain upon the morale of our troops,' wrote Buchan.[8]

The lull, however, did give the British commander-in-chief, Sir Douglas Haig, time to train his field army for a new kind of warfare, with less familiar weapons such as bombs and grenades. British capacity in munitions grew considerably during the first few months of 1916, in the wake of insufficiencies during the Allied offensives of the previous year. The output of heavy guns increased sixfold; the weekly production of machine guns and rifles increased fourteen- and threefold, respectively; and the production of high explosives was 66 times greater than in the beginning of 1915. By June 1916, Britain was providing weekly to the Western Front as much as its whole pre-war stock of land-service munitions.[9]

On 29 April, Haig inspected the South African brigade, and for the next two months the men were initiated in the methods of trench warfare. Lance-Corporal Alf Mandy of the 2nd Regiment headquarters recalled his first experience of the trenches, which was during instruction at Ploegsteert, in Belgium:

> Owing to the nature of the ground there, it was not possible to dig trenches and we were protected from the enemy, a hundred yards or so away, by sandbag walls built on the crest of a ridge. It was therefore quite safe to walk anywhere behind the front line without fear of being hit by a machine gun or rifle bullet. We then took over a sector of the line adjoining that of the regiment commanded by Winston Churchill and one day I had the pleasure of seeing him riding in the rear of his command.
>
> At that time of the year, May and June, things were very quiet, and as an HQ signaller I spent most of my time on routine duties in the adjutant's office in an old farmhouse, which was supposed to be immune from shelling because the Germans occupied a similar building.
>
> One day, however, the Huns strafed us good and solid for a couple of hours, but as we took refuge in funk-hole trenches in the post we escaped with no serious casualties. The nearest I came to being hit was when our guns started retaliating. A howitzer shell was fired prematurely and pitched into the middle of our group, fortunately without exploding. But it wasn't pleasant to realise that we were not safe from our own guns.[10]

On 14 June, the 9th Division finally received orders to move to the Somme, a department in the Picardy region of France, located in the north of the country, which takes its name from the River Somme.[11] The South African brigade was quartered in Ailly-sur-Somme, a commune in the Somme Department, from where parties of officers and NCOs could visit the front line in the Maricourt region. According to Mandy, the men were glad to leave for the Somme:

> The routine life in a quiet part of the line was not particularly interesting, and it was quite a relief to move off to the Somme. We marched

much of the way, and after divisional manoeuvres en route, we detrained at Amiens, where we camped for a few days before marching to Bray-au-Somme, a few miles behind the lines. From there we marched up to Maricourt each day to do an eight-hour fatigue carrying munitions to forward positions in preparation for the big push on July 1.[12]

Now all they could do was wait for the campaign to begin. In the meantime the 2nd and 3rd South Africans were attached to the 30th Division to assist in preparing for the British Expeditionary Force and French Army's joint offensive.

They didn't have to wait long. Silberbauer recalled:

In the middle of June 1916, I found myself at the front. I was posted to the 6th Battalion, C Company, Leicestershire Regiment. The 6th, 7th, 8th and 9th battalions were brigaded together as the 110th Brigade ... Young Cyril Bam was in the 7th Battalion and Toby Moll, captain of the Gardens Football Club [in Cape Town], was in the 9th Battalion ... We were billeted on a French family, who were very kind to us. All the male members were on active service, and three of their sons had been killed. I settled down to get to know my platoon and to learn all there was to know about the trenches. The village was not under shell fire, but our guns would fire on Gommecourt and the bang of the 9,2 has to be heard to be believed. The sector seemed to be relatively quiet and it was difficult to realise that a couple of miles away was trench, barbed wire, snipers, trench mortars and sudden death. We were rehearsing for a trench raid when, to our relief, we received orders to pack up. Trench raids are beloved of the Staff and the lads behind the line lay out what they think is an exact replica of the enemy trenches, created from aerial photographs (which were, in their infancy, quite exceptional) and from reports, and the blanks were filled in from their imaginations. The unhappy subaltern goes back to the headquarters with his raiding party and they go through the drill and there appears to be no trouble in taking the trenches, scuppering a few 'Huns', and returning with prisoners and useful information.

The men began the march south, heavily burdened by all they had to carry:

> A fully equipped soldier carries a lot of kit: a rifle, a pack full of things (including the emergency bully beef and biscuits), gas mask, entrenching tool over his tail, haversack at his side (which can be most uncomfortable), and 60 rounds of ammunition. In addition, the officer carries his binoculars, compass and map case. Every 55 minutes, the men fall out and rest for five minutes, before continuing at an average of 2,5 miles an hour [4 km/h]. At the end of the day, you have had quite enough of soldiering and wish that you were home again. Then you really hate, not fear, the enemy.

Along the way, they saw both beauty and horror:

> The country we passed through on the way to the Somme was very lovely and had not been touched by the War. We stayed on the banks of the Somme for too short a time and then pushed on towards Albert. There we saw the famous figure of Christ hanging from the Church. There was some legend that the enemy would never take the town while the figure hung there. Most of us were new to war conditions and the trenches at Albert were those that had recently been occupied by the Germans. They certainly built for comfort and security. Outside the trenches were many unburied dead, ours and theirs – a sight to which I never became accustomed. It is strange how impersonal these figures become, and that is just as well, or the average person would go off his head. The officer has an advantage over his men in that he must steel himself against any feeling that might impair his efficiency, or do anything that might appear at all weak in their eyes. It is that knowledge and the realisation of his responsibilities which sometimes lifts the NCO and the officer above himself.
>
> We had no sooner settled down in those nice German dug-outs when we experienced our first real shelling. I did not like it and was never more scared in my life, but I took comfort from my company sergeant-major, who said that it was nothing to worry about and it was

just bad luck if you were hit. We all stayed put, but then the Germans started to use tear gas and it was ridiculous to see a platoon of men with tears running down their cheeks. Tear gas does not cause much harm to the infantry, but the gunners hate it. Eyes soon recover and there are no ill effects. Of other types of gas, the less said the better. I never personally experienced a gas attack, but the 2nd Leicesters did, and after that they never took any prisoners – and they were justified in that. War is a rotten business and you might say that it is just as bad to kill a person one way than another. Men get their limbs blown off and the most horrible wounds from the recognised gentle methods of warfare, but the sight of soldiers who have been gassed is awful and it is an everlasting shame on the Germans for having used such a loathsome weapon.[13]

On 23 June, the South African brigade moved to Corbie and Sailly-le-Sec, within a few kilometres of the line, and the next morning the main bombardment started. It was a grey, cloudy day with showers of rain. Buchan captured the scene:

The South Africans, as they moved east from Corbie along the Picardy downs, beheld a landscape which, in the heat and dust of midsummer, must have recalled their own country. The Somme, with its acres of swamp and broad lagoons, was not unlike some river of the bushveld. The 'tawny ground,' which Shakespeare's Henry V had summoned his men to colour with their blood, had something of the air of the highveld – yellow-green ridges and slopes falling away to an infinite distance. As they topped the hill behind Meaulte and faced the long lift of land towards Bapaume, they had the kind of spectacle which is common enough beyond the Vaal. In the hollows around the watercourses was the light green of crops; then a great stretch of unfenced country patched with woods, which were curiously clean-cut like the coppices in the park of a country house. It was such a view as a man may see from Haenertsberg, looking north towards the Woodbush. The weather, too, was the soft, shimmering mist which one meets on the edge of the Berg. Our bombardment had only just begun, and the countryside was not yet devastated. Fricourt was still a pleasant woodland village, Bernafay and Trônes were as yet little forests, and the spire of Mametz church was more than a tooth of masonry.[14]

Even though the Germans had failed at Verdun and lacked immediate reserves, they occupied strong positions between Arras and the Somme, where they mainly held the higher ground with many fortified woods and villages in the rear that could be linked together into reserve lines. The Allies, having realised the depth of this fortified zone, were working on the principle that an attack should proceed by stages, with large artillery bombardments and fresh troops for each stage. In this way 'the Battle of the Somme struck a blow at the heart of Germany's strength from which she never wholly recovered'.[15]

On 30 June, the day before the battle began, the four infantry regiments of the South African brigade, the 64th Field Company Royal Engineers, the 28th Brigade Machine Gun Company and the South African Brigade Trench Mortar Battery moved to Grove Town, on the outskirts of Bray-sur-Somme. The 9th Division remained in general reserve to Congreve's XIII Corps, whose main tasks were to capture the ridge running from Waterlot Farm (south of Delville Wood) to Bazentin-le-Grand; to take Montauban and surrounding trenches; to secure Montauban Alley; and to reach Bernafay and Trônes woods.

Arthur Betteridge of the 4th Regiment, C Company, recalled this period:

> July 1st found the brigade at Grovetown, receiving fighting equipment and watching German prisoners being escorted to the cages: two nights later we occupied some small French dugouts in Billon Valley...
>
> The Frenchies manned heavy guns and let many of us watch the huge projectiles from their guns travelling in the air on their missions of destruction...
>
> The following day we entered the line and found a wounded Frenchman as happy as a sandlark. A sympathetic South African

officer had given the fellow a stiff dose of rum, and a missing arm held no terrors for the wounded man who was happily looking for a casualty clearing station.

At the Glatz Redoubt, a cement dugout made cosy by the Germans who had been there for more than a year, a wardrobe containing women's clothing, apparently used for amateur theatricals, was found. Many strange sights were seen when the troops arrayed themselves in sundry pieces of intimate female attire. This joke soon ended when one of the company picked up a German helmet attached to a bomb. Several members of the SAI [1st South African Infantry Brigade] lost their lives as a result of 'booby traps' of this kind.[16]

The German first line was pushed back almost all the way from the Ancre southward. Success was especially notable in the XIII Corps's area of operation – they had taken Montauban and advanced to the edge of Bernafay Wood.

For the next few days, the centre of the British offence battled to take the communes of Ovillers-la-Boisselle and Contalmaison, while Congreve, on the right flank, worked in cooperation with the French to clear Trônes and Bernafay woods. These lay between the first and second German positions. The 27th Brigade quickly took Bernafay Wood on the night of 4 July, but Trônes Wood proved much more difficult to conquer. It was commanded from the south by the Maltzhorn Farm ridge and from the north by the German position at Longueval, and, although the Allies took most of it, they could not hold it. As Buchan put it, 'The place became a Tom Tiddler's ground, which neither side could fully claim, since it was at the mercy of both the British and German artillery fire.'[17]

In *The Old Front Line*, writer and poet John Masefield captured the dramatic assault:

In the early morning of the 1st of July, 1916, our men looked at them as they showed among the bursts of our shells. Those familiar heaps, the lines, were then in a smoke of dust full of flying clods and shards and gleams of fire. Our men felt that now, in a few minutes, they would see the enemy and know what lay beyond those parapets and probe the heart of that mystery. So, for the last half-hour, they watched and held themselves ready, while the screaming of the shells grew wilder and the roar of the bursts quickened into a drumming. Then as the time drew near, they looked a last look at that unknown country, now almost blotted in the fog of War, and saw the flash of our shells, breaking a little further off as the gunners 'lifted,' and knew that the moment had come. Then for one wild confused moment they knew that they were running towards that unknown land, which they could still see in the dust ahead. For a moment, they saw the parapet with the wire in front of it, and began, as they ran, to pick out in their minds a path through that wire. Then, too often, to many of them, the grass that they were crossing flew up in shards and sods and gleams of fire from the enemy shells, and those runners never reached the wire, but saw, perhaps, a flash, and the earth rushing nearer, and grasses against the sky, and then saw nothing more at all, for ever and for ever and for ever.[18]

Sergeant Louis Leonard Aarons[19] of the 1st Regiment, D Company, recalled:

On July 1st, preceded by a fierce bombardment lasting seven days, the first attack was launched from the British trenches, in front of the village of Maricourt, whilst the French operated in conjunction on our right. A well-known division took the first part, and went over the parapet. It is said that the preceding night the boys spent singing, and so eager were they that they actually leapt over the parapets four minutes before the appointed time, and whilst our artillery were still bombarding … That night our boys lay in the 'Happy Valley', otherwise known as 'Death Valley', waiting to move off. When our division went in I was attached to Brigade Headquarters, in charge of one of the carrying parties to and from the firing line, continuously under shell fire … I personally saw thousands of German prisoners brought down in the valley, just guarded by a few men. My, they looked demented. Our artillery had done its work … How well the British treat prisoners – a pattern to the world. I saw our fellows give them smokes and water, and the Huns were grateful ... For four days they had neither water nor food, so splendid was our artillery fire ... I must also state – give the devil his due – some of their captured doctors worked like Trojans among our wounded, remarking that 'our work is with the wounded, whether enemy or not.'

On July 3 and 4 the weather was simply awful. Rain! rain! rain! and we were simply washed out, without any hopes of shelter, and it impeded operations. The roads were impassable, and if one wants to see mud – well, a visit to the trenches will be quite interesting; one emerges simply covered and that does not tend to make things too comfortable.[20]

The South Africans joined the battle on the night of 2 July, when the South African brigade moved forward to Billon Valley to relieve the 27th Brigade, which was advancing into the line. On 4 July, Major-General Furse ordered General Lukin to relieve the 21st Brigade in divisional reserve and the 89th Brigade in the Glatz sector of the front. The relief was completed by 3:15 on the morning of 5 July.

Private Walter Giddy's diary entries from this time record the scale of death:

4th July 1916: Still lying low in Suzanne Valley. The artillery are quietly moving up. We shifted up behind our old firing line, where the advance started 2 or 3 days ago. The dead are lying about. Germans and our men as well, haven't had time to bury them. The trenches were nailed to the ground, and dead-mans-land looked like a ploughed field, heaps must be buried underneath ...

5th July 1916: ... it rained last night and we only have overcoats and waterproof sheets, but I cuddled up to old Fatty Roe, and slept quite warmly. There are no dug-outs where we are at present, and the shells are exploding uncomfortably near.

Had a man wounded last night for a kick off. The Huns are lying in heaps, one I noticed in particular had both legs blown off, and his head bashed in. Some have turned quite black from exposure. They are burying them as fast as possible. Brought an old fashioned power horn, Hun bullets, nose-caps of shells, etc., back with me, but I suppose they'll be thrown away.[21]

By now the 1st and 4th South African regiments held the line from the junction with the French to Briqueterie Trench, east of Montauban; the 2nd was in divisional reserve at Talus Boise; and the 3rd was in support in the old British and German front-line trenches immediately to the north-west of Maricourt. While the French attacked towards Maltzhorn Farm, the British 30th Division was struggling to secure Trônes Wood on the right. The South Africans were stationary except for a contingent assisting the 30th. Being close to the angle of the Allied front where it bent southward, they were exposed to sniping and gunfire from both front and flank.[22]

Sergeant Aarons recalled:

July 5 saw our boys take up their position in the old line German trench as reserves. Our new lines were already beyond the village of Montauban, or to be explicit, ruins… Well, I took my party over the old lines of the Huns. Shrapnel fell very near to us, and in the distance they were sending shells all over the village and woods. Our artillery was simply wonderful; nothing could live under so fierce a bombardment. The ground on our part was simply ploughed; every inch was struck by shells, no sign of trenches, dug-outs were simply blown in, and I might state that the German dug-outs are very deep. I feel certain that there must have been thousands of Germans dead buried by shells.[23]

According to Giddy, they were told 'to hold [themselves] in readiness, expecting an attack'.[24]

Over the next two days, there was heavy shelling, and the 1st and 4th South African regiments suffered some 20 casualties. Eventually, on the afternoon of 7 July, in the pouring rain, the 1st South Africans were relieved by the 18th Manchesters of the 21st Brigade. That evening, preliminary orders arrived for the second stage of the Battle of the Somme. For the 9th Division, it meant an attack on the German line at the village of Longueval.

By 8 July, the members of the 4th South African Infantry Regiment were the only South Africans on the line where the Briqueterie Trench and the section from Dublin Trench to Dublin Redoubt were being held. The 2nd South Africans, still held in reserve at Talus Boise, were ordered to relieve the 12th Royal Scots and the 6th King's Own Scottish Borderers of the 27th Brigade, who were holding a portion of Bernafay Wood. A and C companies were called up, to be joined the next day by D Company. During this short period on the line, the 2nds were exposed to extremely heavy shelling and suffered some 200 casualties, including Captain H.E. Clifford. On 10 July, they were replaced by two companies of the 4th South Africans, who were about to be drawn into the battle for Trônes Wood.

Two days previously, the 30th Division had dug in there in the face of heavy counterattacks. On the morning of 9 July, A Company of the 4th South Africans was sent to support the 90th Brigade and a platoon was despatched to the garrison at the Briqueterie. The 3rd South Africans were held in reserve to the 30th Division.

Giddy's diary entries for 8 and 9 July captured the ensuing nightmare:

8 July: 3rd S.A.'s were relieved by the Yorks who went over this morning 400 strong and returned 150 strong. Then our S.A. Scottish went over with a couple of the Regiments and took the wood, and I believe lost heavily, but are still holding the wood. Seaforth, Black Watch, Cameron, P.A., G.P.S. are going over in the morning, so there will be some bloodshed, if they get at close quarters with cold steel. Hun sent over some Tear Shells, which made our eyes smart, but were too far to cause much trouble. Two of our companies were up to the firing line ... I'd love to see the four 'Jock' Regiments go over in the morning. The Huns hate them like poison, yet I do not think their hate exceeds their fear.

9 July: Shall never forget it, as long as I live. Coming up the trench we were shelled the whole time, and to see a string of wounded making their way to a dressing station [first-aid post], those who can walk or hobble along; another chap had half of his head taken off, and was sitting in a huddled up position, on the side of the trench, blood streaming on to his boots, and Jock lay not 5 yards further with his stomach all burst open, in the middle of the trench. Those are only a few instances of the gruesome sights we see daily. As I am writing here, a big shell plonked into the soft earth, covering me with dust, one by one they are bursting around us. I am just wondering if the next will catch us (no it was just over). Oh! I thought one would get us, it plonked slick in our trench and killed old Fatty Roe, and wounded Keefe, Sammy who was next to me, and Sid Phillips, poor beggar, he is still lying next to me, the stretcher bearers are too busy to fetch him away. The Manchesters had to evacuate the wood below us, and we the one along here. I'm wondering if we will be able to hold this wood, in case of an attack, as our number is so diminished. I've seen so cruel sights today.[25]

The attack to clear Trônes Wood was launched at dawn on 10 July 1916, when troops of the 30th Division, along with A Company of the 4th South Africans, advanced through the southern half of the wood. By the afternoon, a German counterattack had deprived them of most of their gains and, returning to the trenches, the Allies were subjected to heavy shelling. Arthur Betteridge recorded:

Enemy machine gunners were well entrenched in the wood and some of them supported their snipers hidden in the trees. The 2nd Regiment lost five officers and 200 men before the wood was cleared the next day. Captain Russell, commanding D Company of the Scottish and 40 men were killed before the wood was cleared, and handed over to the Liverpool Regiment.[26]

A and C companies of the 4th South Africans, in the neighbourhood of Glatz Redoubt (Headquarters and B and D companies were in Bernafay

Wood), were subjected to a tremendous barrage from the Germans, who were preparing for their counterattack. It came as a big blow when the experienced and beloved Lieutenant-Colonel F.A. 'Fatty' Jones, the commanding officer of the 4th South African Infantry Regiment, was killed by a shell splinter. Jones had served in the Boer War with the Welsh Regiment and in German South-West Africa. Betteridge recalled that a German shell hit the dug-out he had just left, as Jones and an orderly were climbing up its steps:

> As the shell exploded, both of them were killed instantly and several in the dugout wounded and shocked. I rushed down the dugout after the explosion and assisted in bringing the Colonel's body to the road where we placed it on a stretcher and covered it with a ground sheet. The body of that popular Officer Commanding was taken to a nearby cemetery. This loss was felt by all ranks of the Scottish.[27]

The command of the regiment was now handed to Major D.M. MacLeod.[28]

At this stage neither side could fully claim possession of Trônes Wood, as it was still at the mercy of both British and German artillery fire. On 13 July, Sir Douglas Haig ordered an attack on the German second line. The 4th South Africans were relieved by the 2nd Royal West Surreys and the 7th Middlesex of the 55th Brigade, and the whole South African brigade was now concentrated at Talus Boise as the reserve brigade of the 9th Division. Their stint on the front line had cost them dearly, with the 1st Regiment suffering 50 casualties, the 2nd 205, the 3rd 91, and the 4th 191. By far the most losses were from shell fire. Seven officers had been killed and nine wounded.[29]

At dawn on 14 July, Haig launched his attack against a six-kilometre section of the Germans' second position, from a point south-east of Pozières to Longueval and Delville Wood. Congreve's XIII Corps was tasked with taking Bazentin-le-Grand, Longueval and Delville Wood, clearing Trônes Wood and forming a defensive flank. They carried all their objectives from Bazentin-le-Petit to Longueval, over a front of more than five kilometres and at one moment they had all but penetrated the Germans' third position at High Wood.

Harold Silberbauer recalled the battle:

All this time the battle seemed near. On the night of 12 July, we marched up to our launching place and were guided through the outskirts of Mametz Wood. The dead were everywhere and the men became tired and depressed as we slogged towards the battle. However, once we were in position, a kind of excitement gripped us all and most of us acknowledged afterwards that we had wondered what it would be like to be dead.

Our task was to take three successive lines of trenches and the artillery barrage would lift at definite times to allow us to go forward. The noise was infernal and bewildering – darkness was shattered by ghastly flashes of light and explosions erupted all around. Trees, men, earth, all seemed to be blown to bits around us, but so far, 'C' Company had suffered no casualties. We all crouched in the grass waiting for zero hour at 02.15. The night was mild, but the men were shivering and sweating. Our last meal had been at 19.00 the night before.

All watches were synchronised and zero hour was near. Then our artillery crashed down and I never imagined that such a row was possible. I suppose 'hell let loose' almost describes it. The Germans also increased their fire, and casualties mounted. We were not allowed to do anything for the wounded – that was the stretcher bearers' duty… Their work, and that of the doctors, was a revelation to me of endurance, kindness and sheer bravery.

At zero hour, the barrage lifted and forward we went! Our captain was killed almost immediately. I thought one had to dash ahead as in a story book charge, but soon realised that that was no good. The main rule was to keep the men together, to be with them and to lead them to the objective at a steady walk, or perhaps a trot. The shelling was very heavy – shrapnel and high explosives – but we arrived at the first trenches in fairly good order, to find the enemy gone.

I collected my platoon and a few stragglers from other units and waited for the next jump. On time, the barrage lifted again and on we forged, but now machine gun bullets started to inflict heavy casualties. Despite the fact that daylight was near, it was very difficult to keep in touch in a wood that was being blasted by both sides at once – fallen and falling trees were everywhere.

We struggled on and now began individual fights with stray enemy, most of whom seemed quite bewildered, although the usual brave and tough types had to be dealt with. One of our officers was badly wounded, but refused to give in. I soon lost touch with him and heard later that he had been killed. Gallant deeds were being done all around, but in the chaos there was little time to note special cases, especially names, as I was new to the battalion and at the time knew very few of the officers and men.

We – what was left of us – pushed on to the last objective before the village, but came under terrific fire from our own side, as well as from the enemy. I found out afterwards that this was due to one of those mistakes that should not happen, but do. The barrage on a certain line had been marked 'cancelled' on the infantry maps, but not on the artillery ones. That was one of my nastiest moments in the battle.

We were now out of that nightmare wood in what was once a village – the village of Bazentin-le-Petit, and the day was 13 July. We had achieved our objective, and fondly believed that the Germans were on their way back to Berlin. We received orders to consolidate. The village was a shambles and nothing remotely resembling a house was to be seen. Here I came across an old friend from Hamilton's [Rugby Club], Toby Moll, who told me that Cyril Bam had been killed. No trace of him was to be found. Soon after this, Toby was hit by shrapnel when he was quite near me and I saw at once that there was no hope. It was hard to see Toby go – everything else was impersonal, almost unreal, but with Toby one was up against it.

I collected those I could and went to the end of the village, where there was a sunken road. It seemed to be a good spot to rest and also from which to observe. We all felt very tired and hungry and thirsty, so

> I ordered the emergency rations to be eaten. It was impossible to find out who was in command and the only thing to do was to improvise and allow matters to sort themselves out.
>
> The enemy appeared to be preparing for a counter-attack, and I found myself enfiladed from the right flank, so I pulled the men back to better cover in the village.[30]

They were able to stop the Germans with the Lewis gun, but the men's rifle shooting was poor. One soldier was firing at the Germans some 50 metres away, but his sights were set at over 450 metres. They managed to hold the enemy until, to their relief, fresh troops – the Warwickshires – came advancing to their right. When the Germans saw this they fell back, urged on by bursts of fire from Silberbauer's group.

In spite of their casualties, they were eager to give chase and it was then that Silberbauer was wounded, a bullet ricocheting off his leg 'in a peculiar way'. He discovered afterwards that a big steel knife that he had lost and later found at Trekkoppies, in South-West Africa, had taken the impact. He kept the knife in his pocket over his groin. Another bullet went through his elbow and the wound bled profusely. Soon stretcher-bearers arrived and took him away.[31]

According to Buchan, this section of the battle front was the most difficult:

> To begin with, we were fighting in a salient, and our attack was under fire from three sides. This enabled the enemy to embarrass seriously our communications during the action. In the second place, the actual ground of attack presented an intricate problem. The land sloped upwards from Bernafay and Trones Wood to Longueval village, which was shaped like an inverted fan, broad at the south end, where the houses clustered about the junction of two roads, and straggling out to the north-east along the highway to Flers. Scattered among the dwellings were many little enclosed gardens and orchards. To the east and north-east of the hamlet stretched the wood of Delville, in the shape of a blunt equilateral triangle, with an apex pointing northward.

The place, like most French woods, had been seamed with grassy rides, partly obscured by scrub, and the Germans had dug lines of trenches along and athwart them. It had been for some days a target for our guns, and was now a mass of splintered tree-trunks, matted undergrowth, and shell-holes. The main German positions were to the north, north-east, and south-east, at a distance of from 50 to 200 yards from its perimeter, where they had strong entrenchments manned by machine guns.[32]

Haig's aim was to carry Longueval and make it the flanking buttress of his new line, from which a defensive flank could be formed running south-east to the junction with the French. It was obvious, however, that the whole of Longueval could not be held unless Delville Wood was also taken, as the northern part of the village where the road climbed towards Flers was commanded by the wood. Nothing short of holding the complete village would provide an adequate pivot and, with the wood still in German hands, there would not be a sufficient jumping-off point from which to press outward in the direction of Ginchy and Guillemont.[33] The task of carrying Delville Wood was going to be difficult, as the XIII Corps had to take on the experienced 16th Bavarian Infantry Regiment and the 6th Bavarian Reserve Infantry Regiment of the 10th Bavarian Infantry Division.[34]

3

Longueval

THE ATTACK ON Longueval, on the morning of 14 July 1916, was entrusted to the 26th Brigade of the 9th Division. The 8th Black Watch and the 10th Argyll and Sutherland Highlanders would lead, the 7th Seaforth Highlanders would be in support, and the 5th Queen's Own Cameron Highlanders would be in reserve. Behind them, the 27th Brigade would 'clean up'. It was General Congreve's aim to secure Longueval, as well as Delville Wood.

Shortly after dawn, General Lukin received orders to put a regiment at the disposal of the 27th Brigade to assist in clearing the streets of Longueval. For this purpose, he sent out the 1st South African Infantry Regiment. The 3rd South Africans in the meantime had been allotted to the 26th Brigade, but this instruction order was later cancelled. Buchan recorded the attack as follows:

> The assault of the Highlanders was a most gallant performance. They rushed the trenches outside the village, and entered the streets, where desperate hand-to-hand fighting took place among the houses, for the enemy made a resolute defence. Before noon all the west and south-west part of Longueval was in our hands; but it had become clear that the place in its entirety could not be held, even if won, until Delville Wood was cleared.[1]

At 13:00 the 9th Division's commander reported: '12/R Scots [12th Royal Scots] pushed through Northern half of Longueval Village but were forced back by a machine gun about N.W. corner of Delville Wood. Artillery is being turned on to machine gun. FOO [Forward Observation

Office] reports "German artillery shelling Waterlot Farm. No troops of 9th Div believed to have reached this point".'[2]

Walter Giddy's diary entry for 14 July captured the mood among the men:

> News very good this morning. Our troops driving the Huns back, and the cavalry have just passed, they look so fine. The Bengal Lancers were among them, so I was told. We're under orders to shift at a moment notice. It rained heavily this morning. I hope it does not hamper the movements of the cavalry. If this move ends as successfully as it has begun, it will mean such a lot to the bringing of the war to an end. Our chaps are getting so tired of the mud and damp. There's such a change in the sunburnt faces of Egypt, and this inactivity makes one as weak as a rat. The cavalry have done excellent work, now it remains to us infantry to consolidate the positions. We're just ready to move forward.[3]

Arthur Betteridge recalled:

> Several Scottish Regiments of the 9th Division attacked the village of Longueval, captured it and a small portion of Delville Wood alongside the village. The S.A. Brigade was in support. As we advanced I saw many dead kilties, one of the Cameronians had rammed his bayonet into the chest of a German when both were killed by the blast of a German shell. This was a gruesome sight among many others in the vicinity of Longueval village.
>
> That afternoon we moved up to the fringe of Longueval, digging shallow trenches when time allowed. The Germans had started a frightening barrage on our exposed positions and sent over a gas attack. Captain Farrell was gassed and wounded and Lieutenant Taylor was among others taken by stretcher to the field hospital erected at the side of Bernafay Wood. This hospital was within range of the German heavy guns and carried on attending to the thousands of wounded under shell fire … our advance had caused a huge salient, resulting in Longueval

and Delville Wood coming under fire from three directions, a most unpleasant and dangerous situation. Delville Wood was on high ground, commanding a view of the Germans in a shallow valley. It was imperative that this important wood should be held at all costs. The safety of our other divisions depended on it.[4]

Private Sidney Martin Carey, a 21-year-old serving in D Company of the 1st South African Infantry Regiment, vividly recalled his experience of the fighting that day:

> We all knew that we were going against a pretty tough enemy – but we didn't expect anything like what actually happened. While going up to Longueval my friend next to me [Private G.F. Greenwood] said, 'Man, but there're a damn lot of bees around here!' I said, 'Bees be blowed! Those are bullets flying around.'
> Unfortunately about four minutes afterwards a bullet caught him and killed him right out. Then I began to see that things were getting bad. Then another went over. Then another. Then I thought, 'It's my turn next.' There were machine gun posts at the flour mill at Longueval and we got it very heavy from there. I got hit at the beginning of the wood. The lower part of my jaw was shot away, they reckon by a ricochet. It felt like a mule-kick.[5]

Second-Lieutenant Clive Featherstone of Aberdeen in the Eastern Cape served in the 1st Regiment, B Company, when the advance took place.

> We were in first-line support all day, so we came in for plenty of punishment and tear shells. These are decidedly unpleasant; they make the eyes burn so that you weep freely. The smell is somewhat similar to chloroform.
> By about 2.00 p.m. we became front-line, and we lay down for a time under steady whizz-bang and machine gun fire. But cover was good, with large shell holes and, as the trajectory of the shells was very low, there were few casualties.

After a time we began the advance in earnest and met heavy machine gun fire. Losing men steadily from that and sniping, we pressed steadily forward and made good our advance.

The enemy was putting up strong resistance, and we had to fight for every yard. The fighting lasted for days [Delville Wood included]. There was no rest, night or day, and we were subjected to gunfire incessantly.[6]

General Furse, who had command of the 9th Division, informed Lukin that, as soon as the other two brigades had taken Longueval, the South Africans should capture and consolidate the outer edge of Delville Wood. The entire South African brigade, minus the 1st South African Infantry Regiment, was available to achieve this. Lukin scheduled the attack for 17:00, but the time was later pushed back to 19:00 and then to 19:30. Eventually, because the village was not entirely captured, Lukin's orders were suspended. After a mission to ascertain the position in Longueval, a South African brigade staff officer, Lieutenant P.R. Roseby, had reported that the northern part of the village was not in British possession, and that therefore it would be impossible to form up on a line west of Longueval and advance to the attack from there.

Following a conference with Furse at Montauban, it was decided that the attack would take place at 05:00 the next morning. Furse said the wood had to be taken at all costs, and that the advance was to proceed even if the 26th and 27th brigades had still not captured the northern part of the village.[7]

Lukin instructed his regiment commanders that if on arrival at Longueval they found the northern part still in German hands, they should attack Delville Wood from the south-west corner, moving forward on a one-regiment front. The assault was entrusted to the 2nd and 3rd South Africans, with the latter leading. The 4ths would be in support.

In the meantime, the 1st South Africans, under Lieutenant-Colonel Frederick Dawson, had been heavily engaged in Longueval, having deployed along the line held by the two Scottish brigades. The regiment had been instructed to attack the remainder of the village, and its leading companies, A and B, reached their first objectives at about 16:00 on 14 July. Due to machine-gun fire from the front and flank, however, they were unable to advance. During the night three parties were sent out to capture the enemy posts that were checking their advance, and they found that the whole northern part of the village was a nest of German machine guns. In the morning, once the other three South African regiments had started their advance on Delville Wood, the 1st South Africans returned to Lukin's command.[8]

It was overcast on the morning of 15 July when the South Africans moved forward from Montauban two hours before dawn. Buchan describes the scene:

> As the sun rose the sky lightened above the Bapaume Ridge, and men noticed amid the punctual shelling how small birds still sang in the ruined coverts, and larks rose from the battered ridges. Before them on their right front lay the shadow which was Delville Wood, and the jumbled masonry, now spouting like a volcano, which had been the hamlet of Longueval.[9]

During the march, orders arrived from the division headquarters for the South African brigade to put two companies at the disposal of the 26th Brigade in Longueval. The B and C companies of the 4th Regiment were ordered to report to the officer commanding the 5th Queen's Own Cameron Highlanders. The rest of the brigade, under Lieutenant-Colonel William Tanner, moved over the broken ground under heavy fire until they were close to the southern edge of Longueval.

Tanner's patrols reported that the Germans still held the northern part of the village and part of the wood adjacent to the streets. The situation in the rest of the wood, however, was uncertain. Some of the 5th Camerons were holding a trench running into Delville Wood from the south-west corner, and in the rear of this trench the 2nd and 3rd South African regiments assembled at about 06:00.

Typical of the common practice of using familiar names to identify battlefield locations on British Army maps, the existing roads in Delville

Wood at the time of the Battle of the Somme were given names of streets known to the soldiers. Tanner decided to occupy the wood by first clearing the area south of Princes Street and then pushing north from there to occupy the Strand and the perimeter of the wood from its northern end round to the south-west corner. This would gain him the whole of Delville Wood, except the north-west corner.[10]

The attack went swiftly at first, and by 07:00 the 3rd South African Infantry Regiment and one company of the 2nd held all ground south of Princes Street. The remaining three companies of the 2nd were sent to occupy the Strand and the northern perimeter, but this proved a difficult task. The three weakened companies reached their target area, but were forced to hold a front of some 1.2 kilometres, along which it was almost impossible to maintain connection. The men did their best to dig themselves in and wire the ground they had gained, but as soon as they reached the edge, the whole wood was heavily shelled by the Germans. At the same time, they were subjected to heavy machine-gun and rifle fire from the strongly entrenched German lines around the perimeter.

While this was going on, two patrols of the 3rd South Africans under the command of Captains Medlicott and Tomlinson managed to sneak up on the Germans in the southern and eastern parts of the German trench and capture three officers, 135 other ranks and a machine gun.

At 14:40, Tanner reported to Lukin that he had taken the whole of Delville Wood, except for some strong positions in the north-west abutting Longueval and the northern orchards. The first part of the general's task had been completed admirably, but, as later events would show, the problem with Delville Wood was that it proved far less a task to occupy it than to hold it. It had been Lukin's plan to thin out the troops in the wood as soon as the perimeter was reached, and leave it to be held by small detachments of infantry backed by machine guns. This plan was rendered impossible, however, by the Germans' counterattack, as every available man was needed to hold them off.[11]

At around 15:00, sections of the German 6th Bavarian Reserve Infantry Regiment of the 10th Bavarian Infantry Division launched an attack from the east, but solid rifle fire from the South Africans drove them back. Almost two hours later, Tanner reported that the Germans were also preparing for an attack at the northern end. At around 18:30, he again reported a German concentration to the north and north-east. Tanner had suffered heavy casualties, one company of the 2nd South Africans having been virtually destroyed, and therefore requested some reinforcements. Having already received a company of the 4th South Africans, another company of the 4ths was now sent forward to strengthen the 3rds. And with the 1st South Africans now having returned to Lukin's command, one of its companies was despatched to reinforce the 2nds.

As the sun went down, the intensity of the German bombardment increased. As Buchan dramatically described it, 'the darkness of night was turned by shells and liquid fire into a feverish and blazing noon. The German rate of fire was often as high as 400 shells a minute.'[12]

That evening, Lukin sent a staff officer to determine the full situation of the regiments' positions in the wood. The officers commanding the 2nd and 3rd regiments were urged to dig in properly in view of the heavy shell fire that was expected in the morning, and Dawson, commanding the 1sts, was instructed to detail special carrying platoons to keep up the supply of ammunition. To command the southern edge, a Vickers machine gun and a Lewis gun were set up at the south-west corner of the wood.

By nightfall, the north-west corner of the wood was in German hands, while the north-east corner was held from left to right by one and a half companies of the 2nd South African Infantry Regiment, with one company of the 1st in support, and by one company of the 3rd, with a company of the 4th in support. The south-east corner was held by two companies of the 3rd, and the southern edge from left to right by one company of the 2nd, one company of the 3rd and a company of the 4th. A half company of the 2nd held the western third of Princes Street, while two companies of the 1st formed a defensive flank on the side of the village. The headquarters of the 2nds and 3rds was at the junction of Buchanan and Princes streets. Ten machine guns were in position around the perimeter at the northern apex, the eastern end of the north-eastern edge and in the eastern half of the southern edge. Therefore, 12 weakened infantry companies were holding a wood with an area of slightly less than two square kilometres, on which every German battery was accurately ranged. As the Germans held the north-west corner, they had a covered approach into the wood.

At this stage, the only South African reserves were one company of the 1st and two companies of the 4th, which were due to return the following morning. The latter had been involved in the British attack on Waterlot Farm. After the 18th Division had cleared Trônes Wood on 14 July, they had established their line up to Maltzhorn Farm, joining up with the 9th Division near Waterlot Farm, where the Germans had fortified their position with heavy Maxim machine guns. On the morning of 15 July, when the 5th Camerons had attacked this point, the two companies were used as troops to follow and consolidate. Major Hunt, who was in charge of the companies, sent a platoon from each company to occupy the trenches close to the farm. This they did under heavy fire from concealed German posts to the south and east. Waterlot Farm was not taken until the following day. At about 18:00 that evening, an enemy force was seen coming from Guillemont, but it was countered by the artillery barrage. An hour later, the two companies were ordered to fall back and construct a strong point. At 2:30 on the morning of 16 July they were relieved by the Camerons and withdrawn to the sunken road behind Longueval.[13]

During all of this, the 1st South African Field Ambulance and its stretcher-bearers had struggled to remove casualties. Staff Sergeant Tom Welsh recalled:

> The road from Longueval to Bernafay Wood was in an indescribable condition. It was impossible to carry from the front of the Regimental Aid Posts in Longueval, owing to the sniping, which was at times very severe and accurate. The rear was a mass of ruins, wire entanglements, garden fences, fallen and falling trees, together with every description of debris and shattered building material. It is one thing to clear a path along which reinforcements may be brought, but quite another to make a track on which four men may carry a stretcher with a modicum of comfort to the patient... Besides this road there was a narrow sunken

lane, which at first afforded some safety, but later became so pitted with shell-holes that the bearers were compelled to take to the open. In addition to these difficulties, it must be remembered that these roads were shelled heavily day and night. At times the enemy would put up a barrage with heavy stuff, which meant that no stretcher-bearing could be done until the fire was over. Parties who were unfortunate enough to be caught in one of these barrages spent moments of nerve-racking suspense, crouching in shell-holes or under banks, or wherever cover was available. One of the worst experiences of this kind was when it was decided to shell Longueval once more. Very short notice was given to clear all the Regimental Aid Posts, and only two men per stretcher could be spared. Padres, doctors, and odd men were pressed into service to enable all patients to be removed. As the party left, the bombardment began on both sides. Scrambling, pushing, and slipping amid a tornado of shell-fire, they headed for Bernafay Wood. It was impossible to keep together, and in the darkness squads easily became detached and lost touch. The noise of bursting shells was incessant and deafening, while the continuous sing of the rifle and machine-gun bullets overhead tried the nerves of the hardiest. To crown all, it was raining, and the roads were almost impassable for stretcher work. In fact, had it not been for the light of the German star shells, the thing could not have been worked at all. As the night wore on squad after squad of tired, soaked, and mud-covered men stumbled into Bernafay Wood. Here came a medical officer covered with grime and mud from top to toe, carrying a stretcher with a kilted Scot. Then a tall parson, unrecognizable under a coating of mud, with a stretcher-bearer as partner, whose orders he obeyed implicitly. When word was passed round in the morning that all had returned alive, some were so incredulous that they started an inquiry of their own.[14]

4

Delville Wood

BEFORE THE ASSAULT, Delville Wood was a beautiful, scenic area. This is how Lance-Corporal Ernest Solomon of the 3rd South Africans described it:

> Delville Wood covered a large area; its trees, closely set, towered to a great height, where the leafy branches intermingled and formed a screen so thick that, in parts, the view of sky was almost obscured. Here and there was a clearing, here and there a narrow road, here and there a footpath; but for the most part nothing but trees and thick undergrowth.[1]

By the end of the battle, this idyllic setting would be obliterated by shell, rifle and machine-gun fire.

Three regiments of the South African brigade were tasked to attack Delville Wood. They were to be led by Lieutenant-Colonel Tanner, the officer in command of the 2nd South African Infantry Regiment. Judging by what his men said about him, he was the right man for the job.

> A man of iron and a strict disciplinarian. He was about the most brilliant soldier sent out from SA. His records at the British Military Staff College prove him to be an exceptionally keen student. He gave the impression of being a master at the game. Would go to any amount of trouble to explain difficulties to puzzled 'subs' [subalterns].[2]

One of the soldiers under his command at Delville Wood recalled:

> Tanner took us in and he stayed with us there. His headquarters was Longueval, right on the edge of the wood. He was a man's officer. You

could go to him, or the corporal could, or the lieutenant, and he'd listen. He was our friend. We'd have followed him through any fire, anywhere. He was a trim, wiry man, and a great smiler: I never think of him but I think of his smile.[3]

According to Tanner, General Lukin had allowed him a great deal of latitude in the planning and execution of the attack on Delville Wood.

Two hours before dawn the 2nd and 3rd Regiments left Montauban for Delville Wood followed by the 4th Regiment which was to support the attack. The exact position of our own troops in Longueval was still unknown as Lieutenant Roseby [the brigade intelligence officer] had not returned from his difficult reconnaissance and the probable impossibility of executing the existing order was still a difficulty. In the circumstances I was instructed by General Lukin to ascertain the position of affairs in Longueval and to base the plan of attack upon the result of this reconnaissance.[4]

For easier reference, the South African forces allocated English place names to the locations in Delville Wood. Tanner established his headquarters at Buchanan Street. Lieutenant-Colonel Edward Thackeray stayed with him, moving his 3rd Regiment to the far side of the wood, while Tanner's 2nd Regiment followed them to the east before branching off to the north. C Company of the 2nd Regiment occupied the southern perimeter, close to Longueval.

Private Hugh Mallet of C Company, facing Waterlot Farm, clearly recalled his experiences on that day:

We arrived at the edge of the wood at about dawn, everybody on tenterhooks and just as the last man got in old Fritz opened fire with big and little guns, rifle and machine-gun fire. What a time we had! Our men were being rolled over like ninepins, but on went the boys and by 8.30 we had accomplished our task. We gave old Fritz the time of his life. I took a slow and steady aim and made every shot tell. My only regret was that I did not get my bayonet into him. Later there was a lull and it was during this lull that I was hit. I was on guard at the time and it was my duty to keep a sharp lookout over the parapet. I had only been on a few minutes when old Fritz sent a huge shell right in front of our trench. It blew away a portion of the trench and knocked a tree over on top of us.

One of the splinters of the shell landed me one on the right cheek, which of course put me out for a few moments. It made a nasty hole. I did not wish to leave, but I was told to take another wounded man into safety. We were shelled all the way to the dressing station, but I got him away without any further mishap. On my way through the wood I saw many of our brave lads dead ... Both my captains [H.E. Clifford] and [W.J. Gray] are killed and my platoon lieutenant is seriously wounded – hit in eight places, I hear. He is a brave fellow. I hope he gets over it.[5]

All through the night of 15 July the troops in Delville Wood worked for dear life on entrenchments, using tools that looked like fire shovels. According to Buchan, it was rumoured that the South African soldiers were 'a little negligent in digging, trusting rather to their courage and their marksmanship than to trenches'. But he believed this criticism was unjust:

> No soldiers ever worked harder with the spade, but their task was nearly impossible. In that hard soil, coagulated by incessant shellfire, and cumbered with a twisted mass of roots, wire, and tree trunks, the spade could make little way. Nevertheless, when the Sunday morning dawned [16 July], a good deal of cover had been provided.[6]

The rifle pits the men dug were connected to form a trench with strong points at the salients, and the whole was later deepened to minimise the effects of shrapnel. Private Geoffrey Lawrence recalled how his company (1st Regiment, C Company) struggled from the night of 15 July to the early morning of 16 July to dig their trenches because the tree roots made digging difficult. Lance-Corporal Ernest Solomon (3rd Regiment,

A Company) described how he and his comrades had to lie on their stomachs to dig because of constant enemy shelling and rifle fire.[7]

With the main trench finished, the South Africans had to dig supporting trenches in Princes, Buchanan and Strand streets, as well as a strong point about 140 metres north-east of the junction of Princes and Buchanan. These trenches were the lifeline, so to speak, for the South Africans in Delville Wood. Without them they would have suffered many more casualties.[8]

A 20-year-old private, Ronald Talson Murray Rawbone, of 1st Regiment, D Company, described in a letter to his father the misery of entrenching:

> We then started to dig ourselves in, each man digging his own little place. I dug mine pretty deep, and I am glad I did so, as they turned their machine guns on to us, and the bullets were just going over my head. We were then told that the Germans were massing for a counter-attack; the first attack came off about 12.30, but they were driven off by our machine gun fire. All this time it was pouring with rain, and I was wet through and covered with mud from head to foot. It must have been at about 2.30 when they attacked us again; this time they managed to get right up to us.[9]

(At this point Rawbone was wounded in the arm and sent to Rouen Hospital.)

In the afternoon, Lukin received orders from the division to block the northern entrance into Longueval at all costs. To ensure this, his brigade had to complete the capture of the northern perimeter of Delville Wood and then advance westward until they linked up with the 27th Brigade. North Street was a continuation of the main street of Longueval from the point where Flers Road branched off to the north-east, and between these roads was an orchard. The 27th had to capture the orchard, as well as other enclosures east of North Street, before they could join up with the South Africans on Flers Road. This was to be the work of the 11th Royal Scots, while two companies of the 1st South Africans, forming a defensive flank at the south-west corner of the wood, were to push north from the Princes Street line.[10]

The advance started on the morning of Sunday 16 July 1916, but it failed completely as the Royal Scots were obstructed by a well-wired stone redoubt and the South Africans encountered heavy machine-gun fire from the orchard. A South African bombing party under Lieutenant Arthur William Craig attempted to rush over some 40 metres of ground between the British and German trenches. Most of this party were either killed or wounded by heavy rifle and machine-gun fire. A wounded Craig, unable to move, lay exposed in the open midway between the two lines of trenches. Private William Frederick Faulds of Cradock, accompanied by two other men, climbed over the parapet, rushed into the open, picked up the injured lieutenant and carried him back to safety. For his bravery, Faulds was awarded the South African brigade's first Victoria Cross. Two days later he went out again, alone, under heavy artillery fire, to bring in a wounded man, whom he then carried nearly a kilometre to a dressing station.[11]

Following this failure, the attacking troops fell back to the trenches midway in the wood, and for the rest of the day endured a steady concentrated fire to which they had no means of effective reply. It was hot and dusty, and the Germans' barrage of shells made it almost impossible to bring food and water or to remove the many casualties.[12]

The intensity of the fighting is evident from the reminiscences of Gunner Ivan McCusker, 3rd Regiment, B Company, the No. 1 gunner on a Lewis gun, in a letter to his father dated 25 July 1916:

> The Germans were, of course, shelling us all the time, and we were losing a lot of men. Meanwhile they were massing about eight or nine regiments for a tremendous counter-attack... My no. 2 [on the gun] was Charles Hugo, from Beaufort West. He was as game as a fighting-cock. Well, I managed to fire over 3,500 rounds into Germans in massed formation at ranges varying from 300 to 800 yards. So I guess I put over 300 Germans out of action with my little Lewis before I was hit;

the targets were too good to miss, and the Lewis is very accurate. It is a fine gun, and is aptly described as 'the hose of death'. Well, the shelling was getting heavier and heavier; shells were bursting all around us and very, very near. I said to Hugo: 'Charles, our numbers are up.' He just grinned. Not long after (about 4 p.m.) a 5.9-inch shell plunged right amongst us, and put my whole gun team out of action. What happened to the brigade after this, I don't know much.[13]

Private William Walter Daniel Ryan, a boilermaker from Salt River, in Cape Town, serving in the 1st Regiment, D Company, recalled:

We came back into the second line – this was Saturday [15 July] – and had a pretty hot time of it, as the Germans put up a counter-attack, and did not half shell us, but the boys hung on splendidly and drove them back in disorder… On Sunday morning [16 July] they started to shell us, and one did not know where to stand. They seemed to follow one all over the show. Well, the unlucky one came along and it fell about six yards from me. I was sitting in a dug-out I made, and all of a sudden I was buried alive, and my chums had to dig me out (my officer and six men were wounded in my platoon). When I got out there I felt a bit shaky and faint, but it all wore off and I carried on. Then my sergeant told me and another fellow to take a box of ammunition up to the front line. We had just got round the corner of the trench when another shell came along and fell about four or five yards from us and threw the two of us twelve yards along the trench, and that finished me. It was about 10 o'clock in the morning, and I was unconscious till 4 o'clock that afternoon, to find myself in a dug-out used as a dressing station.[14]

In the afternoon on 16 July, Lieutenant-Colonel Dawson, commanding the 1st Regiment, met Lukin in Longueval. Dawson reported that his men were exhausted and asked for an early relief, but Lukin reiterated his divisional commander's instructions that Delville Wood had to be held at all costs. He was, nevertheless, so alarmed with the signs of strain and fatigue among the men that he referred the matter to General Furse, in command of the 9th Division.

It was a desperate situation. Longueval and Delville Wood had proved far too well held to be captured at the first attack by one division, and, until they were taken, the stability of the whole right wing of the new front was in danger. As fresh troops could not yet be spared for the task, the same exhausted and depleted regiments had to attempt it again. 'It was a vicious circle,' wrote Buchan. 'Longueval could not be won and held without Delville; Delville could not be won and held without Longueval; so what strength remained to the 9th Division had perforce to be divided between two simultaneous objectives.'[15]

Entering and fighting in Delville Wood was a terrible ordeal for the South African soldiers. At first, it was difficult to orientate oneself and visibly communicate with comrades because of the dense vegetation. Thereafter, it was utter desolation. 'When we went into the wood the growth was so dense you could hardly see ten yards in front of you,' described Corporal Hermann Bloom of the 2nd South Africans, 'but before long there was neither a bough nor a leaf left; the bare trees stood out riddled with lead, and the wood a mass of dead and wounded – it was awful!'[16]

Private J. Simpson of the 4ths described the confusion on entering the wood: 'Here things were terribly confusing, for fighting was going on there at the time, and no one seemed to know just what direction to fire, and fellows in trenches in the centre of the wood did not know which direction from which to expect an attack.'[17]

Arthur Betteridge was another one of the men who lived through the drama of 15 and 16 July.

> At 2 a.m. on the 15th, B and C companies of the Scottish attacked a small orchard alongside the Cameronians [5th Queen's Own Cameron Highlanders]. Our boys were led by Major [Donald Rolfe] Hunt and I accompanied them as signaller, carrying a rifle and ammunition, hand grenades, shovel and trenching tool with a small haversack on my back filled with emergency rations, a few personal possessions, small towel, hair brush and comb and my diary. I was wearing an overcoat owing to the rain. A and D companies led by Lieutenant-Colonel [Donald] MacLeod at the same time moved rapidly into

Delville Wood on our right. Our artillery had been brought forward and put up an intensive barrage on the enemy infantry advancing from Guillemont. Many of our field artillery fired with open sights and inflicted serious damage on the attacking infantry.

From this day onwards German gunners drenched Longueval, Delville Wood and the back areas with shells, almost obliterating the wood and reducing the houses in the village to rubble. Within 24 hours no wall of any house was higher than three feet. All of the hundreds of trees in the wood were reduced to a tangle of greenery and stumps. Not one tree was intact. The whole area was a shambles. Under this unbelievable rain of shells we had to clear paths and small communication trenches of rubble to bring up ammunition and what replacements we could find for the casualties. It was not possible to bring out the wounded for hours at a time, and then a lot of them were killed or wounded again on their way to the back lines.

In the wood itself the few men still surviving repulsed numerous counter-attacks of the enemy. Germans recaptured a small portion of the wood, but all of them were killed by the South Africans still standing and capable of firing a rifle or using a bayonet. For a time there was a shortage of hand grenades, but somehow or other supplies were brought through that hellish hail of shells ...

By this time we had become thoroughly fatalistic. So many of our pals had been killed or wounded, we simply carried on, half-dazed by the interminable shell fire, doing just what we had been trained to do. We lived mostly on our emergency rations and surprisingly enough a cup of hot tea brewed somewhere in the wood by our chaps. Only rarely was food or tea safely delivered from the rear. Many of the attempts to bring rations through ended in the carriers becoming casualties in that continuous rain of shells on what was left of the wood.

Lack of sleep, after hours of continuous action was beginning to take its toll. On the night of the 16th our platoon was relieved by a platoon of the 2nd Regiment. We staggered back to the support line behind Longueval, only to find the shelling there was nearly as intense as in the village and wood. Through it all, we did manage to get a hot meal from our field kitchens and a welcome cup of really hot tea, before collapsing to sleep for nearly six hours.[18]

On that Sunday evening a decision was made to have another go at the north-west corner of the wood the following morning. Orders were received to withdraw all the infantry in Longueval to a line south of Princes Street, and all the infantry in Delville Wood to an area east of the Strand, so that the north-west corner of the wood and the north end of Longueval could be bombarded. The bombardment would cease at 02:00 on Monday morning, 17 July. The 27th Brigade and two companies of the 1st South African Infantry Regiment would then once again attack the target they had gone for on the Sunday, and Lieutenant-Colonel Tanner would order the 2nd South Africans, by then holding the Strand, to move slowly forward to narrow the front of the 1sts attacking from Princes Street.

The attack was futile, as once again machine-gun fire from the enclosures blocked any advance from the west or south, with the Germans in force just inside the angle of the wood. The 2nd South Africans met fierce resistance and were forced to fall back to their original position.[19] Eventually, the 3rd Division, under Major-General Aylmer Haldane (an old friend of Winston Churchill from the Boer War days), replaced the depleted 27th Brigade.[20]

Betteridge recalled:

By the 17th July there were only three officers remaining in the wood. Lewis gunners in the front line lost 80 per cent of their men, but the remainder still inflicted serious damage on the numerous German troops who made repeated attacks, some of them in close formation when their ranks were decimated. It was evident that a handful of men holding higher ground had a great advantage over far greater numbers attacking over open ground. This day every available man was pressed into service. Batmen, headquarters sanitarymen even some of the cooks were given rifles and hand grenades to replace the large number of casualties. The few inexperienced new arrivals from Bordon had already been rushed up as replacements, many of them became casualties within hours of their first taste of war.

The previous night our boys had been able to erect a few strands of barbed wire in front of the trenches. This proved helpful when a Regiment of Prussian Guards attacked in daylight in massed formation from German trenches half a mile away. Gunners took a heavy toll of these massed troops. Our chaps fired incessantly into the bunched infantry. A handful managed to reach those few strands of wire before being killed. This was one of the most stupid attacks made by brave, determined soldiers. The valley was strewn with dead and dying men who had been repulsed by a handful of tired but resolute South African troops. It was clear illustration that the High Commands of both sides were willing to send their best troops to certain death in order to secure negligible results. In spite of their ferocity we had to admire those brave men who carried out orders without breaking line in their abortive attack.[21]

On the morning of Monday the 17th, Lukin visited Delville Wood to discuss the serious position with his commanding officers, all of whose troops had been in action for at least 48 hours. The South Africans had rarely had the opportunity to engage the enemy in close quarters – for the most part they had had to sit tight under a continuous barrage of machine-gun and artillery fire. Lukin was concerned about both the men's fatigue and 'the impossibility of making the wood anything but a death-trap'.[22] Back at Brigade Headquarters, he discussed the situation with Furse, but there was still no hope of relief or reinforcements, and General Congreve's orders stood: Delville must be held at any cost.

In the meantime, the suffering of the South African troops continued. Betteridge recorded:

Whenever possible, troops frantically dug their shallow trenches deeper to avoid the deadly shrapnel shells. Cries for stretcher bearers were heard from every quarter, but these Red Cross men had also sustained serious casualties. Most of the seriously wounded lay unattended for several hours. Quite a number of slightly wounded men stayed in the wood helping the dwindling number of their pals still firing at those persistent Germans, or assisting Machine Gunners reload their hot guns. Some of the less seriously wounded men did a good job of work trying to assist those unable to move. Lots of the latter simply lay where they were hit and fell asleep from exhaustion.[23]

There was still no change later that afternoon. If anything, the situation had worsened. On a forward mission to gain information, the brigade intelligence officer, Lieutenant Percy Roseby, was mortally wounded, and during the evening Tanner was wounded too. Tanner was replaced by Lieutenant-Colonel Thackeray of the 3rd South Africans.

News arrived that the 9th Division was drawing in its left flank, and that the 3rd Division, under Haldane, was to attack Longueval that night from the west.

At about 19:30, Lukin received orders to take the German trench parallel to and about 180 metres distant from the south-east edge of the wood before the next dawn. Two companies of the 3rd South Africans held the perimeter of the wood facing this trench. Their commanding officer reported that the enemy trench before them was strongly manned with several machine guns, and added that he could not furnish more than 200 men for the attack without endangering the whole position. Consequently, Furse cancelled the proposed operation.

At 22:30 that evening, Headquarters informed Lukin that as soon as the 3rd Division under Haldane had completed the occupation of the village, they would establish machine-gun posts on the north-west edge of the wood to protect his men. The attack was to take place the following morning at 05:45 and was to advance as far east as the Strand. In preparation, during the night all available reinforcements were moved up to the perimeter of the wood.

In the southern part of the wood, the Germans advanced as far as Buchanan and Princes streets, driving the South Africans out of some of their new trenches. The ground was cleared in a counterattack, but at the cost of heavy casualties. At 03:45 on 18 July, the 76th Brigade of the 3rd

Division obtained a footing in the orchard between Flers Road and North Street. At 08:00, Thackeray was ordered to send up patrols to get in touch with the 76th Brigade. For this purpose, D Company of the 1st Regiment, which was then occupying the Strand and the western part of Princes Street, was instructed to move forward. Facing no strong opposition from the Germans, they joined the 1st Gordons just west of the orchard.

D Company's arrival at the edge of the wood was the signal for the Germans to open a terrific bombardment, with them shelling every part of the area, but most intensively around the perimeter of the wood and down the Strand. The company's commander, Major Edward Burges, was wounded and shortly afterwards killed. At the same time, the 76th Brigade was driven in and the Germans began to enter the wood on the South Africans' exposed left flank. At around 09:00, an officer and 50 other ranks arrived as reinforcements, and all through the morning the company held out as best they could, but weariness was taking its toll and their numbers were rapidly depleting.[24]

Recalling this period, Betteridge wrote:

> On the morning of the 18th, only 50 men of the 250 in B and C companies of the Scottish remained. They were mustered to join similarly depleted ranks of the 1st and 3rd SA Regiments holding the wood. Some stray Highlanders from other Regiments of the Division were ordered to accompany our boys. German shellfire again rose to an unbelievable peak and many of these chaps never reached the front line itself, where they were woefully required to strengthen the depleted ranks. At that time, on the evening of the 18th, there were no officers to give orders, the few N.C.O.'s still alive carried on half stupid from fatigue and lack of sleep. There were enough emergency rations collected from the haversacks of dead companions but hot meals and tea had not reached the wood for three days.
>
> During the whole of the battering not a single telephone line was kept intact from the front line to Battalion Headquarters. Every important demand for replacements, etc. had to be conveyed by runner. Only half of these messages reached their destination.[25]

The bombardment lasted for seven and a half hours, and at times the incidence of explosions was seven per second; 20 000 shells were fired in an area of less than two square kilometres. Frank Marillier (2nd Regiment, C Company), who had been sent to the northern perimeter of the wood as a Lewis gunner, recalled the day's events:

> We were holding the most advanced post in the wood. We did not realize that a couple of days earlier the survivors had been told to withdraw. In the circumstances this was understandable enough. The conditions were appalling. I have never known such shelling and how any of us lived is still a mystery.[26]

Private John Lawson of the 3rd Regiment vividly described the fight on the 18th, when the garrison was forced back to the south-west corner. That morning, Thackeray was holding the wood with nine and a half companies, about 1 500 men, but two days later he would have only 140.

> Our little party had to wait in their cramped position of tortured suspense till nearly 3 p.m. for the only relief we now looked for – the relief afforded by the excitement of desperate fighting against great odds. The enemy now launched an attack in overwhelming numbers, amid the continued roar of artillery. Once more they found us ready – a small party of utterly worn-out men, shaking off their sleep to stand up in the shallow trench.
>
>   As the Huns came on they were mowed down – every shot must have told. Our rifles smoked and became unbearably hot; but though the end seemed near, it was not yet. When the Huns wavered and broke, they were reinforced and came on again. We again prevailed, and drove them back. Only one Hun crossed our trench, to fall shot in the heart a few yards behind it. The lip of our trench told more plainly than words can how near they were to not failing. Beyond, in No Man's Land, we could do something to estimate the cost of their failure ... Exhaustion now did what shell-fire and counter-attacks had failed to do, and we collapsed in our trench, spent in body and at last worn out in spirit. The

task we had been set was too great for us. What happened during the next two hours or so I do not know. Numbed in all my senses, I gazed vacantly into space, feeling as if the whole thing had been a ghastly nightmare, out of which I was now only awaiting complete deliverance. From this state of coma I was awakened by a shell which exploded just over me, and instantaneously I passed into unconsciousness. When I regained consciousness a few minutes after, my first sensation was that of having been thoroughly refreshed by sleep. But on moving I found that the fight for me was over ... I tried to rouse my friend, who had fallen face downward beside me. Getting no response, lifted his head, calling upon him by name, but I could not arouse him. I then began with pain and difficulty to walk down the line. I found that the last two hours of shelling had done their work – only six remained alive in the trench. I aroused one sleeper, and told him I had been badly hit, and was going to try and walk out. He faced me for a second, and asked me what he was to do. I said there was nothing to do but carry on, as the orders of Saturday morning had not been countermanded. His brave 'Right-o!' were the last words I heard there – surely fitting words as the curtain fell for me.[27]

Nineteen-year-old Private Hallam Wills Sampson of the 3rd Regiment aptly conveyed the desperation of their situation in a letter to the *Cape Times* written from the City of London Red Cross Hospital on 9 August 1916:

It wasn't so much the taking of a position as holding it. You'd get a withering machine-gun and rifle fire when charging; but when you got the position, it was so well marked that they could drop shells right into it. Shrapnel, lyddite, high explosive, tear and gas shells. Jove! What I prayed for, and I think what we all prayed for, was an instantaneous death. The sufferings of the wounded round us quite unnerved me. I never for one moment expected to come out alive. And there we sat: no food nor water: nothing could get through: friends dying all round.[28]

On the afternoon of the 18th, Lukin advised Thackeray that he had been superseded as commander of the forces in Delville Wood:

> Col Dawson is being sent up on orders of Divisional Commander with the troops he can get together. He will take over command of our South African troops in the Wood. He has orders to arrange a systematic examination of our front line by officers and to report as soon as possible how it is held and the present positions of our machine- and Lewis guns. Please show this to Col Dawson when he arrives.[29]

The situation had become desperate. Dawson was ordered to take forward as reliefs all the men available under his command, a total of 150 from the 1st South Africans. They had just been withdrawn after seeing continuous action for four days without rest. Dawson positioned his men in a trench at the south-east corner of Longueval and then went into the wood to find Thackeray.

After 14:30, the rate of shelling decreased and Lieutenant Edward Phillips and 79 men of his South African Light Trench Mortar Company were sent from Montauban as infantrymen and placed at Dawson's disposal. Many military historians believe that Phillips's arrival in Delville Wood was instrumental in the success of the South African defence. Although severely wounded on the night of 18 July, Phillips remained at his post and was conspicuous in leading bombing counterattacks.[30]

Dawson found Thackeray in dire straits. In many parts of Delville Wood the garrisons had been utterly destroyed. Everywhere north of Princes Street, the few survivors had been forced back. Thackeray was holding only the south-west corner defined by Buchanan Street and the western part of Princes Street. The trenches were filled with wounded men, as it had become impossible to remove them because all the stretcher-bearers of the 3rd South Africans were casualties and no men could be spared to replace them. Dawson sent Phillips and his men to reinforce Thackeray, and through the division procured additional stretcher-bearers from the cavalry, in addition to those from the 1st Regiment.[31]

The following desperate communication from 3rd Regiment, A Company, was typical of the urgent requests for relief made by all companies. An early-evening message from the company commander, Lieutenant Owen Thomas, to Thackeray read:

> Delville Wood. Mr [Second-Lieutenant] Pearson has just been wounded and is proceeding back. I am now the only officer left in A. Coy. One Lewis Gun crew have been blown up. Can you send another crew? I have wounded men lying all along my front & have no stretchers left, and they are dying for want of treatment, my field dressings being all used up. Can you obtain stretcher bearers? Urgent. I consider the position is now untenable, and have had my breastworks all blown in. It is impossible to spare men to take wounded away, and my front is now very lightly held with many gaps. To save the balance of men it will be necessary to withdraw. Most of the men here are suffering from shell shock and I do not consider we are fit to hold the position in the event of an enemy attack.[32]

Later that night, Lukin reiterated the 9th Division order that Delville Wood had to be held at all costs. Their orders were to assist in every way to recover lost ground, and if the wood was retaken that night the 1st South African Infantry Brigade would be relieved by the 26th Brigade and the men withdrawn. By midnight the work had been partially carried out, and portions of the two companies of the 1st Regiment and the two companies of the 4th were withdrawn.

Private John Lawson recorded his impression of Delville Wood on the morning of Tuesday 18 July 1916:

> It was as if night for ever refused to give way to day. A drizzling rain was falling in an atmosphere unstirred by a breath of wind. Smoke and gases clung to and polluted the air, making a canopy impervious to light. What a contrast was this Tuesday morning to the morning of the previous Saturday, when we first entered what was then a beautiful sylvan scene, but now everywhere a dreary waste![33]

The Germans had pushed up a new division, the 8th of the IV (Magdeburg) Corps, which made repeated attacks against the Buchanan Street line, and for two days and two nights the few men under Thackeray held the south-west corner of the wood. The German attack involved pushing forward bombers and snipers, then advancing in massed formation from the north, north-east and north-west simultaneously. These attacks were repelled with heavy losses, but in the last assault the South Africans were bombarded from three sides. After his adjutant, Captain Albert McDonald, had been wounded, Thackeray was left with only two officers, Lieutenant Garnet Green of the 2nd Regiment and Lieutenant Phillips of the 3rd. Both were wounded but at least able to stay on their feet.[34]

Despite the odds, the men fought gallantly. Thackeray, for his part, twice saved Captain Claude Browne of the 4th South Africans. On the 18th, Browne was lying out in the open, exposed to sniper fire, when Thackeray pulled him to safety. The following day, Browne was again lying in the open, this time on a mound of earth at the back of a trench. He was covered with earth after shells had fallen next to him. Once again Thackeray pulled him to safety. Thackeray was wounded six times and knocked over three times by artillery fire and bombs during their last stand in the wood.[35]

Field-ambulance records reveal the dedication and gallantry of another brave man, Captain M.B. Lawrie, who had established a regimental aid post in Longueval. With the shelling of Longueval on 18 July, Lawrie had found it quite impossible to move all the stretcher cases, and so decided to remain behind in his station. He barricaded the windows and doors with mattresses, furniture and anything else that might stop a bullet. For about nine hours, shells poured into the village, but somehow the regimental aid post did not get a direct hit. Dressing the wounded was carried out under great difficulty, as only a small electric torch or candle could be used. In the background, Captain E. Hill managed to keep up a constant supply of tea and coffee.[36]

All through the days of 19 and 20 July, the desperate handful of South Africans endured incessant shelling and sniping. The sniping now came from much closer quarters, and still no relief came. Early morning on the 19th, Lukin replied to one of Thackeray's requests for relief:

> Your report timed 3.50 am received at 5.10. DLI [Durham Light Infantry] was NOT to relieve units in line. There is another Brigade relieving. It has gone up and should be there now. Whether it will be possible for it to carry out the relief before clearing the enemy out of the Wood – which it has orders to do – is uncertain.[37]

In the south-east corner of Delville Wood, the Germans commenced their advance at 06:00 on the morning of 19 July. Their force comprised elements of the 153rd Infantry Reserve Regiment and two companies of the 52nd Infantry Reserve Regiment. Upon reaching the southern perimeter, they swung left and attacked B Company of the 3rd South African Infantry Regiment, eventually overrunning the position. Captain Richard Medlicott recalled the dramatic events that led to his capture and that of the survivors of B Company:

> Dawn 19th. Exhausted machine-gun ammunition. Drove off attack from wood but had to chuck it [surrender] soon after 8 am. Many of our buried were exhumed by our heavy artillery which hindered us at the wrong moment – at my trench east of wood. Damn those artillery garrisons. Handed back, sorry to say, all German prisoners captured during the day. I got not a wink of sleep for four nights. Could not sleep on the night of the 18th. Got Lieuts Guard and Thomas in a safe place (both wounded) with German prisoners – Irony. I was satisfied at our marksmanship, so many dead Germans round us in the wood. Notes: Germans useless as rifle shots, bar trained snipers, at over 300 yards. Their bombers trained to throw. [They] do not fancy coming on with bayonet, even knowing we had run out of ammunition. I could judge by their eyes. I was too busy waiting for the moment of attack which was maturing during the day.
>   The enemy shell fire was chiefly 5.9. Too intense to think of retiring. If [only the] other troops had avoided text-book rot, i.e. entrenching 15–30 yards inside the wood. I had entrenched deep and narrow, bang up flush with the edge of the wood. We could have withstood that attack which drove in [our] right and left flanks. This is the opinion of all officers with me.

The Germans were rattled with our gun fire. Our men, who at that time owing to want of water and sleep were cold and stiff, were calm and had a 'don't's care a damn' appearance. Many Germans wanted to surrender but were afraid owing to a watch kept on them by comrades and machine-guns turned on them.[38]

Private Victor Wepener was one of the B Company survivors taken prisoner. Wepener was a signaller in the company and also a runner in Lieutenant Guard's platoon. He had two brothers serving with him in Delville Wood, Eric and Horace, while another brother, John, served as a corporal in the 9th Lancers. Both Eric and Horace were wounded in Delville Wood and evacuated. Wepener recalled:

> The 2nd (Natal) Regiment were decimated and left a large gap on our left flank. The Germans eventually came through there. Capt Medlicott's headquarters was in the front line, not in the rear as is usual. We were shelled from all sides. At times men were killed next to me while I was talking to them. Though I always had ammunition, the rain and mud got into our rifle bolts and caused them to jam. Our RSM, incidentally, was killed in the fighting.[39]
>
> When the Germans eventually overran us, I was impressed by a very aristocratic officer who wore a cap instead of a steel helmet. He kept his hand over his pistol holster whilst we 'remnants' were being collected in an open glade. A German soldier with a bandaged head and his rifle and bayonet slung over his shoulder called me 'Kamerad' (comrade). I didn't quite know what to say as I didn't fancy being his comrade. The German soldiers on average were jolly good chaps ... I then helped carry Lieut Guard who had been shot in the leg. Some of the wounded had to be left behind. I was one of the few to escape unscathed. We were then marched through their lines and we saw many Germans lying there waiting to attack. A couple of our chaps carried a German with a stomach wound on a groundsheet. Our artillery opened up and we were amused to see our guards ducking away and running for cover. After what we had been through we didn't worry about shellbursts anymore.[40]

From the south-west corner of Delville Wood, Captain Stephen Liebson, the medical officer of the 3rd Regiment, sent an urgent message to Thackeray: 'Am still at Dressing Station, left centre village. Very few of our brigade wounded come here now, chiefly Durhams, Norfolks, Camerons, Black Watch. Germans advanced to my dressing station yesterday. Heard and I got Naseby [Naisby] away safe. Please send word of relief.'[41]

On the southern perimeter, 2nd Regiment, C Company, was still holding its position. The acting command sergeant-major, James MacAulley Thomson, sent a message to Thackeray: 'As Lt Green [Second-Lieutenant Garnet George Green] was wounded yesterday I am in charge of C Coy 2nd Regt. We are holding our original position [on South Street] with 15 men, one Lewis gun. Are there any rations to draw? Or any orders further than hold tight.'[42]

Encouraged to hear that there were still others grimly holding on, Thackeray replied:

> Thanks for note. Am only officer left as far as I know in forward line since yesterday afternoon. Like you am just about finished but thank God our fellows here have all held on to the finish. They have had a terrible time and the big majority have gone under. Am hoping relief today early – will let you know when we move Brigade HQ. You have done splendidly together with the rest of the Reg and I hope I may see you today. Am informing Bn HQ about your position and relief.[43]

Thackeray's desperation and frustration with their situation are clear from his message to regiment headquarters at around 13:15 on 19 July:

> Our heavy artillery shelled our Buchanan trench some two hours and ground on either side east and west – injured several [of] our men and buried several. This in addition to enemy's fire which already killed two officers Lt Bell and Connock [Second-Lieutenants C.S. Bell and Joseph G. Connock, both killed on 18 July] and many men ... five days continuous work and fighting is becoming beyond endurance and as I have now only Lt Phillips [Lieutenant E.J. Phillips] and one or two

NCOs I do not feel that we can hope to hold the trench in the face of any determined attack. The enemy attacked last night and this morning snipers and artillery casualties are continuing. I cannot evacuate my critically wounded or bury my dead on account of snipers. Four men have been hit helping one casualty. If the wounded cannot be moved, could not some medical assistance be sent up. My MO [medical officer] is far too busy at station and is completely exhausted. Will you manage his relief together with ours as soon as possible. There is some hold up re our relief as OC 19th DLI [officer commanding of the 19th Battalion, Durham Light Infantry] did not get any direct orders but [was informed] that 19th would be relieving. They have now gone forward East and I don't think they will be available. This relief is most important in view of enemy's close proximity, some 100 yards … They snipe continually and have MG [machine guns] both on west and east. I think they have hidden dugouts. So far the SAI [South African Infantry Brigade] have held on but I feel the strain is becoming too much so trust some special effort may be made. The stretcher bearers who came last night only moved our wounded men and left Capt Browne [Captain Claude Melville Browne], 4th Regt when Lt Style [Lieutenant S.W.E. Style] was hit in neck. There is a gap between my left on Princes St and the Village. Artillery observation from here is a farce.[44]

At 01:00 on the morning of 20 July, Thackeray sent a desperate message to Lukin:

Urgent. My men are on their last legs. I cannot keep some of them awake. They drop with their rifles in hand asleep in spite of heavy shelling. We are expecting an attack. Even that cannot keep some of them from dropping down. Food and water has not reached us for two days – though we have managed on rations of those killed … but must have water. I am alone with Phillips who is wounded and only a couple of Sgts. Please relieve these men today without fail as I fear they have come to the end of their endurance.[45]

Finally, at 18:00 that evening, the 76th Brigade of the 3rd Division was able to take over what was left of Longueval and the little segment of Delville Wood. Thackeray marched out of the wood with only two officers – Lieutenants Edward Phillips and Garnet Green – both of whom were wounded, and 140 other ranks, made up of details from all the regiments of the brigade. Lieutenant Green was right at the rear and the last South African to leave the wood. Thackeray spent the night at Talus Boise and joined the rest at Happy Valley the following day.[46]

One of the last four soldiers to walk out of Delville Wood was Frank Marillier of 2nd Regiment, C Company, who recorded his impressions of that final day, including the efforts of the Royal Welch Fusiliers to relieve the South Africans:

> Heavy hand to hand fighting still continues. SA boys, though only a handful left, still hold enemy back. Royal Welsh Fusiliers [*sic*] retire … Col Thackeray splendid. Orders them to return and hold the line or he would shoot [i.e. those who retired].
>
> We have been without rations and water for two and a half days and no sleep for six days and nights … after getting a good way back from the battle we number off and find only 52 of 2nd Regt have come out whole and all other SA Regts about the same. Col Thackeray thanks us and tells how very valuable our services have been in a few words … Oh! It's been a terrible week and it is to be marvelled at that anyone at all came out safe and sound. Thanks to God for my safe return.[47]

William Thorne served with the 4th Regiment in Delville Wood and was only 19 at the time of the battle. Decades later he reminisced about the events of 14 to 20 July 1916:

> A lot has been written about the Battle of Delville Wood, and a lot will still be written, but no pen can ever properly describe the bloodbath of those seven days. The heavy smell of blood filled the air, and every moment you had this intense fear that the next bullet was meant

for you. The real hell broke loose on 17 July when the Germans directed their bombardment at us, the South Africans. For some eight hours the shells rained upon us at a rate of 400 per minute. To make things worse, the British artillery that had to provide cover for us, were very inaccurate and many of the shells landed amongst us and caused havoc. A third of our men died on the 18th July, as the nine divisions of the Germans, regarded as the cream of the German Army, attacked throughout the night. In between, the sweet, disgusting smell of gas drifted upon us like a slight drizzle of rain. Most of us were young men and it had been our first experience of gas. Our equipment was quite primitive and it was a struggle to get the gas masks off our faces again.

The Germans and us were so close to each other in the wood that at times we fought with bare fists. Heaven knows where we got the strength and courage from to move forward yard by yard. Perhaps it was because it had been drilled into us beforehand that the honour of the South African soldier was at stake here. On the 20th July we stumbled from the wood. I stopped and looked back at Delville Wood. Of the forest only one tree remained. I thought of my comrades of whom some were so mutilated that they couldn't be recognised. Big men around me started sobbing bitterly.[48]

Walter Giddy's diary entries between 17 and 20 July also described the horror:

The Huns started shelling us, and it was just murder from then until 2 o'clock of the afternoon of the 18th, when we got the order to get out as best you can. I came out with Corporal Farrow, but how we managed it, goodness knows, men lying all over shattered to pieces, by shell fire, and the wood was raked by machine guns and rifle fire. Major McLeod of the Scottish was splendid. I have never seen a pluckier man, he tried his level best to get as many out as possible. We fell back to the valley below, and formed up again. I came on to camp and was ordered by the Doctor to remain here, having a slight attack of shell shock. I believe the 9th took the wood again, and were immediately relieved, but the lads are turning up again in camp, the few lucky ones. If it was not for a hole in my steel helmet, and a bruise on the tip, I would think it was an awful nightmare ... The lads stuck it well, but the wood was absolutely flattened, no human being could live in it.

Major McLeod was wounded, and I gave him a hand to get out, but he would have I was to push on, as I would be killed. Many a silent prayer did I send up, for strength to bring me through safely. I found a Sergeant of the 1st all of a shake, suffering from shell shock, so I took his arm and managed to get him to the dressing station. Just shaken hands with my old pal John Forbes. He is wounded in the arm and is off to Blighty. I quite envy him.

A sad day of S.A. ... They say we made a name for ourselves but at what a cost. All the 9th are resting on a hillside. Small parties of 25 to 40 men form the companies, which were 200 strong a short two weeks ago. We have taken back several miles.[49]

Lance-Corporal Frederick Charles Lee[50] was the only surviving NCO in the 3rd Regiment, C Company. In an emotional letter to his mother on 21 July, Lee captured the utter desperation and weariness of the survivors. He described the suffering of a close friend, Angus Brown, who died of his wounds. Lee was unable to stay with him until the end because he had to go back to the front line, 'where we were being hard pressed ... I've had a real good cry, I couldn't help it.'[51] Lee wrote:

When we got the order to get back to a certain rallying place, all we could muster of our company was 29. Out the fine S.A. Brigade that went into action about 4,000 strong only approximately 300 are left. Of course quite a lot are wounded. We have no officers left, Captain Jackson and Captain MacLachlan[52] and two Lieutenants killed, and the other two wounded. Not one officer of the 3rd Regiment has arrived so far. I'm the only NCO in C Company who went into action left, and I'm only a Lance-Corporal and action O.C. C Company. Now you can try and judge what we have gone through, and all just for a small wood.

You know what a wood looks like when the trees are in bloom –

well, that is what it was like when we first drove them out. Since then they have continually bombarded it with hundreds and hundreds of guns, until now it is just like one or two poles stuck in the ground.

Yesterday they gave us ten solid hours bombardment with guns of all sizes and kinds – tear shells, gas shells, etc, and some Jack Johnsons[53] that threw you thirty yards away when they landed near you. How I'm alive, mother, I can't say, and I am – I'm not ashamed to say it – one of many that prayed to get shot, absolutely worn out, nothing to eat or drink for two days, thanks to the enemy curtain fire, and no sleep for a week. I'm going to turn in very soon for a well earned rest. I haven't had a wash or a shave for three weeks, and my face is drawn so that I'll wager that I could stand in front of you for inspection and you would not know me.[54]

Private Johann Otto of St James, Cape Town, served in the 1st Regiment and was wounded on 18 July. In a letter to his mother, he described the 'continual dungeon of smoke' in which they found themselves, and how they fought until weariness overtook them:

Some of our boys were so tired they stood sound asleep with their rifles at the shoulder. The enemy made many fierce rushes, and at one time we were shooting them at a range of ten to fifteen yards ... How I got through everything untouched will always be a miracle to me.

Half dazed by shell-fire and enraged at seeing your pals lying motionless around you, you simply carry on with murder in your heart, and I now realise the truth about men going half mad when in the thick of the fight ...[55]

It was not just the Allied troops who were deeply affected by what they saw. In his diary, one German officer described the horrible scene after the perimeter had been taken: 'The wood was a wasteland of shattered trees, charred and burning stumps, craters thick with mud and blood, and corpses, everywhere. In places they were piled four deep. Worst of all was the lowing of the wounded. It sounded like a cattle ring at the spring fair.'[56]

In the aftermath of the battle, General Lukin expressed his sincere gratitude to the men of the South African brigade.

> General Lukin had us gathered round him, and thanked us for the splendid way in which we fought in Delville and Bernafay Woods. He said we got orders to take and hold the woods, at all costs, and we did for four days and four nights, and when told to fall back on the trench, we did it in a soldier like way. He knew his boys would, and he was prouder of us now, than even before, if he possibly could be, as he always was proud of South Africans. All he regretted was the great loss of gallant comrades, and thanked us from the bottom of his heart for what we had done.[57]

And in a later report to Lukin, Thackeray concluded by expressing his own pride in his troops:

> I am glad to report that the troops under my command carried out your instructions to hold Delville Wood at all costs and that not a single detachment of this regiment retired from their position, either on the perimeter of the Wood or from the support trenches.
> I regret they were not strong enough to drive back the enemy on the perimeter, where they were all wiped out, but trust that by holding the support trenches in Princes and Buchanan Streets with the aid of the few men left of the 1st, 2nd and 4th Regiments and TMC [Trench Mortar Company], our losses were not in vain.[58]

For the 1st South African Infantry Brigade, the battle for Delville Wood cost a great many lives. At midnight on 14 July, when Lukin had received his orders, the brigade had numbered 121 officers and 3 032 men. A week later, when Thackeray finally marched out of the wood on 20 July, 143 men remained. The total number ultimately assembled in Happy Valley was about 750. Of the officers, 23 were killed and seven died later of their wounds, 47 were wounded and 15 were taken prisoner or missing. All the commissioned ranks of the 2nd and 3rd regiments who were in the wood became casualties, as did all the officers of the 28th Brigade Machine Gun Company attached to the brigade. Casualties numbered 558 for the 1st Regiment, 482 for the 2nd, 771 for the 3rd and 509 for the 4th. In total, from 1 July, there were 2 815 casualties, of which 502 were killed, 1 735 were wounded and 578 were listed as missing.[59]

Among all the death and destruction, there were the occasional glimpses of light. Robert Grimsdell, wounded on 16 July and left for dead, later managed to crawl from shell-hole to shell-hole, with shrapnel in his neck and a bullet in one leg, until he finally found a dressing station. After the war, a moustachioed and slightly heavier Grimsdell looked up an old comrade at the Johannesburg Municipality, Foreman Carpenter. When he introduced himself as Bob Grimsdell, Carpenter replied, 'Now look, I'm sick and tired of you bums coming with the old soldier trick and trying to make an easy quid, you just fuck off before I throw you out – it happens that I was next to Bob Grimsdell when he was killed at Delville.' So Grimsdell left. From then on it became a family joke. When someone asked, 'Were you in Delville Wood?' Grimsdell would reply, 'Yes, I was killed there.' A fine golfer, Grimsdell finished runner-up in the 1932 South African Open and later served as a club professional, first at Metropolitan in Cape Town and then at Royal Johannesburg, before becoming a well-known golf-course designer.[60]

Delville Wood was finally taken on 25 August 1916, when the 14th (Light) Division cleared it for good, despite the Germans sending their best troops against them: successively, the 10th Bavarian Infantry Division, the 8th Division of the IV Corps and the 5th Division of the III Corps.

In *The History of the South African Forces in France*, John Buchan summed up well the magnitude of the events of Delville Wood when he wrote,

> The six days and five nights during which the South African Brigade held the most difficult post on the British front – a corner of death on which the enemy fire was concentrated at all hours from three sides, and into which fresh German troops, vastly superior in numbers to

the defence, made periodic incursions only to be broken and driven back – constitute an epoch of terror and glory scarcely equalled in the campaign. There were positions as difficult, but they were not held so long; there were cases of as protracted a defence, but the assault was not so violent and continuous. The closest parallel is to be found, perhaps, in some of the incidents at Verdun, and in the resistance of units of the old British regulars at the point of the Ypres salient in 1914; but even there we shall scarcely find an equal feat of tenacity, and certainly none superior.[61]

Sir Henry Rawlinson, the commander of the Fourth Army, wrote that 'in the capture of Delville Wood the gallantry, perseverance, and determination of the South African Brigade deserves the highest commendation'.[62]

Underscoring these words, Lieutenant-Colonel Tanner's final report read:

Each individual was firm in the knowledge of his confidence in his comrades, and was, therefore, able to fight with that power which good discipline alone can produce. A finer record of this spirit could not be found than the line of silent bodies along the Strand over which the enemy had not dared to tread.[63]

In spite of the praise that the deeds of Delville Wood elicited, military historian Ian Uys – arguably the most knowledgeable South African historian on the subject – highlights their futility:

It is virtually the unanimous opinion of military authorities that the losses incurred by the South African Infantry Brigade at Delville Wood were indeed in vain. The most costly defence of the Wood served no strategic purpose whatsoever (Neither; indeed, did the overall Somme offensive, of which Delville Wood formed but a part).[64]

The men on the ground were perhaps the first to realise the pointless nature of the offensive in which they were fighting and dying:

Delville Wood is a name, even now, full of sadness and the suppressed agony of thousands who had to make its acquaintance. Probably nearly as many men remained in it as came out of it whole, and no one fortunate to escape from this hell can think of it without recalling hours of suffering and the names of many good comrades now no more. Towards the end of September 1916 there seemed to be a lull in the Battle of the Somme. The glory of the first great achievements had somewhat faded with the realization of their cost and the doubtful value of their gains. One supposed that the High Command knew what they were doing, though even that is doubtful now. Most of us hoped that the lull meant a discontinuance of the battle, which seemed a hopeless hammering at a resourceful enemy in one of his strongest sectors. It was, however, not for us to argue why the strong rather than the weak positions were always to be attacked.[65]

This was the lament of Captain S.J. Worsley, a member of the North Staffordshire Regiment, who served in France until the end of September 1918, when he was wounded by a bullet through both lungs during an advance around Hill 60 and the Bluff, near Ypres.

5

Life in the trenches

THE FIRST WORLD WAR was expected to be relatively short, and a war of great movement, but instead it was characterised by years of stalemate exemplified by happenings on the Western Front between the northern-hemisphere autumn of 1914 and the spring of 1918.

The opening salvos of the war had been dramatic, as the German Army swept through Belgium and France en route to Paris, but trench warfare soon set in and the war stalled, neither side being able to gain the advantage.

For those thousands of men eager to get to the front, what they found was not what they had expected. Victor Packer, a member of the Royal Irish Fusiliers, for one, was quickly disillusioned:

> I had heard about the previous battles but I couldn't get there fast enough. We had been brought up on the history of the Boer War and patriotism and heroics and everything, and we thought the war was going to be over before we could get there. However, in about half a minute all that had gone. I wondered what the devil I'd got into because it was nothing but mud and filth and all the chaps who were already there, well, they looked like tramps, all plastered with filth and dirt, and unshaven.[1]

The families back home also had little idea of what their sons had to endure. As Private Norman Demuth of the 1/5th Battalion London Regiment commented:

> They didn't know – how could they? They knew that people came back on leave covered with mud and lice, but they had no idea of what

kind of danger we were in. I think they felt the war was one continual sort of cavalry charge; that one spent all day and night chasing Germans or them chasing us. Had they realised the strain of sitting in a trench and waiting for something to drop on one's head, I don't think they would have considered it was just play.[2]

Someone who did know what was happening out there was Winston Churchill, then a battalion commander on the Western Front. On 23 May 1916, he told fellow members in the House of Commons:

I say to myself every day, what is going on while we sit here, while we go away to dinner or home to bed? Nearly a thousand men – Englishmen, Britishers, men of our race – are knocked into bundles of bloody rags every twenty-four hours, and carried away to hasty graves or to field ambulances.[3]

English writer J.R.R. Tolkien, best known for the classic fantasies *The Hobbit* and *The Lord of the Rings*, lived through months on the Somme, and summed up his experiences in the trenches as 'animal horror'. In a BBC programme many years later, his daughter surmised that the Dead Marshes in *The Lord of the Rings* were in fact based on the battlefield in Flanders, a deadly mud swamp in which numerous soldiers had drowned in water-filled shell-holes.[4]

Decades later, in the introduction to the second edition of *The Lord of the Rings*, Tolkien wrote: 'It seems now often forgotten that to be caught by youth in 1914 was no less hideous an experience than to be involved in 1939 and the following years. By 1918 all but one of my close friends were dead.'[5]

Few works in the South African World War I historiography deal with the experiences of the South African troops on the front and there is no comprehensive work on the social history of these soldiers. The best understanding we have of the few joys and much suffering endured by the men on the Somme can be gleaned from looking at their day-to-day

LIFE IN THE TRENCHES

experiences and activities in and around the trenches in which they 'lived'. From their accounts of trench life, we can answer questions such as: What were the conditions like? How did the constant shelling and the deaths of comrades affect them? What did they eat? What did they wear? What did they have to carry? What did they do apart from shooting at the enemy and hiding from the shells that rained down on them? What happened to the wounded? What happened to the dead?

Life in the trenches for the soldiers of the British Expeditionary Force, which included the South Africans, was cyclical. Typically, a regiment would be expected to serve a spell on the front line, followed by a stint in support, and then on the reserve lines, after which a normally short period of rest would follow – before the whole cycle would start all over again. These cycles were determined by the necessities of the situation. Even in a period of rest, men could find themselves busy with duties that placed them in the firing line; others could spend far longer on the front line than usual, depending on the degree of battle.

John Masefield, who served briefly as a hospital orderly in a British hospital for French soldiers in France in 1915, described troops making their way into the trenches on the Somme for the first time:

> Near the lines they had to leave the roads for the shelter of some communication trench or deep cut in the mud, revetted at the sides with wire to hinder it from collapsing inwards. By these deep narrow roads, only broad enough for marching in single file, our men passed to 'the front', to the line itself. Here and there, in recesses in the trench, under roofs of corrugated iron covered with sandbags, they passed the offices and the stores of war, telephonists, battalion headquarters, dumps of bombs, barbed wire, rockets, lights, machine-gun ammunition, tins, jars, and cases. Many men, passing these things as they went 'in' for the first time, felt with a sinking of the heart, that they were leaving all ordered and arranged things, perhaps forever.[6]

Writing to his mother from the Somme, Australian private John Alexander Raws described the trenches:

> The fortification consists of breastworks, built up high to the front, with just a little shallow trench dug behind. The reason is that drainage is so difficult. These breastworks are made of millions of tightly-made sand-bags laid one upon the other, packed well together. Every eight yards there is an island traverse, a great mound of earth and sand-bags strengthened by rivetting [sic], round which the trench winds. This is to localise the explosion of shells or prevent an enemy who might reach the flank being able to pour fire right down the length of the trench. There are communication trenches back every few yards and innumerable succeeding lines for the main army. The whole network extends in most places for three or four miles. The dug-outs are all in lines, but mostly along the communication trenches.
>
> When there is no excitement there are about two sentries to every sector of say 9 yards on watch, and one officer for the company. The rest are in the dugouts. When a bombardment comes or there is a gas alarm, everyone rushes out and takes what cover one can in the front trench, awaiting developments. Against the front breastwork we have a step, about two feet high, upon which men stand to shoot. When there is a bombardment nearly everyone gets under this step, close in against the side.[7]

The daily routine in the trenches began with the morning 'stand to', when, an hour before dawn, everyone was woken up by the company orderly officer and sergeant to climb up on the fire step with their bayonets fixed to guard against a dawn raid by the enemy. The Germans also followed this practice, so both sides were prepared for a dawn attack. Then, as it got lighter, both would relieve the tension of the early hours with machine-gun fire, shelling and small-arms fire directed into the mist in front of them. This action was called 'the morning hate'.

Some men would then be assigned to sentry duty on the fire step for up to two hours, while the others would get on with the daily chores. These included refilling sandbags, repairing duckboards on the trench floor and draining the trenches. With the front line constantly under surveillance by snipers and lookouts during the day, movement was restricted until nightfall, when the men were free to read and write letters home. Often patrols would be sent out into no-man's-land, the area between the opposing trenches, to repair or add barbed wire to the front line. When enemy patrols met face to face in no-man's-land it became a matter of hurrying on their separate ways or engaging in hand-to-hand fighting.

Masefield continued:

Much of the relief and munitioning of the fighting lines was done at night. Men going into the lines saw little of where they were going. They entered the gash of the communication trench, following the load on the back of the man in front, but seeing perhaps nothing but the shape in front, the black walls of the trench, and now and then some gleam of a star in the water under foot. Sometimes as they marched they would see the starshells, going up and bursting like rockets, and coming down with a wavering slow settling motion, as white and bright as burning magnesium wire, shedding a kind of dust of light upon the trench and making the blackness intense when they went out. These lights, the glimmer in the sky from the enemy's guns, and now and then the flash of a shell, were the things seen by most of our men on their first going in.

In the fire trench they saw little more than the parapet. If work were being done in the No Man's Land, they still saw little save by these lights that floated and fell from the enemy and from ourselves. They could see only an array of stakes tangled with wire, and something distant and dark which might be similar stakes, or bushes, or men, in front of what could only be the enemy line. When the night passed, and those working outside the trench had to take shelter, they could see nothing, even at a loophole or periscope, but the greenish strip of ground, pitted with shell-holes and fenced with wire, running up to the enemy line. There was little else for them to see, looking to the front, for miles and miles, up hill and down dale.

The soldiers who held this old front line of ours saw this grass and wire day after day, perhaps, for many months. It was the limit of their world, the horizon of their landscape, the boundary. What interest there was in their life was the speculation, what lay beyond that wire, and what the enemy was doing there. They seldom saw an enemy. They heard his songs and they were stricken by his missiles, but seldom saw more than, perhaps, a swiftly moving cap at a gap in the broken parapet, or a grey figure flitting from the light of a starshell.[8]

To make matters worse, the man in the trench had quite a weight to carry. The kit of the South African soldier at Delville Wood weighed between 26.3 and 36.3 kilograms, and included weapons (rifle, bayonet, bombs, grenades) and ammunition, a shrapnel helmet, two tube helmets, smoke candles (to discharge smoke to conceal the movement of troops), an overcoat, a haversack (filled with rations, personal extras, knife, oil tin, cap comforter), a waterproof sheet, a water bottle, field dressings, iodine, various tools for digging the trenches (entrenching tools, sandbags, pick, shovel, wire cutters, wire) and, in case of a gas attack, a gas mask.

As can be imagined, this heavy load made climbing over parapets during assaults on enemy trenches especially difficult. And when the weather was bad, like it was during the assault on Longueval and Delville Wood, when the ground was covered in mud and the rain made it more slippery, the weighed-down soldier battled even more.[9]

The soldiers' diet consisted of bully beef (tinned corned beef), dog biscuits (the popular name for hard army biscuits), preserved meat, jam and Oxo stock cubes. Tinned sardines were popular, but considered something of a delicacy. Liquid rations consisted of water and sometimes rum or tea. Each platoon received two cans of water. This was kept in water bottles, which the soldiers carried with them. Tobacco was also included in the soldiers' rations.[10]

Some troops were tasked with serving as couriers, or runners, who brought food and ammunition to their comrades on the front line. This was a dangerous business, as they were exposed to enemy fire and shelling. As a result, many of these brave men became casualties. On 16 July 1916 at Delville Wood, Lieutenant Francis Somerset of the 3rd South Africans disregarded the danger in the wood by carrying rations, water and letters to his men on the front line.[11]

As it was often impossible for even the bravest to deliver rations, and when their emergency rations in their haversacks ran out, the men had to improvise. Four privates of 1 South African Medical Corps, carrying wounded men from Longueval to Bernafay Wood, kept their stomachs full by eating bits of biscuit that they found on dead soldiers. Private Betteridge of the 4th South Africans recorded that during the fighting on 18 July at Delville Wood, the South Africans supplemented their food rations by collecting bully beef and dog biscuits from their fallen comrades' haversacks.[12] Private Lawson of the 3rd South Africans told a similar tale: on the same day a fellow soldier named Breytenbach collected food and water from dead soldiers to give to his comrades.[13]

The weary and hungry men who were relieved in Delville Wood had the privilege of a hot meal of boiled eggs and a cup of tea from the field kitchen. Tea was popular and was brewed in Delville Wood even during fierce fighting. It was sometimes given to the wounded and those suffering from shell-shock, while the able-bodied men received rum to keep them warm.[14]

Physical wounds from gunfire, shrapnel and gas were just the beginning. The emotional and psychological trauma caused by the never-ending threat and presence of death was equally debilitating.

Death was a constant companion in the trenches. It was in the bodies of dead comrades, in the shells raining down from the sky, in the bullets of the German snipers. It made life unbearable for many of the soldiers, and, inevitably, a number just 'cracked'. In a letter to his brother from north of Pozières on the Somme in August, Private John Raws wrote:

> It was impossible to help the wounded at all in some sectors. We could fetch them in [to the trenches], but could not get them away. And often we had to put them out on the parapet to permit movement in the shallow, narrow, crooked trenches. The dead were everywhere. There had been no burying in the sector I was in for a week before we went there.
>
> The strain – you say you hope it has not been too great for me – was really bad ... many other fine men broke to pieces. Everyone called

it shell shock. But shell shock is very rare ... I felt fearful that my nerve was going at the very last morning. I had been going – with far more responsibility than was right for one so inexperienced – for two days and two nights, for hours without another officer even to consult and with my men utterly broken, shelled to pieces ... We lived with all this for eleven days, ate and drank and fought amid it; but no, we did not sleep. Sometimes, we just fell down and became unconscious. You could not call it sleep.[15]

Less than two weeks later, Raws was killed along with three privates when a shell burst near them. It was said that his body showed no injuries, and a friend concluded, 'so probably he died from shock instantaneously'.[16]

Many soldiers suffered from shell-shock, a condition today known as post-traumatic stress disorder. Symptoms include fatigue (neurasthenia), nervousness, instability, depression, emotional numbing and nightmares. Private Simpson of the 4th South Africans said that 'a fellow with shell-shock is just like a frightened child, trembles violently, weeps, and requires someone to take charge of him'.[17] Lance-Corporal George W. Warwick, from the same regiment, described how one shell-shocked soldier in Bernafay Wood 'was lying in front of me and his leg trembled. I urged him to pull himself together, not realising that he was suffering from shell-shock. His legs continued to tremble, so I flung myself on his legs.'[18] The soldier cried and trembled but refused to leave the wood.

For those not incapacitated by shell-shock, the situation was equally grim. In the wake of rain on 5 July 1916, Walter Giddy of the 2nd South Africans 'cuddled up' to Fatty Roe for warmth. Not four days later Fatty Roe was dead, killed nearby in the trench when a shell fell on him.

As if the constant shelling were not enough, German snipers also posed a severe threat. Newcomers to the trenches were warned against their natural inclination not to peer over the parapets into no-man's-land. Harold Silberbauer, a South African serving as an officer with the Leicestershire Regiment, recalled wandering along winding communications trenches marked at places with notices saying 'Keep down, Snipers'.[19] But, despite the warnings, many men died on their first day from a sniper's bullet.

From his hospital bed in London, Private Weldon Broughton wrote about a German sniper who seemed to be quite good at his job:

> Another fellow, a sniper, was pretty daring. He crept up and got in a shell-hole just in front of us; could barely see his head. From there he watched and pulled down chap after chap of ours. He had some goes at me, but missed. He was a beautiful shot; got about nine fellows, nearly all in the centre of the head. I think it was he that eventually got me in the hand.[20]

Private R. Richards of the Royal Engineers also had experience of German snipers while at Dickebusch, in Belgium: 'The Germans were only about fifty yards away and they had highly specialised snipers, which made life pretty unbearable. We could never retaliate properly because this sort of warfare had taken us completely by surprise – we had nothing to lob back at them.'[21]

In his diary entry for 15–16 July 1916, Giddy recorded the additional threat of snipers in Delville Wood, where the South African brigade was under heavy bombardment: 'We drove them off, as they would come back and counter attack. Then snipers were knocking our fellows over wholesale, while we were digging trenches, but our chaps kept them off. I got behind a tree, just with my right eye and shoulder showing, and blazed away.'[22]

Frank Marillier also referred to the hazards of snipers in Delville Wood:

> Return to the trenches (centre wood) and managed to hold on to first line, but oh! what a death-trap. We made our way back, joining Col Thackeray and about 70 survivors in a reserve trench. Here we set up our Lewis gun with tragic results. In succession ten of my mates were killed and it looked as if my own turn was next.
>
> Whilst at the gun, one bullet grazed the side of my face, near the eye. Another hit the stock [of the Lewis gun]. But the bullets were not coming from the direction our gun was facing. After our tenth comrade had been killed, one of our chaps thought he saw a slight

movement in a tree, some distance to our rear. We gave the tree a burst, and out dropped a German sniper. A brave man, he must have crept into the wood in the darkness of the previous night, and set himself up, well hidden, in the branches.[23]

Hand-in-hand with the stress and lack of sleep came chronic fatigue, and a psychological disorder known then as neurasthenia. Thought to result from exhaustion of the nervous system, neurasthenia was a common occurrence in soldiers who sometimes had to fight day and night, like the South Africans at Delville Wood. Betteridge wrote that on 18 July the remaining troops in the wood were 'half stupid from fatigue and lack of sleep'.[24] Similarly, John Lawson wrote that on the night of 17 July the men of D Company, 3rd South Africans, had been 'tried beyond all endurance' and were now 'deaf to the roar of hundreds of guns and explosions of shells all around'. They were so exhausted that most fell asleep.[25]

Then there was the gas. The Germans used two kinds of gas shells: lachrymatory (tear gas) and asphyxiating. The former primarily affected the eyes, causing considerable irritation, while the latter affected the lungs. Asphyxiating gas was more volatile but dissipated quicker.

Sergeant J.W. Adams of the 4th South African was wounded in Delville Wood on 16 July 1916 and described the pain caused by the tear gas: 'Before attacking they sent over tear shells, which blind your eyes with tears, tears streaming down your face. The pain is awful.'[26]

In describing a German tear-shell attack in Delville Wood on 18 July, Lawson wrote that 'three-fifths of their shells were tear shells. We shed tears copiously.' He added that 'our gas-masks became stuffy and suffocating, and had to be discarded'.[27]

Arthur C. Stanley of the machine-gun section described the effects of asphyxiating gas in the Battle of Delville Wood: 'The pain is not bad, only a tired feeling and suffocation, alternating with violent fits of coughing that do not remove the obstruction.'[28]

Animals used for transport were of course not immune to these gas attacks and suffered as well.

Collecting the wounded and removing the bodies of dead comrades from the trenches were among the worst tasks. Stretcher-bearers, who evacuated the injured from collecting posts to dressing stations, often had to retire to dug-outs when shelling and firing became too severe. Horse-drawn ambulance wagons were used to transport so-called 'sitting-up cases', soldiers who were not too badly wounded but who could not walk.

Only seriously wounded soldiers were treated at advanced dressing stations, some of which were very near the action. Those less seriously wounded, the 'walking wounded', were treated at medical clearing stations further away from the front line. From there, they were taken to dressing stations in the rear and then sent on to field hospitals. Troops spoke of receiving a 'blighty', a wound serious enough to see them sent back to England to recover.

Caring for the wounded was the responsibility of the South African Medical Corps, but on occasion regular soldiers also had to evacuate the wounded. Lance-Corporal Arthur McLauchlin from Woodstock, Cape Town, serving in the 1st South African Field Ambulance, recalled 'doing nothing else but carrying wounded day and night' during the battle. His whole body was scratched by shrapnel.[29] On 18 July in Delville Wood, the 3rd South Africans had no stretcher-bearers left due to casualties, so Lieutenant-Colonel Dawson sent 16 men of the 1st South Africans to act as bearers for the 3rds.[30]

For the walking wounded, it was often harrowing trying to reach the dressing station, as Private Will Peggs of the 1st South Africans found. He was buried twice by falling debris on his way to the dressing station. 'Trees were falling all round us, likewise shells ... [I felt] as though the whole German artillery were trying their best to blot me out ... that was hell to me, and it lasted for half an hour, until I arrived at the dressing station.'[31]

The macabre task of removing the bodies of fallen comrades was traumatic to say the least. Lawson recalled how he and his fellow soldiers in D Company had to remove their dead and temporarily lay them in shell-holes before burying them.[32]

When they weren't battling the enemy, the soldiers were battling the poor weather conditions, which rendered the trenches unbearable. Rifleman Henry Williamson of the London Rifle Brigade, who was involved in the first Battle of Ypres, recalled:

> We had to go on working parties at night in the woods, and then after four more nights we were in the trenches again, back slithering into the trenches and doing it all over again ... The condition of the latrines can be imagined and we could not sleep, every minute was like an hour. The dead were lying out in front. The rains kept on, we were in yellow clay, and the water table was 2 ft below. Our trenches were 7 ft deep. We walked about or moved very slowly in marl or pug of yellow watery clay. When the evening came and we could get out of it, it took about an hour to climb out. Some of our chaps slipped in and were drowned. They couldn't even be seen, but were trodden on later.[33]

Lieutenant Ulrich Burke of the 2nd Battalion, Devonshire Regiment, complained, 'Oh, the conditions were terrible. You can imagine the agony of a fellow standing for twenty-four hours, sometimes up to his waist in mud, with just a couple of bully beef tins or his mess tin trying to get the water out of this shell-hole. And he had to stay there all day and all night for about six days, that was his existence.'[34]

Harold Silberbauer recalled a frightening episode in the mud of the Somme during a bombardment:

> Nothing much happened in October [1916] – all seemed quiet and we were able to visit Bethune ... Then came winter and the trenches were soon rivers and pools of icy mud. We lived in cold clay mud and feet suffered from perpetually wearing gum boots. One horrid night, on a lone visit to a forward sap, mortars began falling about me and it was impossible to move out of the sticky mud of that Hohenzollern Redoubt. It was a nasty moment, being stuck and hearing 'rum-jars' [mortar bombs] coming in our direction.[35]

Frederick Barratt of the 2nd South Africans recorded abominable weather in August 1916. Due to heavy rains, at one stage the men were standing in about 60 centimetres of water and in the last few days before the division left the sector it rained so heavily that the parapets crumbled, and every available man had to be employed to repair them.

By October the autumn rains had started to fall steadily, hampering the movement of men and supplies. Shelled woods, fields and roads became seas of mud in which bodies, and body parts, lay submerged but unburied, and the smell of death fouled the air.

The winter that followed was the most severe Europe had experienced since 1839. Snow, strong winds and hard frost prevailed throughout January and February. The men in the trenches nevertheless had better protection from the bitter wind than those in the bare and draughty buildings of Arras.[36]

Writing about conditions in the trenches at the Hohenzollern Redoubt, which they had left before Christmas 1916 and returned to in early 1917, Silberbauer recalled, 'Things were not too bad during February and early March as everything was frozen stiff, including the mud, but then came the thaw. Sandbags burst and mud and slush were feet deep. In places, it ran over the tops of our gum boots, thighs, and was awful.'[37]

At times like this trench foot became a problem. Trench foot is a medical condition affecting the feet caused by prolonged exposure to damp, cold and unsanitary conditions, like those found in the World War I trenches. If not treated, feet could turn gangrenous and would have to be amputated. Burke recalled:

> A further great problem was trench fever and trench foot. When a fellow got a very high temperature, you could tell he'd probably got trench fever. It wasn't dysentery exactly, but it was constant diarrhoea and left him weak and listless. Trench foot was owing to the mud soaking through your boots and everything. In many cases your toes nearly rotted off. We lost more that way than we did from any wounds or anything.[38]

Besides the obvious health risks caused by the wet and muddy conditions, the soldiers also had to put up with appalling smells from various sources. The Somme battlefields were littered with thousands of rotting corpses. Those that weren't lying exposed were in shallow graves. The offensive stench from overflowing latrines vied with the smell of disinfecting agents like creosol and chloride of lime, which were used to counter the constant threat of disease and infection. As Burke recalled, 'Another extra chore was that lime had to be spread on the back of the posts because open excreta was being chucked out and if you didn't put down lime then when you came crawling out you'd be covered in it.'[39]

All of this mingled with the unpleasant odour of unwashed bodies as thousands of men were denied baths or showers for weeks, and even months, on end:

> It was a ghastly existence there in the middle of what remained of the Loos battlefield. The place was unhealthy and stank. Everyone had to be on the alert all the time and boots were never taken off during the three-day spell. In wet weather, the men had to parade in the support line and rub their feet with whale oil … a nasty smelling process. Platoon commanders had to ensure that [their] men's feet were healthy.[40]

In addition, the trenches were infested with huge numbers of big rats, gorging themselves on human remains. Fusilier Victor Packer wrote with dismay:

> Then there were the rats, of course, rats. You would not kill rats because you had no means of getting rid of them, they would putrefy and it would be worse than if you left them alive. I think they lived in corpses, because they were huge, they were as big as cats, I am not exaggerating, some of them were as big as ordinary cats, horrible great things.[41]

Private Tom McIndoe of the 12th Battalion, Middlesex Regiment, exclaimed:

Rats! Oh crikey! If they were put in a harness they could have done a milk round, they were that big, yes, honest. Nearly every morning, a bloody great thing would come up and stand on its back legs and gnaw at something. I used to line the sights up and give them one round of ball. Bang! And blow them to nothing.[42]

And Gunner Leonard Ounsworth of the 124th Heavy Battery, Royal Garrison Artillery, wrote, 'The rats used to pinch your rations at night, they'd gnaw through anything you put them in unless it was in a metal container. But the gas attack finished them. In the morning there were dozens and dozens of these rats crawling about on their bellies.'[43]

The rodents were a real nuisance, spreading infection and contaminating food. Soldiers attempted to rid the trenches of them by bayoneting, shooting and clubbing them to death, but it was to no avail. The rat problem would remain for the duration of the war.

Lice and fleas were another never-ending concern. They bred in the seams of filthy clothing, causing the men to itch continuously. In his diary, Frederick Barratt – who arrived at the front after the Battle of Delville Wood – recounted how the newcomers picked up lice from the survivors of the battle. The men spent much of their free time hunting lice in the seams of their trousers. Barratt tells of how he applied Harrison's Pomade and Keating's Powder, sent to him by relatives in England. Hot baths and fumigating their clothing brought some relief, but it meant standing around naked in chilly breezes after the bath while clothes were treated.[44]

Lice were the cause of trench fever, a particularly painful disease that began suddenly with severe pain followed by a high fever. It took up to 12 weeks to recover away from the trenches. Trench fever brought J.R.R. Tolkien's war to an end. Then a second-lieutenant, he was first sent to the officers' hospital at Gezaincourt. He spent the rest of the war convalescing back home in England.[45]

Private Clifford Lane of the 1st Battalion, Hertfordshire Regiment, wrote:

> Fleas, yes. Every man in the front line ... had fleas after about two or three weeks. Fleas used to get into the seam of your underclothes, and the only way to get rid of them was to get a candle and go along the seams with the candle and you could hear the eggs crackling. And the extraordinary thing is these lice were so bad in places, I've seen men taking their shirts off with the skin of their backs absolutely raw where they'd been scratching. And there was no way of getting rid of them at all. We used to have sent out a chemical called Harrison's pomade. We used to use that but it wasn't very effective. Lice were a curse, were a real menace to us. For one thing, you had very few chances of getting a good sleep anyway, and when you had the lice with you there to irritate you, drive [you] into a sort of frenzy almost – the whole thing was that the lice were in the dugouts.[46]

As Lane noted, sleep was elusive anyway. At night, everyone was on alert in anticipation of trench raids. Silberbauer recorded:

> It was a ghostly vigil to stare across No Man's Land, through barbed wire, with a few remnants of humans out in front. All was silent ... Suddenly a flare would shoot up into the sky and drop slowly, flickering, to earth, lighting up the nightmare torn ground; machine guns would rattle and dull crashes from mortars would shake the world. Suddenly, it would be quiet again, for a while, until the sentry thought that he saw something (or perhaps he did see something) and bursts of rifle fire would break out and all would be hell again. One of our patrols might have been out in front and we would have had to be very careful not to shoot them. Everyone was on edge for those three days in the front line.[47]

Sergeant George Ashurst of the 2nd Battalion, Lancashire Fusiliers, recalled a Christmas armistice with the Germans, who were just 180 metres away in their trenches. A corporal from his company went all the way to the German trench where they were waving a newspaper, and when he got there they shook his hand, wished him a merry Christmas and gave him the paper. Although the armistice officially ended at one o'clock that afternoon, there were still men from both sides walking about at five o'clock, and not a shot was fired.

> It was so pleasant to get out of that trench, from between those two clay walls, and just walk and run about. It was heaven. And to kick this sandbag about, but we did not play with the Germans. Well we didn't, but I believe quite a lot did... Eventually, we got orders to come back down into the trench.[48]

As awful as they were, for Captain Charles Carrington of the 1/5th Battalion, Warwickshire Regiment, the trenches became the men's whole world:

> This world of the trenches, which had built up for so long and which seemed to be going on forever, seemed like the real world, and it was entirely a man's world. Women had no part in it, and when one went on leave one escaped out of the man's world into the women's world. But one found that however pleased one was to see one's girlfriend, one could never somehow quite get through, however nice they were. If the girl didn't quite say the right thing one was curiously upset. One got annoyed by the attempts of well-meaning people to sympathise, which only reflected the fact that they didn't really understand at all. So there was almost a sense of relief when one went back into the man's world, which seemed the realest thing that could be imagined.[49]

Those who experienced the trenches struggled to come to terms with the ordinariness of life back home. Writing to his mother, a despondent John Raws told her,

> How we do think of home and laugh at the pettiness of our little daily annoyances!

We could not sleep, we remember, because of the creaking of the pantry door, or the noise of the tramcars, or the kids playing around and making a row. Well, we can't sleep now because –

Six shells are bursting around here every minute, and you can't get much sleep between them;

Guns are belching out shells, with a most thunderous clap each time;

The ground is shaking with each little explosion;

I am wet, and the ground on which I rest is wet;

My feet are cold; in fact, I'm all cold, with my two skimp blankets;

I am covered with cold, clotted sweat, and sometimes my person is foul;

I am hungry;

I am annoyed because of the absurdity of war;

I see no chance of anything better for to-morrow, or the day after, or the year after.[50]

6

The Butte de Warlencourt

THREE DAYS AFTER their relief in Delville Wood, the South African brigade marched to Maricourt, where they were transferred by train to Hengest. They arrived in the Frévillers area, north of the main road between Arras and Saint-Pol-sur-Ternoise, on 27 July 1916. The first priority was to reorganise the brigade – drafts numbering 40 officers and 2 826 men of other ranks had been sent from Bordon during July.[1]

One of these newcomers was Frederick Barratt (2nd Regiment, C Company), who had originally travelled to South Africa from England in 1901 during the Anglo-Boer War with the intention of teaching. He ended up doing blockhouse duty near Cradock with the Grahamstown Volunteers instead.

Barratt's group had left their training camp at Rouen by train. When they got closer to the front, they alighted and marched the rest of the way, spending a night at Happy Valley, near Bray-sur-Somme. The next morning, they were joined by the ragged remnants of the men who had fought at Delville Wood. In due course they were transported by train to Estrée-Cauchy, north-west of Arras. As it was peaceful compared to what they had been through, the men renamed it 'Extra Cushy'. Barratt recalled those few weeks as 'a time of resting, doing a bit of training, eating French bread, wandering through the cornfields, spending evenings in estaminets and quarrelling over pickled onions'.[2]

With the horrors and trauma of the battles of Longueval and Delville Wood behind them, the 9th Division left the Somme and was transferred from the XIII Corps of the Fourth Army to the IV Corps of Sir Charles Monro's First Army. The IV Corps was commanded by Lieutenant-General Sir Henry Wilson.

Monro inspected the South African brigade on 5 August. At that stage, it numbered 62 officers and 2 523 men. A week later, at Frévillers, they were honoured with a visit from King George V.

By mid-August, the brigade was regarded as sufficiently rested and reorganised to once again take its place on the front line. On 23 August, they took over the Berthonval and Carency sections of the Vimy area from the 26th Brigade. The Germans held the crown of Vimy Ridge, while the British line ran along its western slopes. Various regiments of the South African brigade held the first-line trenches along Vimy Ridge until 23 September. The weather was abominable for most of that time – during the last few days of the action at Vimy Ridge, thanks to perpetual rain, the men stood in almost a metre of water surrounded by crumbling trench parapets.[3]

On 29 August, Barratt recorded that they had stayed in the village of Camblain-l'Abbé for four to five days and had a 'very wet and slippery march' to the trenches for working-party duties. And while 31 August was 'a miserable wet cheerless day', they had been 'literally washed out' of their dug-out the previous day due to a thunderstorm.[4]

While Vimy Ridge had seen some ferocious battles in the summer of 1915, now it was a relatively quiet area. The most action the South Africans saw there was when parties from B and D companies of the 2nd Regiment raided the German trenches on the night of 13 September. Led by Lieutenants Percy Lilburn (wounded at Delville Wood) and F.G. Walsh, the raiders managed to reach the German side of the British wire without being observed. Covered by their artillery, the men doubled across no-man's-land and jumped into the German trenches, bombing dug-outs and taking prisoners. They killed at least a dozen enemy soldiers and took five prisoners, and suffered only two casualties themselves.[5]

Barratt recalled the days in the trenches and the night of the raid in his diary:

Have had spell of a week now in reserve trenches: mostly trench-repairing work, shifting sandbags (3 shifts: 10 p.m. to 6 a.m.: 6 a.m. to 2 p.m.: 2 p.m. to 6 p.m.) Creighton, Cullis and [name indecipherable] are all on the night shift and sleep all day. I have been most of the time on light duty and have had a soft time, my only duties being connected with sanitation. Rations have been rather low and parcels from home welcome. Fritz has bombarded us at intervals, and a good many casualties. Last night quite successful raid on German front line – result 5 prisoners, and 7 killed [in actual fact, it was more than that]. Our losses one killed [name indecipherable] (whom I knew very well) and one wounded. We had to get up before 4 and hold ourselves in readiness – very cold morning. Shelling very heavy. Trench mortars etc – showers of shrapnel. Comparatively few hit.[6]

On 23 September, the South African brigade was relieved. Two days later they moved to a new training area with the Third Army, and on 5 October the 9th Division was restored to the Fourth Army. By now, the autumn rains had started to fall, and men and machines struggled to make their way to their destinations in the soggy countryside. An obviously anxious Barratt recorded:

We left Vimy Ridge on the 18th expecting to go into billets, have hot bath etc. Instead we are moved back to reserve trenches where crowded into a wretched rat-run of a shelter. Cannot sleep for rats running over us. Washing almost impossible. Very heavy rain. Nearly all dugouts washed out. My place fortunately dry. Daily fatigues navvy work repairing trenches. My boots give in. Have to wear canoes size 12. Fetch wet shirts at night. Fall into ditch. Improvement in rations… Moving off today to billets at Gouy Servins. Have blankets to carry in addition to other kit. Still rather fed up with the youths with whom one has to mix, but they are at any rate intelligent and observant and make excellent scouts. We are wondering what is to be our fate for the winter. Heaven send it be not the trenches of Flanders![7]

On 7 October the South Africans marched south to the Somme, and the following day, in the pouring rain, they relieved the 141st Brigade of the 47th (1/2nd London) Division in Mametz Wood. Like Delville, the wood was now a bleak, desolate place. On 9 October they moved to High

Wood, where they took over from the 142nd Brigade. The 9th Division was now side by side with the 15th (Scottish) Infantry Division and part of General Pulteney's III Corps.[8]

Since the Battle of Delville Wood, General Haig had taken first Pozières and the high ground at Mouquet Farm, and then Guillemont and Ginchy on the other flank, making the gap in the second enemy line 12 kilometres wide, and giving the Allies the highest ground from which direct observation over the slopes and pockets to the east was possible.

Lieutenant Jack Drummond, a South African serving with the Australians, had taken part in the Battle of Pozières. In a letter to his sister in Plumstead, Cape Town, on 28 July 1916, he wrote:

> Last night we came up to this inferno, made a bit of a headquarters, and sent our guns up, some to the firing line about a mile away. Our guns of all calibres were belching forth their shells from left and right, front and rear, and we trying to get up in the pitch dark, falling into trenches and millions of shell holes. The din is continuous and terrific, and the flashes blinding. To make things worse we had several gas alarms and had to put on our gas helmets... Some artillery men say this beats Verdun... The country here is absolutely ploughed up, both from our shells and theirs. The roads leading up to the front trenches are absolutely shrapnel-swept all day and night.[9]

By 3 September, the Allies between Thiepval and Estrées were facing the German third line, which was based on a string of fortified villages lying on the reverse slopes of the main ridge – namely Courcelette, Martinpuich, Flers, Lesboeufs and Morval. Behind it lay an intermediate line, with strong points at Le Sars, Eaucourt l'Abbaye and Gueudecourt. Further back, a new fourth line covered the villages of Sailly-Saillisel and Le Transloy, and protected Bapaume.

By now the Germans had been considerably weakened, in part due to changes in the German High Command, and the time was ripe for a new attack to accelerate their decline and reposition the British front. To the right, the French had had some notable successes: the Austro-

German forces were being pinned down on the Eastern Front; General Maurice Sarrail had launched an offensive in the Balkans; and Romania had entered the war.

Haig's aim was to break through the German third line and ultimately advance north-east across the upper Ancre River to get behind the enemy positions from Thiepval northward. On 15 September he struck to Ginchy from a point south-east of Thiepval, with a force consisting of Canadians and New Zealanders who were new to the Somme. Also new to the area was the use of British tanks, which Captain D.H. Pegler, then a battery sergeant-major with the Royal Field Artillery, remarked on:

> I have forgotten the 'Land Crabs' – the great armoured cars that took part in the battle of the fifteenth – some are lying on their backs, mangled masses of twisted and broken iron, others are back in their repairing yards, all are more or less crocked, but Gad the execution they did was awful. It struck me as I saw them from the corner of Leuze Wood how symbolic of all war they were. Then one saw them creeping along at about four miles an hour, taking all obstacles as they came, spluttering death with all their guns, enfilading each trench as they came to it – and crushing beneath them our own dead and dying as they passed. I saw one body on a concrete parapet over which one had passed. This body was just a splash of blood and clothing about two feet wide and perhaps an inch thick. An hour before this thing had been a thinking breathing man, with life before him and loved ones awaiting him probably somewhere in Scotland, for he was a kiltie. Nothing stops these cars, trees bend and break, boulders are pressed into the earth. One had been hit by a large shell and the petrol tank pierced. She lay on her side in flames, a picture of hopelessness but every gun on her uppermost side still working with dogged determination. The firing gradually slackened and she lay silent, the gallant little crew burned to death each man at his gun.[10]

In just one day, Haig had advanced to an average depth of 1.6 kilometres on a front of more than 10 kilometres. He took Courcelette, Martinpuich and Flers, and, on 25 September, Morval, Lesboeufs and Gueudecourt. On 26 September, the right wing of Sir Hubert Gough's Fifth Army carried Thiepval and the whole of the crest. Allied fortunes on the Western Front looked brighter, but soon after the attack on the 26th the weather broke. October saw a succession of violent gales and pounding rains.[11] Buchan would record:

> Now appeared the supreme difficulty of trench warfare. For three months the Allies had been slowly advancing, blasting attack, and the result was that the fifty square miles of old battleground which lay behind their front lines had been tortured out of recognition. The little country roads had been wholly destroyed, and, since they never had much of a bottom, the road-menders had nothing to build upon. New roads were hard to make, for the chalky soil had been so churned up by shelling that it had lost all cohesion. In all the area there were but two good highways, and by the third month of the battle even these showed signs of wear. The consequence was that there were now two No Man's Lands – one between the front lines, and one between the old enemy front and the front we had won. The second was the bigger problem, for across it must be brought the supplies of a great army. It was a war of motor transport, and we were doing what the early Victorians had pronounced impossible – running the equivalent of steam engines not on prepared tracks but on high-roads, running them day and night in endless relays. The problem was difficult enough in fine weather, but when the rain came it turned the whole land into a morass. Every road became a watercourse, and in the hollows the mud was as deep as a man's thighs. The army must be fed, troops must be relieved, guns must be supplied, so there could be no slackening of the traffic. Off the roads the ground was one vast bog, dug-outs crumbled in, and communication trenches ceased to be. Behind the British front lay six miles of sponge, varied by mud torrents. It was into such miserable warfare, under persistent rain in a decomposing land, that the South African Brigade was now flung.[12]

THE BUTTE DE WARLENCOURT

The line of the Fourth Army ran southward from a point north-east of Courcelette, along the foot of what the British Expeditionary Force had come to know as the Thiepval–Morval Ridge, to High Wood. From this ridge, a series of spurs jutted eastward into the hollow, one of which was the Butte de Warlencourt, an ancient burial ground immediately west of Flers. The German fourth line lay below the eastern edge of this spur. While the spurs themselves were not part of the main German front, they were held as intermediate positions, as every advantage was taken of sunken roads, ruins and undulations in the countryside. And until they were conquered, no general assault on the main German front could be undertaken. The Butte de Warlencourt in particular would also provide cover for the British forces and their advanced gun positions, as well as protection for supplies moving to the front.

By October 1916, 'the Butte de Warlencourt had become an obsession. Everybody wanted it. It loomed large in the minds of the soldiers in the forward area and they attributed many of their misfortunes to it. The newspaper correspondents talked about "that miniature Gibraltar".'[13] So said 24-year-old Lieutenant-Colonel Roland Bradford.[14]

During that month, various British divisions circulated through the trenches overlooked by the Butte de Warlencourt. An attack on the butte was made on 7 October, when the 23rd Division took Le Sars on the Albert–Bapaume road. A week earlier, the 50th and 47th divisions had taken the Flers line, the strong trench system north of Destremont Farm, and the ruined abbey of Eaucourt. With the attack on Le Sars, however, the 47th Division, on the right of the 23rd, failed to reach the butte. The two divisions were eventually relieved by the 15th and 9th, with orders to carry the butte and the German intermediate line.

On 9 October, the 2nd South African Infantry Regiment, commanded by Lieutenant-Colonel E. Christian and numbering 20 officers and 578 other ranks, took over the portion of the front line to be held by the brigade. During the night, the South Africans brought in a number of the wounded of the outgoing 141st Brigade.

The South African brigade was now on the left of the 9th Division, its boundary running through the ruins of Eaucourt l'Abbaye, beyond which the 26th Brigade held the front, with the 27th Brigade in divisional reserve. B and C companies of the 2nd South Africans held the front line, together with two strong posts on their left and right fronts. A and D companies were in the support trenches of the old Flers line running along the south-west side of Eaucourt l'Abbaye. The German front trenches, known as Snag and Tail, lay just short of a kilometre from the British front line, and beyond them – running through the Butte de Warlencourt – was the main German intermediate position. Due to the confused fighting and rains of the past weeks, the whole front on both sides was indeterminate, and at any one moment it was unsure which trenches were held by the Germans and which by the British. The first task for the Allies was to clear the ground up to the butte to get directly in front of the German fourth position.

The 2nd South Africans' first orders were to link up the two aforementioned strong posts with the ruins of an old mill to the left of their front, but the slow pace of the relief postponed this to the second night when about 500 metres of trench were dug. Despite heavy shelling during 10 and 11 October, their casualties were small. On the 11th, General Furse issued orders for a daylight attack the following day in conjunction with the 26th Brigade on their right and the 44th Brigade of the 15th Division on their left. The attack was to be carried out on a one-regiment front by the 2nd and 4th South Africans (the 2nd leading), with the 3rd and 1st in reserve. They had two objectives: the enemy trenches Snag and Tail, and the main intermediate line through the Butte de Warlencourt.

In drizzling rain on 12 October, the 2nd South Africans crossed the parapets, closely followed by the 4ths under Major Donald Hunt. A tremendous German barrage wiped out the telephone wires to the front line and for some time no reports could be received. To make matters worse, the mist, combined with the smoke that the brigade had laid down around the butte and which was now drifting in their direction, made it impossible to see any distance. The German machine guns caught them at long range across the gentle slope of the field, and before the first objective – Snag and Tail – was reached, the assault faltered.

In the afternoon, Captain Thomas Ross of the 4th South Africans sent a message to General Lukin that he and some details of the 2nd were holding a line of shell-holes and a shallow trench halfway between the old front line and Snag and Tail. He also reported that a company of the 4th Regiment was positioned in front of them near Snag and Tail, with a part of the 2nd farther forward. Having already sent forward a company of the 3rd Regiment to hold the old front line, Lukin ordered two officers' patrols from the company to investigate. Their report-back was disheartening: the brigade was nowhere near its first objective. As the now disorganised 2nd and 4th regiments had already suffered heavily, Lukin ordered the 3rd to relieve them and moved the 1st up in support. By just after dawn on 13 October, the 2nd and 4th regiments had been brought back to High Wood.

Later that day it was discovered that Lieutenants Pearse and Donaldson, and about 60 men were dug in at an exposed point near the German line. Thanks to a reconnaissance by Lieutenant Cruddas, their exact position was ascertained and they were brought back to safety that evening. A new trench, afterwards known as Pearse's Trench, was dug from the old line to the point which he had held, and made a jumping-off point for future operations.[15]

Barratt's diary gives insight into this terrible experience:

October 13. My 39th birthday yesterday. By a miracle I am still alive. Had enough the last two days of the horror of war to last a lifetime. October 10. Came off guard and put on party shifting dead bodies out of trench. Then a ration fatigue. Finally to bed in dugout. October 11. Van Reenen hit twice by shell. I propping him up when hit second time. Died that evening. Shelling of trench continues. Men hit every few minutes. Spent day in dugout. That evening went out digging an advance trench from 7 p.m. to 5 a.m. German sniping. Back to dugout at 6 a.m.

(October 12) No water. Orders to fall in at 12 ready to go over top. Rifles damaged by shell. Fleming hit in leg. Cullis bandaging him hit in back. Parade mustered 20 in platoon 11, 7 in platoon 12. Just before went over shell knocked Creighton and me over unhurt and buried Joubert (taken back with shell shock). Went over at 2.5. I between Treloar and Creighton. Just as I stood on the parapet and was jumping down was hit and fell over, rifle falling away. Crawled into shell hole and eventually decided had not lost my head, but found difficulty in walking. Pitched my shovel off and found I had wound at back of neck. After a time made a dash and got back into trench. Found Sergt Tayfield who had fallen and come back without wounds. Other wounded men came back over trench. Lay in trench for some hours amid continuous fire. Saw some wounded men going along to dressing station and went with them. Went along trenches for miles. Great difficulty in moving on, over corpses etc. After hours emerged on road and then started on long walk along road. Great relief to be out of reach of shells. Had a lift in a wagon and another in motor van and eventually reached Divisional Dressing Station, helping wounded men along the road: one man with eye gone got on horseback. Arrangements at Dressing Station wonderful and all doctors ambulance men very kind. Gave us lots of cocoa and bread and butter and cheese. Then sent on to casualty clearing station. Then had the first proper night's sleep for a long time. Following day put in train with ticket tied to my pocket. Possibly wound not so slight as I had thought.[16]

Early on the night of 14 October, B Company of the 3rd Regiment, under Captain Sprenger, was sent to reconnoitre the Pimple, one of the two German strong points, which was subsequently garrisoned by a party under Lieutenant Medlicott. A short while later, Lieutenant Mallett entered the trench at the Pimple and moved towards Snag and Tail, bombing the enemy until he was driven back by machine-gun fire and severely wounded. But a party under Lieutenants Harris and Estill forged ahead, and succeeded in taking and holding considerable parts of the trenches. That night the place was heavily bombed by Germans, but the garrison of B Company held the Pimple and captured trenches until relieved by A Company the following night. During the operation, Medlicott was killed and Sprenger and Mallett wounded, though the latter later died of his wounds. There were 35 other casualties. On the night of 16 October, the 3rd Regiment retired to the support line, while the 1st, under Lieutenant-Colonel Dawson, took its place.[17]

In the meantime, the communication trench between the Pimple and the front line and back to Flers had been widened and deepened. On 17 October, orders arrived for an attack early the next day on the same objectives that had been unsuccessfully targeted on the 12th. All that evening and most of that night, heavy rain fell, so that the trenches and parapets were 'mere undulations in a quagmire'.[18]

By 03:40, the three attacking companies of the 1st Regiment were formed up in no-man's-land. With C Company on the left, B Company in the centre and A on the right, they began their advance, the men disappearing in the rain. News came through several hours later that C Company, under Captain Jenkins, had been held up by wire in front of the German line and had been heavily bombed from the trenches, the leading platoon almost entirely shot down. An officer and six men of the following platoon managed to enter the German trench, but also fell immediately. Realising the hopelessness of their chances of success, a wounded Captain Jenkins ordered the company sergeant-major to withdraw the survivors to their original line. Of the 100 men of C Company who went out, 69 became casualties.[19]

A and B companies fared even worse. Advancing rapidly, they had entered Snag but the B Company commander, Captain Whiting, was mortally wounded halfway across. Heavily battered by shell fire, the trench outlines had become obscured and, failing to realise that they had reached their objective, the companies continued beyond it. Some 500 metres to their right were Highlanders of the 26th Brigade, but the Germans were filtering in between them and their old front, and only Lieutenant Stapleton with a few men succeeded in making it back. Two officers and 16 others were taken prisoner; the rest of the men of A and B companies were dead.[20]

Lieutenant-Colonel W.D. Croft of the 9th Division recalled: 'One saw a large party of South Africans at full stretch with bayonets at the charge – all dead; but even in death they seemed to have the battle ardour stamped on their faces.'[21]

At daybreak, Major Ormiston, who was in charge of the troops on the Pimple, made an attempt to bomb along the trench leading to the junction of the Snag and Tail trenches (known as the Nose by the British), but the attack broke down under machine-gun fire. A company of the 3rd Regiment, under Captain Langdale, was moved forward to the front line and put at Dawson's disposal, and a company of the 4th was sent to replace it in the support line. Langdale took up position in Pearse's Trench and sent out a patrol to look for A and B companies, which returned in the afternoon with no information. It was now apparent that C Company had failed with heavy losses and that A and B companies had disappeared.

It was obvious to Dawson that the key enemy position was the Nose. He had been asking all day for its bombardment, but because of difficulties with communications, the guns were firing at the wrong point. He ordered another attack at 17:45 – D Company of his own 1st Regiment would attack from the Pimple, and Captain Langdale's company of the 3rd Regiment would advance from Pearse's Trench.

The trenches, however, were now almost impassable, so Langdale set out with just one platoon and two Lewis gun teams. He moved along Snag Trench to the right for some 180 metres, established a block with a Lewis gun and then moved west to a point near the Nose, but came upon three German machine guns. Regarding the posts too strong to attack, he withdrew to the original front line. At the same time, the bombing attack from the Pimple had also failed.[22]

On Dawson's orders, Captain Langdale reoccupied Snag Trench on the morning of 19 October. B Company of the 4th Regiment, under Captain Ross, was also sent forward with orders to make a renewed attack on the crucial Nose. They reached the front line early in the morning, but at about 05:00 the Germans attacked with bombs and flame-throwers. The men were driven out and there were heavy casualties in Ross's company. Ross himself was wounded and Lieutenant Alexander Young, who had been wounded at Delville Wood, was killed. Snag and Tail were still firmly held by the Germans.

In another desperate attempt, C Company of the 3rd Regiment, under Lieutenant Harold Elliott, was sent to enter Snag Trench and make contact with the 26th Brigade on their right, and then to work their way towards the Nose, driving out the enemy. The company entered Snag without difficulty, but failed to advance towards the Nose, apparently owing to insufficient bombs. Beyond the Nose, Major Ormiston was waiting to attack as soon as support from the east showed up, but the situation had become hopeless. Dawson had not a single officer or man fit to send to the front line, while the mud was so thick that rifles, machine guns, and Lewis guns were constantly jamming. Among the little party on the Pimple, there was not one rifle that could be fired. In some trenches, the mud lay a metre deep, so that the wounded had to be dug out at once before they suffocated. That night, Dawson and his men were relieved by the 6th King's Own Scottish Borderers of the 27th Brigade. By the morning of 20 October, all were back in High Wood.[23]

In summing up the battle for the Butte de Warlencourt, Buchan identified all the problems that faced the 9th Division and the South African brigade, and the reasons for their failure:

> The enemy held his ground with admirable skill and resolution. The fighting had not the swift pace and the obvious successes of the earlier battles. We were striving for minor objectives, and such a task lacks the impetus and exhilaration of a great combined assault. Often the action resolved itself into isolated struggles, a handful of men in a mudhole holding out till their post was linked up with our main front. Rain, cold, slow reliefs, the absence of hot food, and often of any food at all, made those episodes a severe test of endurance and devotion. So awful was the mud that each stretcher required eight bearers, and at the end battalion runners, though carrying no arms or equipment, took from four to six hours to cover the thousand odd yards between the front line and battalion headquarters. To show the utter exhaustion of the troops, at High Wood after the relief many men were found lying fast asleep without overcoats or blankets, and stiff with frost. To add to their discomfort, there was a perpetual and inevitable confusion of mind. The front was never at any one moment clearly defined, and officers led and men followed in a cruel fog of uncertainty. Such fighting could not

be other than costly. In the ten days from the 9th to the 19th October the South African casualties were approximately 1,150, including 45 officers, 16 of whom were killed.[24]

On 21 October, with the exception of the 3rd Regiment, which stayed in High Wood in reserve to the 27th Brigade, the South Africans moved to Mametz Wood. Two days later they were informed that they would be in reserve for the 9th Division's attack on 25 October, but this order was later cancelled and the entire division was taken out of the line. At the end of October, the 9th Division moved to the area south of the Doullens–Arras road, and became part of Major-General Aylmer Haldane's VI Corps of the Third Army.

On 5 November, an all-out effort to capture the butte was undertaken by the 7th, 8th and 9th (Durham Light Infantry) battalions of the 50th (Northumbrian) Infantry Division in appalling conditions. Despite heavy casualties, the 9th Durhams managed to take it, only to be driven off by German counterattacks. The Butte de Warlencourt remained under German control throughout 1916, and it was only after the German retirement to the Hindenburg Line in February 1917 that the butte passed into British hands.[25]

7

The Battle of Arras

In november 1916, the 1st South African Infantry Regiment was posted at Duisans, the 2nd at Lattre-Saint-Quentin, the 3rd at Wanquetin and the 4th was billeted in Arras. The 4ths were kept busy by improving Arras's defences, while the other regiments were occupied in training, and the construction of new roads and cable trenches necessary for a planned spring offensive. It was a month of high wind and sharp frost. In between parades and bayonet training, Frederick Barratt of the 2nd Regiment described the conditions: 'Mud and rain. Rain and mud … Have been at Lattre St. Quentin all this time. A lot of new officers whose one object seems to be to make the private's life one long misery.'[1] Lukin, now a major-general, had taken over command of the 9th Division. Lieutenant-Colonel Dawson of the 1st Regiment had succeeded him as South African brigade commander, and Major F.H. Heal had replaced Dawson.

While the men toiled, the Allied Powers held a conference at the general headquarters of the French Army to plan for the 1917 campaign. Sir Douglas Haig wanted to undertake a great offensive in Flanders with a view to clearing the Belgian coast, but before this he wanted to capitalise on the fact that the enemy was penned in the salient between the Ancre and Scarpe valleys. To this end, he proposed an early spring attack from two fronts: the Fifth Army would move on the Ancre front, while the Third Army would attack from Arras in the north-west. At the same time, the First Army was to carry the Vimy Ridge to secure the left flank of the Allied operations farther south. When this was completed, the Flanders campaign would begin with an assault on the Messines Ridge, followed by an attack eastward from the Ypres Salient.

Haig was fully aware of the new German position known as the Hindenburg Line, and did not regard it as good strategy to make a frontal assault upon it. He believed that if they persisted in the tactics of the Somme during 1917, along with reasonable pressure from the Russian front, they would secure victory before the close of that year.

The decision was made for Haig to take over a longer front, and before the end of February 1917 the British right was as far south as a point opposite the French town of Roye. The Germans' subsequent retreat during February and March 1917 destroyed the salient that Haig had intended to attack and, except for carrying the Vimy Ridge, the original plan was scuppered.

The French then proposed a new plan, relinquishing the old method of limited objectives for a large assault by a huge concentration of troops on a broad front to break through the German lines. This assault, which became known as the Nivelle Offensive and was scheduled for the middle of April 1917, would operate against the southern pivot of the Hindenburg zone and required Haig to strike a week before against the northern pillar, east of Arras. This meant that the Battle of Arras, initially regarded by Haig as a mere preparation for the main campaign, would be the principal task of the British Army during the first half of 1917. There was an element of risk to this new plan: if the fighting at Arras was protracted, the chances of the more vital Flanders summer offensive would be endangered. This is exactly what happened.[2]

It was against this background that in December 1916 the 9th Division relieved the 35th Division holding the trenches in front of Arras. According to Barratt, it was 'a fine big town with good buildings. Now in a pitiful state of deserted decay. Hardly a building left intact. Cathedral and town hall a mass of ruins. Still one or two small businesses chiefly butchers, restaurants going.'[3]

The South African brigade held a front of about 1.6 kilometres extending north from the River Scarpe for three months. It was a difficult time, as France was experiencing its severest winter for many years. It rained for most of December, and the first two months of 1917 were marked by heavy snowfalls and bitter frost.

On 3 January 1917, a party of volunteers from the 3rd South Africans, led by Lieutenants B.W. Goodwin and W.F.G. Thomas, made a successful raid on the German trenches. Thoroughly trained for the assignment, they camouflaged themselves by blackening their faces and spoke only Zulu so that the enemy would not understand anything should they have heard them speaking. Following a barrage on the enemy front line, they entered the German trenches, destroyed a number of dug-outs and concrete machine-gun emplacements, and inflicted many casualties.[4]

On 14 January, the 9th Division passed from the VI Corps to the XVII Corps, under Lieutenant-General Sir Charles Fergusson. The 26th Brigade, which was holding a line of trenches south of the Scarpe, relieved certain Canadian units until the whole of the new corps front was now held by the 9th Division, with all three brigades in line. In early February the 51st (Highland) Division took over the section held by the 26th Brigade, and the 34th Division relieved the 27th Brigade. The South African brigade held the 9th Division's front from St Pancras Trench to the Scarpe.

On 4 March 1917, the South Africans were relieved by the 26th Brigade, and moved from Arras to Ostreville, where they began training for the coming offensive. During their stint by the Scarpe, two of their officers and 49 other ranks had been killed, and five officers and 166 other ranks had been wounded.

While the South Africans were training, the Germans were completing their withdrawal from the Bapaume Ridge to the Hindenburg Line. Their position from the northern pivot of the new Siegfried Line to the city of Lens was strong and consisted of three main systems of trenches. A switch line running from Feuchy north across the Scarpe to beyond Thélus acted as a virtual fourth line of defence. In addition, an independent line ran from Drocourt, south-east of Lens, to the Siegfried Line at Quéant as an alternative in case of an assault on the Arras Salient. The key was Vimy Ridge, which was necessary to protect the flank from any advance farther south.[5]

The recollections of Alfred Mahncke, a German staff officer and company commander on the Western Front in 1917, shed some light on life for the Germans:

> We received orders to relieve a battle-worn 4th Guards Infantry Division. Their GSO [general staff officer] 1 was Hauptmann von Papen [later to become *Reichskanzler* under von Hindenburg]. He handed me a trench system stretching along the foot of Vimy ridge near Lens ... It cut through coal country where mines, mining gear and villages had been destroyed in previous battles. In whatever ruins could still be found standing, artillery spotters had settled themselves in to make the opposing soldier's life hell, while they reciprocated in kind ... Far in the distance I could see Vimy ridge enveloped in mist. The ridge had been turned into a wasteland of craters like a moonscape ...
>
> All soldiers had gone underground with the exception of a handful of day sentries. My HQ, under the abattoir, was about 80 m behind the line. The hole also contained a piano. Nobody knew how this piece of furniture had been brought here. It had lost a lot of its former lustre, but it could still be played and attracted visitors who came to play or listen. The rest of the furniture consisted of a rickety table with a cheap candle, a rack for hand grenades and ammunition, and wooden beds for the orderlies and myself. In an alcove, next to the entrance, the telephonist worked, and next to him stood the stretchers for the wounded ...
>
> This was my world. Above, a few hundred square metres of ground to defend; below, this suffocating mousetrap. The land above interested me only to the extent that I could see it, which was not far. Time lost its meaning. Days were divided between day and night and from one ration delivery to the next. Space and time merged into one. It was a world I shared with 122 soldiers.[6]

One of the German soldiers on the Arras front was a young Adolf Hitler, who had entered the German Army in 1914 as a member of the 6th Bavarian Reserve Division. He was a good and brave soldier, although unusual by trench standards, in that he neither smoked nor drank and he did not join in the banter about French women. Having been wounded in late 1916 on the Somme, he returned to the front in February 1917 and fought in the battles of Arras and Passchendaele, earning himself the Military Cross for bravery. Hitler's war ended in October 1918 following a gas attack near Ypres.[7]

The desolated city of Arras lay less than two kilometres inside the British lines. While few buildings had escaped bombardment, it was still habitable, but this would all change towards the end of March 1917, when the streets and lanes were once more full of life, as an endless procession of troops and transport passed under the Roman arch of the Baudimont Gate. Arras's huge ancient sewers were explored and enlarged to accommodate three divisions underground. It was arranged so that the greater part of the VI Corps would assemble for the attack due east of the city. In the third week of March, British heavy artillery started shelling the German back areas and communications, and two days later a steady bombardment was launched against all the main German positions, especially the fortress of Vimy Ridge.

The British front of attack was slightly more than 19 kilometres long, from Givenchy-en-Gohelle in the north to a point just short of Croisilles in the south. On the left, directed against the Vimy Ridge, was the Canadian Corps of Sir Henry Home's First Army, under Sir Julian Byng, with one British brigade. On the Canadians' right was the XVII Corps of Sir Edmund Allenby's Third Army, under Sir Charles Fergusson. Three divisions formed the line – the 51st (Highland), the 34th and the 9th – while the 4th Division lay in support. General Aylmer Haldane's VI Corps made up the centre – the 15th, 12th and 3rd divisions supported by the 37th. On the right was Sir Thomas Snow's VII Corps – the 14th, 56th and 30th divisions in line, and the 21st forming a pivot on the right.[8]

Mahncke recalled this time from the German perspective:

Our division occupied a quiet sector of the trench line, where both sides knew each other's habits. It had a little bit of the 'live and let live' syndrome, although fighting never really stopped. During daytime everything came to a standstill, unless one wanted to invite a deluge of fire from the enemy. Most of the soldiers rested or slept, wrote letters or merely whiled away the time. Life only began at night, and a very high degree of vigilance was observed... At the beginning of April the Allies began their attacks. The British, South Africans and Canadians approached Arras; the French, Soissons and Reims. For weeks the fortunes swung from side to side, with neither party gaining a decisive advantage. For a few metres of worthless, bloody, churned up ground men perished in vain, and the end was again a stalemate. It was terrible fighting... Telephone lines were usually shot to pieces, carrier pigeons or messenger dogs seldom arrived. One could only work at night, guided by runners who knew the trenches intimately.[9]

Things on the Allied side were not much better, according to Harold Silberbauer:

Life in the trenches continued and the great thought was a spot of leave or, better still, a 'blighty' wound that would not hurt too much and might give you a few months at home. To us from overseas, home was very far away. The Army Post Office never disappointed us and letters arrived daily with the rations. The eagerness with which letters were awaited was pathetic to see and there were very few on the Home Front who let their men-folk down. Most of the men gave far more thought to religion than they would have under normal conditions and a good padre was worth a lot... Towards the end of March, when rumours of a contemplated push began to be circulated, we expected much from the tanks. These had not come up to expectation on the Somme because they had been put into action too soon and the conventional general was not keen on this new idea. Had the tanks been properly tested and perfected, they would have run right through the Germans. Aircraft were scarce and we seldom saw any. Far away, at times, there would appear a few planes and then there would be some wholly inaccurate ack-ack fire, but we never saw a fight and were never bombed or machine-gunned from the air.[10]

Members of the 4th South African Regiment marching on the Somme, July 1916

The small French village of Cappy on the Somme (*circa* 1916), which was visited by the 4th South African Regiment

Troops moving to the front during the summer of 1916

British artillery transport crossing a trench bridge onto the Bapaume Road

Members of the 1st South African Infantry Brigade on 14 July 1916, before going into Delville Wood. Private P.P.J. Grobler is marked with an X

All that was left of Delville Wood after the battle

Lieutenant-Colonel F.A. Jones, killed at Bernafay Wood

Brigadier-General W.E.C. Tanner, who led the South African attack on Delville Wood

Lieutenant-Colonel E.T. Thackeray, who took over from Tanner in Delville Wood when the latter was wounded

The late Mr William Thorne in 1974, a survivor of the fierce battle of Delville Wood

Coming and going on the Fricourt–Contalmaison Road, July 1916

A trench at Ovillers, July 1916

Troops getting ready to go up to the front line

John Buchan, *The Battle of the Somme*

A raiding party going over the parapets to attack German trenches

Frank H. Simonds, *History of the World War*

A group of convalescing patients and nursing staff at a military hospital (probably Richmond). The soldier marked with an X is James Gabriel (Jimmy) Brown, of the 4th South African Regiment

Sleighs were used to convey the wounded through the mud

Machine-gunners in action wearing their gas masks

Sergeant-Major Reginald Smith with men from the South African Native Labour Contingent in France

THE BATTLE OF ARRAS

The British divisional guns began their preliminary bombardment on 5 April. The very next day, the South African brigade, excluding the 1st Regiment, which was on the line, was inspected by General Jan Smuts. For the first time, they were to engage in a great forward movement with ample artillery support.

On 7 April, the 1st Regiment was ordered to carry out a daylight raid. Under cover of a gun barrage, a party of five officers and 50 other ranks, led by Captain T. Roffe, reached the German trenches without casualty. Their mission accomplished, they fell back to their own line, sadly suffering four casualties – one dead and three wounded.

That night the rest of the South African brigade marched from the training ground to Arras, where it took up positions on the northern outskirts. The artillery preparation continued until Sunday 8 April, the date originally fixed for the attack. On that clear day, the Germans started shelling Arras, but did little harm, as the troops were waiting comfortably in cellars and underground assembly stations.

The weather changed in the evening, as rain and snow swept in. During the night the South Africans began to assemble in the front and support lines, where the 9th Division was holding almost two kilometres of front from the Scarpe to a point just north of the Bailleul Road. The 26th Brigade was on its right next to the river, the South African brigade was in the centre and the 27th Brigade was on its left. They had three objectives: the Black, Blue and Brown lines. The Black Line, from the Scarpe to Chantecler, represented the last line of the enemy's front system; the Blue Line, lying east of the first objective, represented the Germans' second trench system on the Arras–Lens railway; and the Brown Line, still farther east and running from the village of Athies to Point du Jour, represented the Germans' third system. The Brown Line was some 2.5 kilometres away. If that was taken, General Lambton's 4th Division was to pass through the 9th Division and capture the Green Line, including the village of Fampoux, the last German system before the Drocourt–Quéant Line.[11]

The South African brigade was to attack on a two-regiment front of 550 metres, with the 4th Regiment, under Lieutenant-Colonel Christian, on the left and the 3rd Regiment, under Lieutenant-Colonel Thackeray, on the right, each attacking on a two-company front and supported by their two remaining companies. The 2nd Regiment, under Lieutenant-Colonel Tanner, was to provide support on the left, and the 1st, under Lieutenant-Colonel Heal, on the right. When the first two objectives – the Black and Blue lines – were taken, the two regiments in support were to become the attacking regiments for the third objective, the Brown Line. The two original attacking regiments would remain in support.

During the night, pontoons were thrown across the Scarpe to facilitate the men's march to the assembly area. By 02:00 on the morning of 9 April, all four regiments were in position. The Battle of Arras was about to begin.

The morning was intensely cold and drizzly. At 5:30, the British guns broke into a tremendous fire and the South Africans went over the parapets. 'There were now no enemy front trenches; there were no second-line trenches; only a hummocky waste of craters and broken wire, over which our barrage crept relentlessly,' wrote Buchan, describing the beginning of the assault.[12]

The South Africans advanced to the attack. On the left, the 4ths: C Company (Lieutenant Smith) and D Company (Captain Reid) leading, A Company (Captain Grady) and B Company (Lieutenant Morrison) following. On the right, the 3rds: A Company (Captain Vivian) and D Company (Lieutenant Money) leading, B Company (Lieutenant Elliott) and C Company (Lieutenant Ellis) following. The supporting companies of the 1st and 2nd regiments were close by, occupying some trenches just beyond the German front line.

As the 3rd South Africans crossed the parapet and moved over no-man's-land, they were met with heavy machine-gun fire on their right flank and suffered many casualties. Despite the barrage and screen of smoke, they reached the Black Line in about half an hour. The 4ths on the left had fewer casualties, but their leading companies had approached too close to their own barrage and sustained injuries. The mopping-up detachments of the 4th, 1st and 2nd regiments met with little resistance, and reached the trenches with the first wave. They cleared the dug-outs and took many prisoners.[13]

The advance continued towards the Blue Line, supported by the barrage of 20 machine guns. Their major obstacle was to cross the Arras–Lens railway and descend a slope where a number of wire entanglements had not been fully destroyed. The passes through the wire were commanded by snipers on the edge of the railway cutting, and it was at this point that most of the Allied casualties occurred. Once down the slope, the railway embankment provided some protection. The many machine-gun posts down in the cutting were engaged by the attackers' Lewis guns, but Captain Vivian of the 3rd Regiment and some details of the 26th Brigade cleared out the German machine gunners and snipers, and the Blue Line was consolidated.

For the attack on the Brown Line, the 1st and 2nd regiments replaced the 3rd and 4th, who now became the support. The 1st Regiment numbered 20 officers and 488 other ranks, and the 2nd Regiment 20 officers and 480 other ranks. The German wire in the valley just west of the Brown Line was found to be strong and un-traversable, but by about 14:00 the line was occupied. With the South Africans' task accomplished, General Lambton's 4th Division could now move up to assault the final Green Line, which fell before dark.

The South Africans had lost seven officers, Major H.C. Symmes and Lieutenant Hardwich of the 2nd Regiment; Lieutenants Godfrey, Burrows and Lee of the 3rd Regiment; and Lieutenants Hunt and Dorward of the 4th Regiment. In the 1st Regiment, 15 men were killed and 69 were wounded or missing; in the 2nd, 20 killed and 68 wounded or missing; in the 3rd, 53 killed and 226 wounded or missing; and in the 4th, 57 killed and 186 wounded or missing. Because the advance was so rapid, the stretcher-bearers had a difficult job, having to cover a distance of more than three kilometres across a sea of mud to the nearest collecting post. But by evening, all the wounded had been collected and evacuated by the 1st South African Field Ambulance, which also dealt with casualties from the other two brigades of the 9th Division and from the 34th and 4th divisions.[14]

The Allies had rolled back all the German front positions and had breached their final position short of the Drocourt–Quéant line, on a front of four kilometres. But with the cold, wet and muddy conditions, which caused a delay in bringing up the guns, there was no chance of delivering a final blow, and their gains could only be increased by small additions from day to day.

The South African brigade spent 10 April in the Blue and Black lines, cleaning rifles and equipment, and replenishing ammunition, before they were placed at the disposal of the 4th Division. Early the next day, they received orders to relieve the 10th Brigade holding the Brown Line. Lambton attacked at noon, and the 1st and 2nd South Africans moved up to a forward post behind the Green Line in support. The 4th Division gained some ground, but failed in its main purpose. In the dark, the 1st, 2nd and 4th South Africans took up a position running north-west from Fampoux, with the 3rds in reserve. The Germans were holding a line running south to north from Roeux, through the chemical works and the railway station, along the Gavrelle road.

The next day, 12 April, the 9th Division was to advance against the line between Roeux and a roadside inn situated a kilometre east of the Hyderabad Redoubt. The 15th Division was to hold the front south of the Scarpe, while the 4th Division protected the northern flank of the attack. The objectives were to take the road from the inn to the station; the chemical works and buildings south of the railway; the wood called Mount Pleasant; and the village of Roeux. The South African and 27th brigades were ordered to capture the road from the inn to the station, after which the 26th Brigade would advance south of the railway.

In the afternoon, the 1st, 2nd and 4th South African regiments assembled in Fampoux, but were subjected to a heavy bombardment that cost them many casualties. All three brigades of the 9th Division were exhausted, having had no sleep for four nights, three of which had been spent in the snow without blankets or greatcoats. There was now no chance of a proper advance, and no time for reconnaissance.

The open country between Fampoux and Roeux Station was commanded in the south by a high railway embankment and three woods, all held by the Germans. In the north it sloped gradually to the inn, where the Germans had established strong points. The 1st and 2nd regiments, with two companies of the 4th in support and the 3rd in brigade reserve, were greeted by heavy machine-gun and rifle fire as they emerged from the shelter of the houses in the east end of Fampoux. To make matters worse, the barrage from their own guns fell some half a kilometre east of the starting point and behind the first enemy line of defence, also missing the German machine-gun posts on the railway embankment. Having had to cross a long stretch of open ground before they could reach the German first line of defence, and being exposed to flanking fire from the woods in the south and the south-east, and from the direction of the inn, both brigades suffered heavy casualties. Only a few South Africans reached the station. Their bodies were recovered only a month later when the position was eventually taken.

During these failed operations, the 1st South African Field Ambulance once again had a difficult time. They had a collecting station in Fampoux and the stretcher-bearers were under constant shell fire. On 12 April, Captain Welsh was mortally wounded. From 12 to 15 April, many of the stretcher-bearers worked without rest, carrying on until they eventually dropped from sheer exhaustion.[15]

Casualties for the 2nd Regiment numbered 16 officers and 285 men; for the 1st, two officers and 203 men; and for the 4th, six officers and 200 men. Captain E.C.D. Grady, who commanded A Company of the 4th Regiment, was one of those killed, as were Lieutenants J.M. Ross, Lees and Porteous. As the first part of the attack had failed, the 26th Brigade was never called on, and now they took over the line from the Scarpe to the Hyderabad Redoubt and linked up with the 4th Division. The South Africans withdrew to the Green Line, and were finally relieved on the night of 15 April. Since the 12th, they had suffered 720 casualties.

As scheduled, the French attacks began on 16 April 1917. In what became known as the Second Battle of the Aisne, the French moved against the German-occupied Chemin des Dames ridge, 110 kilometres north-east of Paris. They took about 29 000 German prisoners but failed to achieve their strategic objective, which was to inflict a decisive defeat on the enemy.

Due to the failure of the French attack on the Aisne, the British were compelled to continue in the Arras area, but the South African brigade was to have no further part in the drawn-out struggle that would last well into May. The brigade was stationed in the Monchy-Breton district during the latter part of April, and on 5 May a composite regiment, consisting of a company from each of the 1st, 2nd and 3rd regiments, was formed under the command of Major Webber. From here they moved to Arras, where they were placed at the disposal of the 27th Brigade. They helped hold the British front line until 14 May, when the brigade was demobilised. The following month they were stationed in Arras as a divisional reserve, and on 5 June two composite regiments were formed to assist in the attack on Greenland Hill. The attack by the troops of the XVII Corps was so successful, however, that there was no need to call upon the support troops, and the regiments subsequently rejoined their brigade the next day, 6 June 1917.

By now the numbers of the South African 1st Infantry Brigade had dwindled significantly. During April 1917 it had suffered severe casualties, and many troops were laid low by sickness, which wasn't surprising considering the appalling weather and conditions in the trenches generally. For the proud South African brigade to preserve its highly respected identity on the British war front, it required reinforcements, and in larger numbers than had been previously allocated. Between the end of April and the end of June 1917, 1 448 drafts arrived in France to replenish the brigade. Even with these additional men, however, it remained gravely under strength. By the end of June, the 1st Regiment had 38 officers and 680 other ranks; the 2nd Regiment, 37 officers and 601 other ranks; the 3rd Regiment, 35 officers and 691 other ranks; and the 4th Regiment, 39 officers and 818 other ranks.

The following month, the brigade moved to the Somme for training, and on 27 July was transferred to the IV Corps along with the rest of the 9th Division. On 28 July, the South Africans relieved the 174th Infantry Brigade in the Trescault section of the line, situated north of Havrincourt Wood and along the Canal du Nord. At the time this was a relatively quiet region; apart from a few minor raids, nothing much had happened. While the brigade had experienced good weather during their month of summer training, at the end of July the heavens opened and the rains came pouring down again, evoking memories of the miserable October of 1916, when they had suffered in the trenches of the Somme.[16]

By the end of July 1917, when Haig launched his attack on the Ypres Salient, the nature of the war had changed dramatically. The grand plan for 1917, in which the Somme Offensive had been the preliminary component, had proved impossible. This could be ascribed to the failure of the April offensives at Arras and the Aisne, but, more importantly, to the defection of Russia, following the October Revolution spearheaded by Vladimir Lenin and his Bolsheviks, who took over the government and declared the end of Russia's participation in the conflict. The war of two fronts was now a war of a single front.

While the French on the Aisne required his aid, Haig was compelled to protract the fighting in the Arras region, and the time had come to start looking at the offensive against Germany in Flanders. Not only could success there turn back the northern flank of the whole German defence system in the west and destroy the worst of the German submarine bases, it could also restore to Belgium its lost territory and deprive Germany of a prized bargaining asset.

8

The final push

The Third Battle of Ypres

Before General Haig could embark on his campaign against the Germans in Flanders, he still had to clear his flanks. Between 7 and 14 June 1917, he took the Messines–Wytschaete Ridge in what was known as the Battle of Messines. The offensive was conducted by the British Second Army, under the command of General Herbert Plumer, near the village of Messines in Belgian West Flanders. It forced the German Army to move reserves to Flanders from the Arras and Aisne fronts. The British intended to advance from Messines to Passchendaele Ridge and then occupy the Belgian coast up to the Dutch frontier. The offensive was a prelude to a much larger campaign, the Third Battle of Ypres, which began on 11 July with preliminary shelling.

The German front was now less than three kilometres from the town of Ypres, and included all the hills to the east. Friedrich Bertram Sixt von Armin, who had led the IV Corps at the Somme, was in command. As the waterlogged soil of Flanders made it impossible to construct deep dug-outs and trenches, Von Armin came up with the idea for the 'pillbox', a small concrete fort that could be sited among farm ruins or derelict pieces of wood and raised a metre or two above the ground. Heavily guarded by machine guns, and holding between eight and 40 soldiers, the pillbox would become a deadly and efficient defence mechanism.

Preparation for the battle, in which every part of the Ypres Salient was bombarded by Allied fire, lasted for the greater part of July. The advance from the River Lys to a little north of Steenstraate began on the last day of the month. The first day was hugely successful, as the whole of the first line was taken, as well as great parts of the second. Bad weather, however, prevented a further series of planned attacks.

THE FINAL PUSH

The second stage of the Ypres campaign began on 16 August, with the Fifth Army attacking the German third line, Gheluvelt–Langemarck. It resulted in a stalemate. Once again bad weather put a halt to operations. Only in the third week of September, when the weather had improved, could the third stage of the battle begin.

For this, the 9th Division was brought up from the Somme. It arrived at Brandhoek on 14 September to become part of Sir E.A. Fanshawe's V Corps of the Fifth Army. The assault would be led by General Dawson of the South African brigade and General Frank Maxwell of the 27th Brigade. Their front covered some 1.8 kilometres north of the Ypres–Menin road, with the Ypres–Roulers railway running through its centre. The 9th Division formed the right of the Fifth Army, with the South Africans on the left and the 27th Brigade on the right, while the 26th Brigade was held in reserve. The 3rd South African Infantry Regiment, led by Lieutenant-Colonel Thackeray, was supported by the 1st, under Lieutenant-Colonel Heal. The 4th Regiment, led by Lieutenant-Colonel MacLeod, was supported by the 2nd under Major Cochran. On 17 September, they moved onto the front line, relieving the 125th Brigade.[1]

The battle commenced on 20 September 1917, and resulted in a limited advance and the capture of 3 000 German prisoners. John Buchan concluded:

> Few struggles in the campaign were more desperate or carried out in a more gruesome battlefield. The mass of quagmires, splintered woods, ruined husks of pill-boxes, water-filled shell-holes, and foul creeks which made up the land on both sides of the Menin road was a sight which, to the recollection of most men, must seem like a fevered nightmare ... Delville Wood was still for the Brigade the most heroic episode in the War. But its advance on 20th September must without doubt be reckoned its most successful achievement up to that date in the campaign.[2]

Two days after the battle, Dawson wrote: 'The regimental officers were an awful sight this morning, haggard and drawn, un-washed and unshaven for four days, covered with mud and utterly tired, but very happy, and exceedingly proud of their men.'[3]

During the assault, Lance-Corporal W.H. Hewitt of the 2nd Regiment earned himself a Victoria Cross. He had attacked a pillbox in his section and, rushing the doorway, found stern resistance from the garrison within. In spite of a wound, he managed to reach the loophole[4] where he was again injured while attempting to insert a bomb. But he eventually succeeded: the bomb dislodged the occupants and he took the position.[5]

The brigade had suffered numerous casualties. In the 1st Regiment, 58 were killed, including Captain J.T. Bain and Second-Lieutenant E. Spyker, and 291 were wounded and missing; in the 2nd, 61 were killed, including Captain F.M. Davis, Lieutenant E.D. Lucas and Second-Lieutenant A.B. Cooper, and 224 were wounded and missing; in the 3rd, 88 were killed, including Captains E.V. Vivian and A.W.H. McDonald, and Second-Lieutenants W.J. Blanchard, C.F. Coxen, N. Cruddas, N.T. Hendry, J. Newbery, W.P. Sweeney and D.A. Williams, and 283 were wounded and missing; and in the 4th, 56 were killed, including Captain D. Gemmell and Second-Lieutenants B.D. Trethewy, A. Aitken and W.G.S. Forder, and 197 were wounded and missing.[6]

According to Second-Lieutenant Geoffrey Lawrence, who led 1st Regiment, C Company, Captain McDonald had had a premonition of his own death: 'He appeared to dread the coming of the dawn and was apparently convinced that he would fall. He was one of the first to be killed by a burst of machine-gun fire after advancing a short distance from our jumping-off line.'[7]

General Maxwell, commander of the 27th Brigade, was killed by a sniper on the morning of 21 September. A survivor of the Boer War, he had won a Victoria Cross at Sanna's Post.

As usual, the field-ambulance posts had been under constant shell fire. This time, however, the Decauville trains, which were run by a section of the South African railwaymen, helped them evacuate the walking wounded.

Early on the morning of 22 September, the South Africans were relieved at the front line, and by 4 October they were in the Houlle area doing general training. A week later, the 9th Division began to concentrate

THE FINAL PUSH

in the forward area of the XVIII Corps where they relieved the 48th Division and entered the support line along the canal bank at Ypres.

On 13 October, the 2nd and 4th South Africans moved up to the front line to take over trenches held by groups from the 26th and 27th brigades. Due to the terrible weather, the whole country had become a bog. Over the next two days, the men were subjected to intermittent shelling as well as bombing from German planes, before being relieved by the 1st and 3rd regiments. But for five more days the South African brigade remained in the front trenches under constant shelling. By 23 October, when they were moved out of the Ypres Salient, the brigade had suffered 261 casualties, dead and wounded.

The 9th Division was next sent to relieve the 41st Division in the Nieuwpoort area on the Belgian coast, where it remained until 20 November. Here the South Africans were able to spend some time in rest billets while new recruits were brought in to replace those lost in the Third Battle of Ypres. During this time, Lieutenant-Colonel Tanner left to take over command of the 8th Brigade in the 3rd Division, and was succeeded by Lieutenant-Colonel Christian.

The struggle at Ypres reached its conclusion in November. On the 6th, the Canadians took the last section of the Passchendaele Ridge and on the 20th, General Julian Byng, commanding the Third Army, struck at Cambrai.[8] Ten days later the Germans launched counterattacks on the British left at Bourlon and on their right between Masnières and Vendhuile.

On the day of Byng's attack, the 9th Division left the Belgian coast for rest billets in the Fruges area. News of the German counterstroke at Cambrai reached them on 30 November, and on the morning of 1 December they set off on a long march southward in heavy rain and wind, followed by snow and frost. By the time of their arrival at Moislains three days later, the men of the South African brigade had experienced the worst conditions imaginable. Ordered to relieve the 2nd Guards Brigade at Gouzeaucourt, the 2nd and 4th regiments took over a section of the front line, with the 1st in support and the 3rd in reserve. The line, which had been established by the British Guards Division after their advance on 1 December, ran along the east slope of Quentin Ridge and extended from Gauche Wood to a point near the head of Flag Ravine.[9]

For the next few weeks, the South Africans were kept busy bringing up material for the area's defence, burying a large number of British and German dead, digging trenches and building shelters. All through the month they were subjected to heavy shelling, during which time Captain E.C. Bryant and Second-Lieutenants V.S. Dickerson and G.J.S. Mandy were killed.

On the night of 8 December, the 2nd and 4th regiments were relieved by the 1st and 3rd regiments. The 4th became the brigade reserve, while the 2nd formed the garrison of the support and reserve lines. The entire brigade left the line on 13 January 1918 and for ten days was billeted in Moislains, Heudicourt, Fins and Sorel-le-Grand. On 23 January, the 2nd and 3rd regiments were moved once again into the line to relieve units of the 26th Brigade. The 1st and 4th regiments followed the next day. Since 4 December, the brigade's numbers had been depleted from 148 to 79 officers, and from 3 621 to 1 661 men of other ranks.

On 31 January, all four regiments moved from the front trenches to a back area, where for a month they trained for another great battle destined for early March. On 17 February, the regiments gathered for a memorial service at Delville Wood. On the south side of the site, towards Longueval, the beloved Padre Eustace Hill unveiled a tall wooden cross made by Sergeant McFee of the 4th Regiment from one of the shattered trees. It held the inscription: 'In Memory of the Officers and Men of the 1st South African Brigade who fell in Action in July 1916 in the Battle of the Somme.'[10]

In the meantime, a decision was made to reduce the British divisions from 13 to 10 battalions. This meant that one battalion (or regiment) had to be cut from each brigade. It was a sad day when, on 18 February 1918, Generals Jan Smuts and Lukin disbanded the 3rd South African Infantry Regiment (Transvaal and Rhodesia), as over the past year it had received the smallest number of recruits. Officers, NCOs and men joined the other South African regiments.

Gauche and Marrières woods

In early March, in order to return home on leave, Lukin handed over command of the 9th Division to Major-General Henry Hugh Tudor, who had formerly commanded the divisional artillery.[11] At this time, the South African brigade once again moved up to the front. On the night of 12 May, it took over the sector east of Heudicourt from the 116th Brigade of the 39th Division.

The 9th Division formed the extreme left of the Fifth Army, with the 21st Division on its right and the 47th (1/2nd London) Division on its left. The 9th held its front with two brigades, the 26th on the left and the South Africans on the right, with the 27th in reserve. The South African sector covered some two kilometres from just north of Quentin Redoubt to just south of Gauche Wood. The brigade covered not only the front line, but all other trench lines to a depth of about 1.6 kilometres. The forward zone, lying west of the village of Villers-Guislain, was held by the 2nd Regiment on the right and the 1st on the left, with the 4th in reserve in the area behind it.

The outpost line had two important points, Quentin Redoubt, in the north, garrisoned by a company of the 1st Regiment, and Gauche Wood, in the south, held by a company of the 2nd Regiment. Apart from the posts in the forward zone, the specially fortified areas of resistance for the 9th Division were the village of Gouzeaucourt and a place called Queen's Cross to its south-east. For the South Africans, it was Revelon Farm or, failing that, the village of Heudicourt. They were aware of a large concentration of German troops well back in the German hinterland, but had no notion of the Germans' real strength.[12]

The attack was scheduled for 21 March. The 19th brought drizzle, and by sunset the next day a thick fog lay over the area. At precisely 16:45, thousands of shells from more than 6 000 German guns started raining down on the British forward zones. The back areas especially were drenched with gas, which hung like a pall in the moist and heavy air. Second-Lieutenant G.G.J. Lawrence recalled the attack:

> Soon amongst the high explosive shells falling all around we heard the unmistakeable plop, plop, as gas shells fell mixed with the others and

the burnt potato or onion smell warned us it was time to put on our gas helmets. One poor chap could not find his helmet, another had his torn across his face by a flying piece of shrapnel. We waited apprehensively for a direct hit any moment but luckily none came and the barrage lifted back to the front line and also to the artillery lines. We then all staggered out to find our battle positions, trying as best we could to see through helmet eye pieces and the dense fog.[13]

Three German armies, consisting of highly trained elite German storm troops, were simultaneously attacking General Gough and his Fifth Army's extended front and half of the front held by General Byng's Third Army on Gough's left flank. Confusion reigned in the British ranks thanks to the thick mist, and many units that survived the massive bombardment got cut off and wiped out. Before those at the outposts knew it, the Germans were in their rear and they were overwhelmed before they could send back warning. The fog enabled the Germans to bypass the strong points manned by machine guns that Gough had established, and as the day wore on, the Allied situation became desperate. They were covering a front of 65 kilometres with 12 infantry divisions and three cavalry divisions while, by the second day, the Germans had unleashed more than 60 divisions. The Fifth Army was forced to begin a retreat as Third Army positions fell to the south.

At Quentin Redoubt, where a company of the 1st Regiment was stationed, there was no attack. The main assault in that area fell upon the left brigade of the 21st Division, and on B Company of the 2nd Regiment in Gauche Wood. Captain Garnet Green, the company's commander, had three strong points inside the wood and one in the open on the south-west side. Also in the wood were two machine guns and a detachment of the South African Brigade Trench Mortar Battery.

The Germans attacked the wood from the east, and Second-Lieutenant Kennedy fought them with his machine gun until all members of his team were either dead or wounded. He himself was wounded and captured. The enemy then began to enter the wood from the north and overpowered the two posts in the east under Lieutenants Bancroft and Beviss, killing Bancroft and most of his men, and wounding and capturing the rest. Beviss, with nearly half his garrison, managed to reach Captain Green, who then withdrew the men of the third post to join the fourth post in the open ground to the south-west. When the mist lifted, the garrison at Quentin Redoubt to the north opened a heavy flanking fire on the advancing Germans, and for the rest of the day Green and his few men held their position on the outskirts of the wood.[14]

Before midday, the Germans broke into the Fifth Army front at Ronssoy, Hargicourt, Templeux-le-Guérard and Le Verguier, and into the Third Army front at Lagnicourt-Marcel and Bullecourt. That afternoon, orders came for a general retirement of all forward troops. During the evening and early night, the South African brigade fell back from the forward zone.

Throughout the following morning, the Germans gradually closed in on Chapel Hill and Revelon Farm, and took both in spite of a brave defence. In the attack, Captain Liebson, a medical officer with the 4th Regiment, was killed. Just after midday, orders arrived to fall back further to the next line and to be ready to retire later to the next line five kilometres in the rear.

With the Germans in the north behind the British front, the three South African regiments could not keep to the original route of retirement. Instead they had to fall back in a northerly direction and then head west. On the left, the 1st Regiment, under Lieutenant-Colonel Heal, withdrew to the village of Fins. As Lieutenant-Colonel MacLeod, commander of the 4ths, was wounded, what remained of the regiment was taken over by Captain Bunce, who led them to the Fins–Gouzeaucourt road and then west away from Fins. Lieutenant-Colonel Christian and a large part of his 2nd Regiment roughly followed the route taken by the 4ths. Tragically, Green's B Company had no chance to withdraw and was wiped out fighting to the last. By 02:00 in the morning, the brigade had dug in along the Nurlu–Péronne road south-east of Moislains, and was now in divisional reserve.[15]

During the first two days of the battle, the South African brigade had lost about 900 men of all ranks. Two decimated companies of the 1st Regiment, under Captains Burgess and Ward, were separated from the rest in the dark of night, and had spent the next day fighting with the 26th Brigade. In the 2nd Regiment, Captain Green and Lieutenants Bancroft and Terry had been killed; Captains Rogers and Stein had been wounded and captured; Captains Jenkins and Pearse, and Lieutenant Sprenger had been wounded; and Lieutenant Beviss was missing. All the senior officers of the 4th Regiment – Lieutenant-Colonel MacLeod, Majors Clerk and Browne, and Captain Mitchell – had been wounded.

When Saturday 23 March 1918 dawned in another cloud of fog, the South Africans were in reserve on the right flank of the 27th Brigade. But in a wavering front, the brigade was ordered onto the front line again. It had to maintain contact with the 21st Division, which had been forced to retire by the withdrawal on its right from the Péronne bridgehead. Dawson fell back from Moislains, and later positioned himself on the ridge south-west of there, where he was heavily shelled.[16]

Lieutenant Lawrence later recalled:

Early on the morning of the 23rd Major Ormiston came up and gave the officers our orders. He said, 'You are now the rear guard to the whole of this front and you are to hold this line. You will fight to the last man and the last round. There will be no surrender and no retreat. All forward troops of ours retiring, will be stopped on this line, if necessary, with your revolvers and you will shoot any man who refuses to stand.' When he left we set about further improving our defences and awaited the approached enemy. It is difficult to describe the feeling that came over me then that this was to be our final sacrifice. No heroics, but a feeling of great spiritual uplift. We few were safeguarding our weary Brigade – here we stand and here we die – a feeling of utter release from the cares of life and things material came over me. It is not possible to convey the uplift and supreme elation of those moments.[17]

Before dark, the Germans had occupied Moislains and Haute Allaines. Péronne, dominating the Somme and its lakes in northern France, had to be abandoned the same day, and the retreat continued towards the old Somme battlefields.

By dawn on Sunday 24 March, the two South African regiments were holding a patch of ground behind the northern point of Marrières Wood, running north-east in the direction of Rancourt. The land sloped east and then rose to another ridge about a kilometre from where the Germans had set up good observation and machine-gun posts. The South Africans' position had one proper trench and several poor ones, and the whole area was dotted with shell-holes. The brigade numbered about 500, consisting of 478 infantrymen, a section of the 9th Machine Gun Battery and a few men from Brigade Headquarters. Some officers from the transport lines had joined them, so the number of officers was out of all proportion to other ranks.

Dawson, who had taken up headquarters some 275 metres to the rear, could only communicate with the divisional headquarters through runners, and he had no contact with the divisional artillery. Isolated, they were in the dark as to what was happening elsewhere. The men were already exhausted, having been shelled continuously and poisoned by gas, and deprived of hot food and tea for several days. They faced a quandary: on the one hand, they had a long, clear field of fire before them, but, on the other hand, it was a dead end from which there could be no retreat. All the land to the west was wide open to enemy eyes. Each man had 200 rounds of ammunition and a good supply of Lewis-gun drums, but one section of the 9th Machine Gun Battery had only four belts of ammunition. Three of the guns with their teams were sent back to the transport lines at Savernake Wood.[18]

Early on that Sunday morning, Germans were spotted assembling troops on the ridge to the east, and at about 09:00 they opened fire with machine guns, followed by artillery. An hour later, some British guns returned fire, unknowingly at the South Africans and especially the Brigade Headquarters trench, compelling Dawson to shift to a nearby shell-hole. The messengers he sent out to tell the gunners about their error did not seem to get through, as the shelling continued for more than an hour, fortunately with few casualties. Only when the guns had retired did the firing cease.

In the meantime, the Germans had intensified their gunfire and advanced to 685 metres from the brigade's front, where they halted. The men had orders to use their ammunition sparingly, and not to use their rifles until the Germans were within 365 metres. At some stage, Dawson received news from General Tudor that the 35th Division, then at Bray-sur-Somme, would take up position about a kilometre to the rear of the brigade – but, as Buchan pointed out, 'It was never during that day within miles of the South Africans.'[19] Dawson's report on the situation to Tudor was the last communication they had with the 'outside world'.

Their situation was critical. At midday, a frontal attack, an attack on the south and a movement in the north had been held off. The Germans had set fire to the dry grass and, using the smoke as a screen, had worked their way to within 180 metres of the brigade's position in the north, but their progress was miraculously checked.[20]

Elsewhere on the front, the enemy was already at Combles, in the north, and at Péronne and Cléry, in the south. The 21st Division had gone, while the other brigades of the 9th Division were being forced back on the South Africans' left. That afternoon, an officer with some 30 men began to retire under the impression that a general retirement had been ordered. Under enemy machine-gun fire, Major Cochran, Captain Beverley and Regimental Sergeant-Major Keith of the 4th Regiment went out to stop them. They immediately took cover in shell-holes on the north flank, but, sadly, Cochran was fatally wounded by a bullet.

Early in the afternoon, with the Germans about 180 metres from his front and closing in on his flank and rear, Dawson sent Major Ormiston out with some 25 men as a flank guard for the left. During the mission, Ormiston was badly wounded. Then, all the wounded who could hold a rifle were ordered back to the front line and remaining rounds of ammunition were collected from the casualties.

By now, the Germans were well to the west of the brigade and snipers had begun firing from that direction. The most dangerous threat appeared to be from the north, so Dawson sent Lieutenant Cooper of the 2nd Regiment with 20 men to position a flank guard in shell-holes 90 metres from Brigade Headquarters. They fought well, but their casualties were heavy and reinforcements had to be frequently sent. Cooper himself was killed by a shell fragment. Also that afternoon, Lieutenant-Colonel Heal, the commander of the 1st Regiment, who had already been wounded twice, was killed.

All afternoon the terrific shell fire from the gun batteries continued, and a number of light trench mortars hit the north-east corner of the brigade's front, causing many casualties. By now, the whole line was being held by only a few isolated groups. At around 16:00, Christian told Dawson that he feared his men could not hold out much longer: with every machine gun and Lewis gun out of action, and the ammunition nearly gone, the men were at the limit of their physical endurance.[21]

Dawson probably still had the faint hope that he could stand his ground until dark and then fight his way out, but he also had his doubts. His orders were to hold his ground at all costs, but was it not a useless sacrifice? In his diary, he later wrote: 'I cannot see that under the circumstances I had any option but to remain till the end. Far better go down fighting against heavy odds than that it should be said we failed to carry out our orders. To retire would be against all the traditions of the service.'[22]

Some time after 16:00, three fresh German battalions were brought up for the final attack, massing to the east-north-east of Brigade Headquarters and executing the assault in close formation. Waiting for them were just a hundred South Africans, some already wounded, with not a cartridge left between them, except for a few rounds in officers' pistols. It was clear the end had come.

As the enemy surged down upon the haggard little group of unarmed men, officers Dawson, Christian and Beverley went out to meet them. Shouts of 'Why have you killed so many of us?' and 'Why did you not surrender sooner?' greeted them. But Dawson just shook his head. One German soldier said, 'Now we will soon have peace.' The officers were allowed to find Cochran's body and rescue a few brigade papers before they were taken into captivity.[23] One of those taken prisoner was Lieutenant Faulds, who had won the Victoria Cross in September 1916. Father Eustace Hill, who had been tending the wounded, refused the freedom offered to him by the Germans and insisted on going with the other prisoners.[24]

The rest of the 9th Division, along with remnants of the 21st, continued to fight north of the Somme behind Cléry. They moved through Trônes Wood to Longueval, where the 35th Division and the 1st Cavalry Division came to their aid. The two companies of South Africans that had gone astray on the night of the 22nd and a few other parties that had been cut off or lost and unable to rejoin their units, gathered that evening at a point halfway between Bray and Maricourt. They were joined by the brigade's details and transport. Over the next two days, the roughly 450 men were formed into a composite battalion of three companies under Lieutenant-Colonel Young, each company representing a regiment of the South African brigade. No. 1 Company was led by Captain Burgess, No. 2 by Lieutenant Jenner and No. 3 by Lieutenant G. Smith.[25] Lawrence wrote:

> On the 26th we were ordered back to the line now being held at Dernancourt on the river. We marched back against the stream on the roads, choked with retiring troops and artillery. We held our heads up and marched proudly with a swinging step as if we were the Guards. I remember the retiring troops looking at us in amazement as if we were going the wrong way. We were singing as we marched, *Mein Gott, mein Gott, what a bloody fine lot, the Kaiser he will say. Who are we? – we are – we are – the SA Infantry*.[26]

They were ordered to report to the 26th Brigade at Dernancourt, where they found the 9th Division holding a line to just south of Albert. The South Africans positioned themselves in the trenches and along the railway embankment south-east of Albert. The Germans tried to drive them out, but they held on until they were relieved by the Australians on the night of 27 March. The entire 9th Division was then withdrawn from the line.[27]

As at Delville, the South Africans had proudly upheld their reputation in the woods of Gauche and Marrières. General Tudor commented: 'This much is certain, that it was shortage of ammunition alone which made the survivors surrender. The division will not seem the same again without them, and it was they who bore the brunt of the fighting of the 9th

[Division] on the 21st and 22nd.'[28] Dawson had similar praise for his men:

> For the two years I have been in France I have seen nothing better. Until the end they appeared to me quite perfect. The men were cool and alert, taking advantage of every opportunity, and, when required, moving forward over the open under the hottest machine-gun fire and within 100 yards of the enemy. They seemed not to know fear, and in my opinion they put forth the greatest effort of which human nature is capable. I myself witnessed several cases of great gallantry... It must be borne in mind that the Brigade was in an exhausted state before the action, and in the fighting of the three previous days it was reduced in numbers from a trench strength of over 1,800 to 500.[29]

The Battle of the Lys

On 25 March 1918, the Germans launched an assault all along the front, forcing the British back from their positions on the Somme Canal. By that evening, the Germans had driven a deep wedge through the old battlefield zone and had advanced as far as the Ancre River near Beaumont-Hamel. Several towns and villages, including Maricourt and Bapaume, fell to them, and when Albert fell a new line was established west of the town.

On 28 March, the Germans launched a big attack on the Third Army at Arras, but despite their superior numbers, they did not succeed. Another assault was launched on 4 April against the British units holding the line at Villers-Bretonneux, with limited success, and in a final attempt to break through to Amiens, a further attack on Villers-Bretonneux commenced on 24 April. This time the Germans were supported by tanks. It was the first tank battle to take place on the battlefields of Europe.[30]

Lieutenant Frank Mitchell, a commander of one of the British tanks, described it thus:

> [A] great thrill ran through us all. Opening the loophole, I looked out. There, some 300 yards away, a round, squat-looking monster was advancing. Behind it came waves of infantry and further away to left

and right crawled two more of these armed tortoises. So we had met our rivals at last! For the first time in history tank was encountering tank! ...

Suddenly, against our steel wall, a hurricane of hail pattered, and the interior was filled with myriads of sparks and flying splinters. Something rattled against the steel helmet of the driver sitting next to me and my face was stung with minute fragments of steel. The crew flung themselves flat on the floor. The driver ducked his head and drove straight on. Above the roar of our engine could be heard the staccato rat-tat-tat-tat of machine guns and another furious jet of bullets sprayed our steel side, the splinters clanging viciously against the engine cover ... as the ground was heavily scarred with shell holes we kept going up and down like a ship in a heavy sea, making accurate shooting difficult ... Nearing the village of Cachy, I saw to my astonishment that the two female tanks were slowly limping away to the rear. They had both been hit by shells almost immediately on their arrival and had great holes in their sides ... We still were lucky enough to dodge the enemy shelling, although the twisting and turning once or twice almost brought us on top of our own trenches.[31]

For a brief time, Villers-Bretonneux was in German hands, but it was reoccupied the next day by the British. Even though fighting continued here and there for some time, the Germans had given up any serious effort on this front.[32]

Meanwhile, on 28 March, the 9th Division had been sent north to join General Plumer's Second Army in Belgium. Travelling by train, they reached the Dickebusch area at the end of the month. Replacements were sent out from England and within a few days the brigade numbered 39 officers and 1 473 other ranks.

The mornings of 9 and 10 April were filled with the rumbling of heavy gunfire from the front line to the east. The Germans' target was now the area on both sides of the River Lys between the La Bassée Canal and the Messines-Wytschaete Ridge. The brigade was soon marched to its deploying positions, its objective being the Messines-Wytschaete road on the crest of the ridge. The 1st Regiment would be on the right, the 2nd on the left, with the 4th in support. Lawrence was once again thrown into the fray:

> We formed into three lines, or waves, of attack. Captain Ward now came up to me and said, 'You know, Lawrence, this is not fair, you and I have been through it time and again – we can't go on like this and get away with it.' I said, 'I know, skipper, it's bad luck,' and to break the tension suggested I should take the front wave and guide our right flank. He agreed and took charge of the second wave with a junior officer, Second-Lieutenant Hopgood, leaving two other junior officers to the third wave ... Machine guns and rifle fire opened up on us at once.[33]

The South Africans made a brave stand at Messines Ridge, which played a vital part in the Battle of the Lys. They held on in the face of superior enemy numbers and heavy firing, and when the Germans were able to occupy the ridge on 12 April, they prevented them from advancing any further for a whole day. South African brigade casualties incurred during the three days of the fighting numbered 639: 89 killed, 270 wounded and 280 missing (most of whom were found dead afterwards). The 1st Regiment, on the right, suffered the heaviest casualties. The 2nd had comparatively fewer, while the 1st lost three officers and nine were wounded, with a proportionate number of casualties from other ranks.

On 16 April, the South Africans took part in defensive operations east of Kemmel Hill as part of the Lys Campaign. The 1st and 4th regiments had 250 men each, and the 2nd, 292 men. On 17 April, the brigade was placed temporarily under the 26th Brigade. The following morning, under cover of mist, the Germans captured the advance posts held by the 1st Regiment, killing Lieutenant Hogg. (By the end of it, 48 men were missing.) On the 20th, the 4th Regiment, in the southern part of the Vierstraat line, was relieved, and two days later the 1st and 2nd regiments were also relieved and moved to Dickebusch. On the 23rd, the whole brigade reassembled in the Hopoutre area.

By now it was clear that the reconstructed brigade could not continue.

The new recruits had already been used up in the heavy fighting on the Messines Ridge, and there were no more reinforcements. Consequently, the men, together with drafts arriving from England, were organised into one battalion and placed under the command of Lieutenant-Colonel H.W.M. Bamford of the 2nd Regiment. The total strength of its four companies stood at 59 officers and 1 527 other ranks. Attached to this composite battalion were the 9th (Service) Battalion of the Scottish Rifles and the 2nd Battalion of the Royal Scots Fusiliers.

The last major episode of the Battle of the Lys began on 29 April, when the Germans launched an attack to capture the Scherpenberg, a hill to the north-west of Kemmel Hill. Throughout the attack the South African lines were shelled constantly and movement during the day was dangerous. The Royal Scots Fusiliers suffered heavily and Lieutenant B.W. Goodwin was killed by shell fire. On the night of 5 May, the composite battalion rejoined the 9th Division, and on 25 June they saw action near Meteren, which they helped to capture on 19 July. In this latter battle, five men of the battalion were killed. Two officers, Lieutenants Harvey and Uys, were wounded along with 21 men of other ranks.

For the northern part of the British line, those summer months were relatively quiet, as the war tide had flowed southward. On 28 August, the composite battalion marched to Lumbres, where it prepared for disbandment. Since its formation on 24 April, the battalion had been almost continuously on the line, and had lost seven officers and 84 men. Of the 11 wounded officers and 329 wounded men, 27 would later die from their injuries. One man was listed as missing.[34]

On 11 September 1918, the battalion was withdrawn from the 9th Division and transferred to the VII Corps, with whom it trained until 22 September, when it joined the 66th Division attached to the First Army. It was once again reorganised into a brigade, this time under the command of General Tanner. The three infantry battalions were joined by the signal company, the South African Light Trench Mortar Battery and the 1st South African Field Ambulance. The 1st Regiment was led by Major H.H. Jenkins, the 2nd by Lieutenant-Colonel Bamford and the 4th by Lieutenant-Colonel D.M. MacLeod.

The reputation of heroes

On 8 and 9 October, the South Africans saw action from the village of Beaurevoir to Maretz. And from 17 to 20 October, they took part in the British attack on the Hermann Line. Between 8 and 19 October, the South Africans took four German officers and 1 238 men of other ranks prisoner. Their own casualties numbered 47 officers (six dead) and 1 229 men (184 dead).

When the armistice came into effect on 11 November 1918, the South Africans were at the forefront of the British advance. The end of the war marked the beginning of many months of demobilisation. Finally, in June 1919, the bulk of the South African brigade's remaining members boarded a requisitioned German liner bound for home.[35]

John Buchan summed up their achievement in *The History of the South African Forces in France*:

> We have seen pasty-faced youths from the slums of cities toughen into redoubtable soldiers, and boys new from office-stool and college classroom become on the instant leaders of men and Berserks in battle. The Brigade had the initial advantage of drawing upon men of a fine physique, and, in many cases, of practical experience in a rough and self-reliant life. Its recruits, too, as I have already said, showed a high average of education, and many who never left the ranks were well qualified for commissions. They developed rapidly a perfect esprit de corps which, because they were so few and so far from home, was more than the solidarity of a fighting unit, and became something like the spirit of a race and a nation. I do not think a more perfect brotherhood-in-arms could have been found on any front … There is one quality of the South Africans which deserves especial mention – I mean their curious modesty … To talk to them after a hard-fought action was to hear a tale of quite ordinary and prosaic deeds, in which little credit was sought for themselves but much given to others. They had that gentle and inflexible pride which is too proud to make claims, and leaves the bare fact to be its trumpeter … They feared very little on earth except the reputation of heroes.[36]

On the road to victory in France, the South African brigade suffered close on 15 000 casualties, nearly 300 per cent of its original strength. Of these, about 5 000 had been killed. By comparison, the South African contingent in East Africa was nearly twice the size of the force in France, but its losses were about a quarter of those on the Western Front. South Africa contributed over 136 000 troops to the Allied cause.

The brave South Africans made a massive contribution to the war effort, but their crowning glory was certainly their achievements in France. Not knowing what awaited them, in the summer of 1915 they sailed to a foreign country. For three years they fought competently with steadfast honour. Never more than a few thousand in number, and regularly short of drafts, they made a name for themselves and for South Africa. At Delville, Marrières and Messines they showed what resolution in defence really means. These men, these volunteers, could have chosen to stay at home, living a life of comfort and ease. They could have avoided the misery, the death and the horrors of the trenches. But they made a choice and, having done so, were fully resolved to endure to the end.

APPENDIX I

Heavy artillery

On arriving in England, the five batteries of the South African Heavy Artillery Brigade were armed with six-inch howitzers and affiliated to the Royal Garrison Artillery, becoming the 73rd, 74th, 71st, 72nd and 75th siege batteries. In April 1916, a sixth battery, the 125th, was formed. Early in 1918, a seventh battery, the 542nd, and an eighth, the 46th, were created, but when they arrived in France they were broken up, and their guns and personnel distributed, the first between the 75th and the 125th, and the second between the 72nd and the 74th. A ninth battery, the 552nd, armed with eight-inch guns, was formed in the autumn of 1918, but the war ended before it could be brought into action.

At first the batteries were independent units, allotted to various corps and heavy artillery groups. It was not until the beginning of 1918 that they were brought together, and two South African brigades formed, the 44th and the 50th. The 44th included the 73rd (SA), 71st (SA), 125th (SA) and 20th batteries; the 50th included the 74th (SA), 72nd (SA), 75th (SA) and 275th.

73rd Siege Battery, Royal Garrison Artillery
After a period of training in England, the 73rd landed at Le Havre on 1 May 1916, under the command of Major Walter Brydon. On 9 May, it reached Bienvillers-au-Bois, in the Somme area, where it took up a battle position under the command of the 19th Artillery Group. On 15 May, it fired its first round for sighting purposes.

On 1 July, when the First Battle of the Somme began, the 73rd covered the infantry advance on Gommecourt, attaining a record of 32 rounds in eight minutes with each gun. On 17 July, it moved to the village of Berles-au-Bois and was engaged in smashing enemy trenches and counter-battery work in the neighbourhoods of Monchy-au-Bois and Ransart. On 25 August, it moved back to Doullens and thence to Albert, where it took up position in the ruins of La Boisselle. Here it supported the attack on Pozières, Courcelette and Thiepval. Major Brydon was wounded while observing for the battery in the front trenches. In October, the 73rd advanced to Pozières, where it suffered considerably from enemy fire and had its fill of discomforts from the weather during that appalling winter.

In February 1917, Brydon returned to duty. On the 15th of that month, two battery officers, Lieutenant Campion and Second-Lieutenant J. Currie, advancing with the infantry to capture Boom Ravine, rallied two companies whose officers had all been killed and captured two strong machine-gun posts. Campion fell in this gallant exploit, and Currie received the Distinguished Service Order.

In March, in heavy snowfall, the 73rd left the Somme and went north to the Arras area. In the Battle of Arras on 8 April, it supported the Canadians' attack on Vimy Ridge. By noon the advance had progressed so far that the battery was now out of range, and so it moved forward to Thélus, where it suffered many casualties. Notably, on 1 May, Brydon was wounded for the second time. Soon after, the 73rd was relieved and retired to Houdain for its first spell out of the line since its arrival in France.

With Captain P.A.M. Hands temporarily in command, the battery returned to Thélus on 28 May, where it remained until the last day of June, when it was transferred to Flanders. At its new position in the Ypres Salient, at the village of Zillebeke and close to Hill 60, the 73rd was exposed to enemy fire within 1 000 yards of the front line. Owing to this, working parties had to be sent up overnight and travel in single file for over three miles, past such dangerous places as 'Hellfire Corner' and 'Shrapnel Corner'.

The guns were in position by 17 July, and on 25 July Major Brydon returned from hospital. The 73rd was bombed night and day by enemy aircraft, and had no means of making shell-proof cover, for the water was only two feet below the surface of the ground. On 29 August the battery was relieved for a short period, but it was not until 1 November that it finally left Zillebeke and the Second Battle of Ypres. During the four months there, the 73rd had nine guns put out of action by hostile fire. On 7 October, Major Brydon had been gassed and sent to hospital for the third time.

The battery returned to Thélus, which was now a quiet area, before moving to Liévin, west of Lens. Here the men had comfortable quarters, but were kept busy preparing positions in anticipation of an attack. The 73rd pulled out to Béthune for Christmas, and on 5 January 1918, took up position at La Loisne, where it received news of its inclusion in the new 44th (SA) Brigade.

APPENDIX I: HEAVY ARTILLERY

71st Siege Battery, Royal Garrison Artillery

The 71st, under the command of Major H.C. Harrison, arrived at Le Havre on 16 April 1916. Destined for the impending offensive on the Somme, its first position was at Mailly-Maillet in the VIII Corps' area of operation. On 2 June, however, it was ordered north to Ypres, where the Canadians were heavily engaged. On 18 June, the battery returned to Mailly-Maillet, where it participated in the first days of the First Battle of the Somme. On 5 July it moved to Bécordel-Bécourt and supported the attack on Mametz Wood, Ovillers, and Contalmaison, and the September attack on Martinpuich and Flers. On 20 September it moved forward to Bazentin, where it fought in the Somme mud until the end of the year.

After a short period of rest, the 71st found itself at Ovillers on 2 January 1917. During February and March, it moved slowly eastward, following the German retreat. In April it was engaged against the Hindenburg Line and had a share in the fierce fighting around Bullecourt.

In July and August, the 71st had a position at Croisilles, some 2 000 yards from the enemy front. One section moved north on 31 August to a position just outside the Menin Gate at Ypres, and the rest followed on 15 September. Here the battery took part in the Third Battle of Ypres, supporting the South African Infantry Brigade's attack on 20 September. This was the first time the 71st saw action with its own infantry. Its position was badly exposed and it suffered many casualties from enemy shell fire and aerial bombing. The battery was relieved on 22 October.

Much worn out, the 71st now moved to Liévin in the Lens area, where the men found some respite. On 8 November, the 71sts swopped guns with the 73rds and went south to Bapaume. From its new position on the outskirts of Gouzeaucourt, the battery participated in the Battle of Cambrai on 20 November. The German counterattack of 30 November came very near its position, and during those stormy days the battery, now under the command of Major P.N.G. Fitzpatrick, did brilliant work under difficult circumstances. Unhappily, on 14 December at Beaumetz, Fitzpatrick was killed by a chance shell. On 18 December, the guns were withdrawn to Beaumetz, and by the end of the month the 71st was on the front between Béthune and Lens, one section going to La Bourse and the other to Beuvry. Here it became part of the 44th (SA) Brigade.

125th Siege Battery, Royal Garrison Artillery

The 125th was organised on 4 April 1916, under the command of Major

R.P.G. Begbie. It arrived at Le Havre on 21 July and reached the Third Army's area of operation on 26 July, during the fourth week of the First Battle of the Somme. The battery was positioned at Sailly-au-Bois, on the extreme left of the battleground, where its principal targets were the German batteries at Puisieux, Bucquoy, and Grandcourt. On 19 October, the 125th moved to the eastern edge of Englebelmer Wood, where it was attached to Sir Hubert Gough's Fifth Army. Here it prepared for and participated in the attack on Beaumont-Hamel on 13 November. This was a difficult task, because the battery's gun positions were far from the road and every 100-pound shell had to be carried some 400 yards through a swamp until a line of rails could be laid.

On 20 January 1917, the 125th moved to a new position on the Auchonvillers road, half a mile north of Mailly-Maillet, where for the next few weeks it was engaged by enemy batteries and a German heavy-calibre naval gun. On 22 February, after suffering many losses, the 125th was moved to better quarters at Beaumont-Hamel.

On 22 March, the battery moved over challenging roads north to Arras, where its first position was beside the Faubourg d'Amiens. On the second day of the Battle of Arras, the 125th moved east to Saint-Sauveur-le-Vicomte, and on 16 April moved forward a mile east of Tilloy-lès-Mofflaines, on the Arras–Cambrai road. Here the battery was too exposed and so, three days later, it was moved back to Tilloy Wood. For the next month its guns were constantly in action day and night. On 11 May, the 125th was pulled out for a much-needed rest, during which time it received reinforcements to bring it up to strength.

On 18 June, the battery moved to Roclincourt in the Oppy sector, where its first leave to England was granted. On 21 July it took up position in Béthune, near Lens, where it fell under the First Army. From 15 to 23 August, the 125th was heavily engaged in supporting the Canadians' attack on Hill 70, east of Loos. On the evening of the 23rd, the battery moved forward into the ruins of Loos and rendered brilliant service in the action of the following day. Its cables were constantly cut by shell fire, and on 5 September it suffered 28 casualties from a deluge of German gas shells. The battery was withdrawn to rest on 8 September, but resumed its work on 21 September until 8 October. When the four guns were brought back to Béthune, it was found that not one was fit for further action.

The battery was now attached to the Belgian Army as one of the 13 siege batteries constituting the XIV Corps Heavy Artillery. It was positioned in

APPENDIX I: HEAVY ARTILLERY

swampy country in the neighbourhood of Steenvoorde and Oostkerke. On 3 December it moved to the La Bassée area and rejoined the First Army, taking up position at Annequin. Following a short respite at the beginning of January 1918, Major Begbie handed over command to Major J.G. Stewart and the 125th became part of the 44th (SA) Brigade.

44th (South African) Heavy Artillery Brigade

On 29 January 1918, South African Defence Force lieutenant-colonel T.H. Blew took command of the 44th (SA) Heavy Artillery Brigade headquartered at Beuvry Castle. The four batteries that made up the brigade were in position east and south of Béthune. As this was a quiet sector during February and March, the batteries prepared detailed reserve positions in expectation of a German attack.

From 1 April, the guns were actively engaged in counter-battery work. One of the main objectives of the German assault that came on 9 April was the right pillar of the British front at Givenchy, held by the 55th Division. All the brigade's battery positions, except that of the 125th, had been located by the enemy, who from the early morning drenched them with high explosives and gas. For a time, all communications with Brigade Headquarters were cut. The falling back of the division on their left allowed the enemy to advance almost up to their gun positions.

The 73rd was in the most hazardous position, and owing to the shelling it was impossible to bring up motor transport to evacuate its guns. Major Brydon, who had returned the month before from hospital to command the battery, was ordered to blow up his guns, but instead he served out rifles and a couple of machine guns to his men and bade them stand to. At one stage he had to send the breech blocks to the rear for safety, but the attack was stayed before it reached the guns and the breech blocks were brought back. Though wounded and gassed, Brydon refused to leave his battery. When he was finally compelled to retire, his men dragged the guns for nearly a mile under cover of darkness. By 02:00 on the morning of the 10th, a new position had been found and the battery was once again in action. The casualties of the brigade that day included 13 men killed, and six officers and 29 men wounded.

The stand on 9 April checked the enemy for a time, and all batteries were able to take up less exposed positions. They suffered, however, from continuous bombardment, and on 12 April the heroic commander of the 73rd was

143

killed by a shell. Brydon had left the doctor's hands when a severe burst of German fire began, hurrying forward to see to his guns. No officer in the British Army had a finer record for gallantry and devotion to duty. His battery was known everywhere on the front as 'Brydon's Battery', and he was beloved by his men, as his only thought was for them.

The 18th of April saw another severe bombardment, when five officers of the 73rd were gassed – Captain Hands, the second in command, and Second-Lieutenants Maasdorp and Brown died of the effects. Since the battle began, the brigade had lost five officers. In addition, the expenditure of ammunition during that period had been enormous: the 71st, for example, fired 11 000 rounds.

The brigade remained on the front until 27 June, when it was brought out to rest. On 27 July, Lieutenant-Colonel Blew relinquished his command. He was temporarily succeeded by Major E.H. Tamplin, who handed over to Lieutenant-Colonel G.M. Bennett, former commander of the 74th, on 17 August.

On returning to the line on 2 August, the brigade took up positions farther south in the neighbourhood of Hulluch. On 22 August, its headquarters was heavily shelled and one member of staff was killed. During August and September, the brigade batteries supported the steady pressure maintained along this sector in anticipation of a German retirement. On 2 October, the enemy fell back three miles to the line of the Haute Deûle Canal, and the advance of the Fifth Army began.

As soon as roads were repaired, the guns moved up to Douvrin, Hulluch, and Wingles, and on 12 October the brigade assisted the 15th Division in capturing Vendin. Because it was so difficult to bridge the numerous canals, siege batteries could only follow slowly, and the Germans were already on the line of the Scheldt River before they again saw action. The enemy kept up a heavy bombardment during the first week of November, and on the night of 6 November 1918 the brigade suffered its last casualties in the war. The bridging of the Scheldt was in rapid progress, and the batteries were preparing to advance across, when hostilities ceased.

74th Siege Battery, Royal Garrison Artillery

The 74th landed at Le Havre on 30 April 1916, under the command of Major Pickburn. It proceeded to Authuille and on 4 May took up position at Bienvillers-au-Bois. On the first day of the First Battle of the Somme, the

74th's four guns fired 1 733 rounds, supporting the infantry's unsuccessful attack at Gommecourt. It then took over the 73rd's position and later, on 27 August, moved to the Martinsart–Aveluy road for the operations against the enemy at Thiepval.

On 7 October, the battery arrived in the orchard at Colincamp, a place without cover and a favourite enemy target. On 7 November, Pickburn was killed. On 20 November, the enemy kept up a severe bombardment all day and four gunners lost their lives. It was the same on the 29th, when an armour-piercing shell penetrated a cellar protected by seven feet of earth and bricks, and killed the three occupants. Despite the position being untenable for a heavy battery, it was held until early December, when a move was made to Auchonvillers.

The battery moved to Gouy-en-Artois, and then to Arras and the Faubourg d'Amiens. In the early weeks of 1917, it went to Rivière, opposite Ficheux, and then back to Arras.

In the Battle of Arras, the 74th supported the South African Infantry Brigade's advance and the fighting in the Oppy, Gavrelle, and Rœux areas. At the time, they were the farthest forward siege guns on the British front. The battery continued its operations until the battle died down. During that time, Major Tamplin, who had taken over from Pickburn, was gassed and sent back to England, and Major Murray-MacGregor took over command. By 5 July, the whole battery had moved to Ypres, where it took up position on the canal bank near 'Shrapnel Corner'. There, during the first stages of the Third Battle of Ypres, the 74th suffered the usual fate of combatants in the salient.

Murray-MacGregor was succeeded by Major G.M. Bennett, and the battery moved to a position on the Verbrandenmolen road, and a little later to Hooge in Belgium. This was its station for the remainder of the battle. The 74th suffered many casualties from shell fire and gas, and the reliefs coming by Menin Road faced an incessant enemy barrage. There were only 17 per shift for all four guns; had three of the guns not been knocked out, the task would have been impossible. When at last the battery was withdrawn, it was reduced to one gun and 70 men. On 21 December, a reinforced 74th returned to the line as part of the 50th (SA) Brigade.

72nd Siege Battery, Royal Garrison Artillery

The 72nd landed in France on 21 April 1916, under the command of Major C.W. Alston. Its first position was at Mailly-Maillet, from where it was sent to Ypres on 3 June along with the 71st to assist the Canadians. When Alston was severely wounded, Captain A.G. Mullins took command. Returning to Mailly-Maillet, the battery took part in the opening days of the First Battle of the Somme, before moving first to Englebelmer and then to Authuille. The latter was an excellent position, with a steep bank in front of the guns and the Ancre River behind. The battery remained here for eight months, until the enemy's retirement enabled it to advance to Thiepval and Grandcourt.

On 22 March 1917, the 72nd moved to the Arras area, taking up position near Berthonval Wood, a few miles east of Mont-Saint-Éloi. From here the battery took part in the battle for Vimy Ridge, after which it moved forward to Souchez, below the northern end of the ridge. On 30 April it retired to Houdain for its first rest since arriving in France.

On 12 May, the 72nd was at Thélus. Four days later it was transferred to the 1st Canadian Heavy Artillery Group, and took up position in the Zouave Valley, near Givenchy. There it remained for three months, supporting the Canadian attack at Lens. On 17 October, Captain C.P. Ward took over command, and on 25 October, the battery went north with the Canadian Corps to Ypres, where it relieved the 73rd battery in a peculiarly unhealthy spot between Zillebeke and Observatory Ridge. During the first 24 hours here, the 72nd suffered 12 casualties.

On 11 January 1918, after a period of rest, the battery took up position behind the Damm Strasse, near Wytschaete. The 72nd was now brigaded with the 50th (SA) Brigade.

75th Siege Battery, Royal Garrison Artillery
The 75th reached France on 24 April 1916, under the command of Major W.H.L. Tripp. It took up a position on the outskirts of Albert, near the hospital, and was attached to the III Corps. The battery participated in the preparation for the First Battle of the Somme, and on 1 July fired 1 312 rounds before noon. On 14 July it moved to Becourt Wood, and on the 29th to a position north of Fricourt Wood. Here it supported the attack of 15 September.

On 21 September, the 75th moved to the wood near Bazentin-le-Grand, where it was in touch with the South African Infantry Brigade during its action at the Butte de Warlencourt. On 29 January 1917, it moved back to Albert, and in early February went south of the Somme into the old French area. There it advanced as the Germans fell back, crossing the Somme at

Péronne on 25 March and occupying ground successively at Templeux-la-Fosse and Longavesnes. On 6 April, at Sainte-Emilie, the battery fired its first shot at the Hindenburg Line, and remained in that area until the end of June, when it moved north to Flanders.

By 13 July, all four guns were in position on the Vlamertinghe–Elverdinghe road, where, owing to the flat topography, the battery had great difficulty finding suitable observation posts. On the night of 30 July, it moved forward to the bank of the Ypres Canal, where it provided support at the beginning of the Third Battle of Ypres. Later it advanced to the Pilckem Ridge, where in a highly exposed position it supported the attack on Houthulst Forest and Passchendaele. The battery was exceptionally fortunate because, between 31 July and 20 December, it experienced only one officer casualty. In the middle of December, the 72nd went south to the Zillebeke Lake, and on 11 January 1918 moved to the Damm Strasse as part of the 50th (SA) Brigade.

50th (South African) Heavy Artillery Brigade

The 50th (SA) Heavy Artillery Brigade was formed in January 1918, under the command of Lieutenant-Colonel Tripp, formerly of the 75th battery. On 28 January, the brigade was attached to the Australian Corps, occupying positions between Zillebeke and Wytschaete. On 26 February, it went to General Headquarters Reserve, encamped near Bailleul. On 6 March, the 496th (SA) Siege Battery arrived and was split between the 72nd and 74th batteries, making them six-gun batteries. On 10 March, the brigade was ordered to prepare positions behind the Portuguese divisions, but these orders were later cancelled. On 13 March, it was attached to Sir H. Plumer's Second Army and on 24 March, after the great German attack had been launched at Saint-Quentin, it began to move southwards. On the 28th, it was at Neuville-Saint-Vaast during the German assault on Arras and on the 30th was attached to the Canadian Corps.

During April, the batteries of the brigade moved into position at Roclincourt, to the north-east of Arras, and settled down to the familiar type of trench warfare. Since the entire military situation was uncertain at the time, preparation of reserve-battery positions was critical. Five series of trenches were selected, varying from three to 15 miles behind those in use. On 1 May, the brigade was ordered north: the 72nd and 74th batteries joining the I Corps near Mazingarbe, and the others going to the XIII Corps in the vicinity of

Hinges. By 3 May, these orders had been changed and the whole brigade was sent to Arras to the XVII Corps. There it remained until the end of August, engaged in the usual trench warfare. On 7 August, Captain E.G. Ridley was promoted to major in command of the 74th battery, to replace Major Bennett, who had gone to command the 44th brigade.

On 26 August, the brigade supported the advance of the Canadian Corps and the 51st Division, which resulted in the capture of Monchy-le-Preux. The batteries now began to move forward along the Arras–Cambrai road, where they were engaged in cutting the wire of the Drocourt-Quéant Switch. On 1 September, the brigade's medical officer, Captain G.R. Cowie, was seriously wounded. He died two days later. On 2 September, the Canadians carried the Drocourt-Quéant Switch. All the guns in the brigade assisted in the preliminary bombardment and the subsequent barrage. The following day, the brigade passed under the XXII Corps, who held the line of the Sensée River, to protect the flank of the Canadian thrust towards Cambrai.

No serious operations took place for more than three weeks, but on the 27th came the great advance of the Canadian and XVII Corps towards and beyond Cambrai, and it became clear that a general enemy retirement was a matter of days away. On 3 October, Major Ridley left for England to form a new eight-inch South African battery, and his command of the 74th was taken over by Major C.J. Forder. On 11 October, the brigade came under the Canadian Corps.

The following day, the batteries advanced first to Tortequesne, and then to Estrées and Noyelle-Vion. On 19 October, they were at Lewarde, and on the 20th a section of the 74th battery moved to Wallers to support the Canadian attack. This was the brigade's last engagement, as it was placed in the army reserve on 24 October, where it remained until the armistice on 11 November.

(All information extracted from John Buchan, *The History of the South African Forces in France*, Edinburgh: Thomas Nelson and Sons, 1920.)

APPENDIX II

South African Signal Company (Royal Engineers)

Inception and organisation, August to October 1915
At the start of the war, communications in the Imperial Army were organised by the Signals Branch of the Corps of Royal Engineers. They provided and maintained all communications, which comprised telegraphs, telephones, visual signalling and despatch riders (horse, motorcycle and bicycle). Towards the end of the campaign in German South-West Africa, the Union of South Africa set about raising a Divisional Signal Company to serve overseas.

The raising of this company was entrusted to Major N. Harrison, engineer-in-chief of the Union Post Office, who had acted as director of signals to the Union forces during both the rebellion and the South-West African campaign. The 230 men he assembled in Potchefstroom during August and September 1915 were fully representative of all South Africa: 53.7 per cent were recruited from the Transvaal, 25 per cent from the Cape, 12.7 per cent from Natal, 6.6 per cent from the Orange Free State, and 2 per cent from Rhodesia and various other places.

Skilled telegraphists and linemen from the Union Post Office, the majority of whom had served in South-West Africa, formed the backbone of the company. Drivers were recruited mainly from the farming population, and included many young Afrikaners. Officers were selected from officials of the engineering branch of the post office and electrical engineers from the Witwatersrand.

On 17 October, the company sailed for England on the *Kenilworth Castle*, with six officers (Major Harrison commanding, and Lieutenants J.A. Dingwall, R.H. Covernton, J. Jack, F.H. Michell and F.M. Ross) and 22 men of other ranks. They arrived at Bordon Camp on 4 November.

Reorganisation and training in England, November 1915 to April 1916
As the South African Infantry Brigade would constitute only one-third of the infantry of an Imperial division, the signal company could not serve with the brigade in the capacity of a divisional signal company as originally planned. The War Office decided to reorganise it into the Corps Signal Company,

which would receive the necessary specialised training at the Signal Service Training Centre in Bedfordshire. The company accordingly left for Hitchin on 23 November, and during the next few days was reorganised.

The Corps Signal Company's task was to provide communications between the headquarters of the army corps and the infantry divisions with their associated divisional field artilleries. In addition, the Corps Signal Company acted as a repair workshop and supply store for the signal material and apparatus required by all units and formations within the corps. It also assisted with signal arrangements and provided electric lighting for corps headquarters. On 17 January 1916, all sections were concentrated in order to continue their training as a company, and were billeted in the small villages of Clifton, Shefford and Broome.

Towards the end of March, the great blizzard of 1916 destroyed much of the post office and railway telegraph systems in the Midlands. All experienced men in the company were called upon to assist with repairs. On 10 April, the company reassembled in Southampton and set sail on the SS *Investigator* for Le Havre, arriving on the 21st. From there it moved to Vignacourt, a village in the Somme Valley between Abbeville and Amiens, now the headquarters of the newly constituted XV Corps under Lieutenant-General Home. On 23 April, Major Harrison was appointed assistant director of Army Signals and the company became the XV Corps Signal Company. It served with the XV Corps for the remainder of the war.

A few days later, the corps moved into the line between the III and XIII corps, becoming part of the Fourth Army under General Sir H. Rawlinson. It took over the sector fronting Fricourt and Mametz between Bécourt and Carnoy. On 30 April, the XV Corps Signal Company took over from the XIII Corps Signal Company at Heilly, near Corbie. BF and EG sections were sent to join the headquarters in the line of the 7th and 21st divisions, respectively. BF Section later proceeded to Ville-sur-Ancre, where Brigadier-General Napier, commanding the Corps Heavy Artillery, had his headquarters. The section took charge of the heavy artillery's communications on 27 April.

The Battle of the Somme, July to November 1916
The start of active operations brought the work of the operators and despatch riders at headquarters and with the heavy artillery to a point of extreme pressure, which was maintained with little variation throughout the months that ensued.

Up to 2 000 telegrams, and an even greater number of Despatch Rider

APPENDIX II: SOUTH AFRICAN SIGNAL COMPANY

Letter Service packets, were received or despatched daily. The telephone exchanges at both corps and heavy-artillery headquarters, with over 60 and 30 connections, respectively, worked hard day and night. The destruction of lines by hostile shelling and traffic was met by the skilful use of alternative routes and by the impressive speed at which the maintenance linemen carried out the repairs.

On 10 July, BG Section, under the command of Lieutenant Covernton, did a notably fine job of laying and maintaining lines through the intense barrages surrounding Mametz Wood. On 14 July, another Allied general assault secured the line along the ridge between Bazentin-le-Petit and Longueval. The memorable struggle of the South African Infantry Brigade for Delville Wood had begun, and over a mile of ground had been gained. The corresponding extension of communications necessarily taxed all sections to their limits. The advanced divisional headquarters moved up to Fricourt Castle, and a 24-wire heavy route was rapidly constructed by the Fourth Army's signal companies from Méaulte to this point, and thence to Mametz, in readiness for the advance. In addition, the wire light route built by the XV Corps Company was extended by the Air Line Section past Fricourt, up Death Valley, to Mametz Wood. Although the next deep advance was not to occur for another two months, the German artillery had destroyed communication lines back to points thousands of yards from the front, so there were a lot of repairs to be done.

As July wore on, the demand for additional forward communication increased, as did the strength of the hostile fire. It was obvious that no satisfactory communication could be secured beyond Fricourt except by burying cables, and so it was decided to bury 16 pairs of armoured cables from the head of the open route at Mametz to the dug-outs at Pommiers Redoubt, where Brigade Headquarters and divisional report centres were now situated. The work was difficult because of the frequent shelling, but they completed the trench and subsequently extended the cables to Caterpillar Trench. During the comparative lull towards the end of July, the shelling of the Fricourt area became so heavy that, pending the next general attack, the headquarters of the divisions in the line were moved back to Bellevue Farm, between Méaulte and Albert, and the opportunity was at once taken to transfer the Corps Exchange in Fricourt into the dug-outs so vacated.

In anticipation of the great attack on 15 September, the necessary labour was made available for a considerable buried communication system, with the first section of a new cable trench to be constructed from Pommiers Redoubt via the Cosy Corner inn outside Montauban and thence to York Trench, to the left of Longueval. The lines were ready in time for the divisions that had moved headquarters up again to Fricourt and Pommiers Redoubt, with advanced headquarters at York Trench, and also for the heavy artillery, most of whose batteries took positions along the Mametz–Montauban ridge. To cope with the steady forward drift of XV Corps units, and to provide another advance maintenance point, a new Corps Forward Exchange was established at Pommiers.

The attack on 15 September proved highly successful, as over a mile was gained, including the villages of Courcelette, Martinpuich and Flers. The advance rendered urgent a further extension of the cable trench, and a section of trench was dug from York Trench through the corner of Delville Wood to Switch Trench. The digging proved a gruesome task, as Delville Wood and the surrounding area had become one huge graveyard. Liaison lines had grown formidably in numbers. Direct lines were now demanded not only between heavy artillery headquarters and the divisional artillery headquarters in the line, but also between the divisional artilleries and the majority of the heavy artillery groups.

On 25 September, the intermediate German line, including the section in the areas of Morval, Lesboeufs and Gueudecourt, succumbed, and the XV Corps once again advanced over a mile. On the following day, the victory was completed by the Fifth Army's capture of Thiepval. Once again the signal company's hands were kept full with preparations for moving all headquarters forward. The weather, however, intervened on the Germans' behalf, and it remained miserably cold and wet. During this period, some heavy batteries of the heavy artillery group headquarters moved up to and in front of Longueval, necessitating the running of many new cable lines. Permanent cable was laid in the second section of the main cable trench up to Longueval, and a third section of trench was dug forward to the sugar works at Factory Corner, near Flers.

At the end of October, the Australian and New Zealand Army Corps (Anzac) relieved the XV Corps. As there was then no other Corps Signal Company in France formed from Colonial troops, it looked like the XV Corps Signal Company would be retained in the line with the Anzacs. Everyone heaved a sigh of relief when it became known that K Corps Signal Company was to take over. The transition happened gradually, and BE Section, the last to leave the line, did not reach the new headquarters at Long until the middle of November. Orders then came for the XV Corps to take over a portion of the French front in the Péronne sector.

The winter campaign on the Somme, December 1916 to June 1917

The move into the line commenced on 3 December and was completed on the 6th. The cable sections moved with the divisional signal companies: BE and BG at Bray, and BF at Maricourt. Headquarters and the Air Line Section joined XV Corps headquarters at Étinehem, on the right bank of the Somme, a mile or so west of Bray. All sections had a most strenuous time taking over communications as they were released by the French. The corps's front extended from the XIV Corps boundary on the north at Combles to near Bouchavesnes-Bergen, and ran in front of St Pierre Vaast Wood.

In early January 1917, orders were received for the XV Corps to extend its front to the right, to Cléry, and to hand over a divisional frontage on the left to the XIV Corps. The divisional sectors were taken over successively, and the move was completed by 22 January. Heavy artillery headquarters with BE Section moved to PC Chapeau, and the Corps Forward Exchange at Maricourt was transferred with BF Section to Suzanne. This change of frontage was a nasty blow to the company, as nearly all along the new routes the same work had to be started afresh in the bitter January frosts.

In the meantime, hostile aeroplane activity had caused a rapid increase in the number of anti-aircraft units with batteries and searchlights now dotted over the area, and the installation and maintenance of a separate system of communication for the anti-aircraft defence of the XV Corps area was now added to the company's duties.

The commencement by the Germans of systematic counter-battery work made it even more difficult to keep the forward lines in continuous operation. A scheme for the forward extension of the buried-communication system was prepared under the greatest transport difficulties. A portion of the material was moved up to Marrières Wood, later the scene of the South African Infantry Brigade's fine stand in the March retreat, but the frozen ground prevented digging. The 8th Division's important local attack on Fritz Trench above Bouchavesnes-Bergen on 4 March therefore had to be carried out without the assistance of the new buried communications, and as most of the above-ground cables were cut, the first news of the assaulting troops was brought by pigeon to the corps loft at Étinehem.

The general German withdrawal began on 15 March. The XV Corps Signal Company had to maintain direct contact between the corps staff and the advanced troops. The difficulties were doubled on 25 March by the sudden withdrawal from the line of the XIV Corps on the right and the consequent extension of the already wide XV Corps frontage that now stretched from Péronne to Le Transloy. A lot of heavy material once again had to be relayed forward by teams from the cable sections over tracks impassable to trucks, and finally carried on sappers' shoulders over shell-shattered ground. Under such handicaps, and in the teeth of continuous blizzards of snow, sleet, and rain, which lasted until the end of April, over 40 miles of poled route was erected, and two successive moves of the corps headquarters completed without any loss of communication.

In early April, the advance reached its limit, held up in front of La Vacquerie and Havrincourt, outlying strong points of the Hindenburg Line. On 17 April, corps headquarters was established near Haute Allaines. During their retreat, the Germans had destroyed all signal communications and the whole of the immense network of communications for stationary warfare had to be reconstituted under continuing supply and transport difficulties. Scarcely was this task underway when orders were received to prepare signal plans for an offensive and to commence the necessary work as early as possible. The position regarding materials was alleviated in May by the organisation of a temporary Corps Signal Salvage Unit, composed of BF Section, a platoon of a labour company, and the necessary horse and motor transport.

Towards the end of May, orders arrived for the XV Corps to hand over operations and proceed to Villers-Bretonneux. The cable sections of the signal company joined various divisions, and at the end of May accompanied them out of the area to unknown destinations. On 3 June, the remainder of the company reached Villers-Bretonneux, where they settled down comfortably. The great and continuing growth in the demands on the signal service had unduly taxed the available personnel, and so a Heavy Artillery Headquarters Signal Section with one officer and 37 other ranks was added to the signal company. At the same time, a signal subsection of one officer and 27 other ranks was formed for each heavy artillery group, and the Signal Section forming part of the headquarters of the South African Infantry Brigade was now affiliated to the company.

In the middle of March, the Corps Signal School was reconstituted at Chipilly, with a separate establishment, and Lieutenant Johnson was seconded as commander with a staff of four sergeant-instructors from the original company. The school continued to function until after the armistice, moving with the corps from point to point.

On 11 June, the XV Corps arrived in Dunkirk and was tasked with taking over the Nieuport sector of the front line, an important stretch running from the sea along the Yser River, which had been held by the French since the First Battle of Ypres. The corps headquarters was established in a casino at Malo-les-Bains, a suburb of Dunkirk.

The Belgian coast and the Battle of the Dunes, June to November 1917
Though for a long period this sector had been quiet, the German artillery concentration on the Yser riverbank opposite was great. The corps headquarters moved to Bray-Dunes on 29 June, but as every approach road was swept by heavy German shell fire, forward communications failed almost at once. It was a most trying day for the signal personnel, as nearly all wire communication was lost in the first two hours and all formations had to fall back on despatch riders and runners. After nightfall, the HA Section staff were forced to move into the sand dunes half a mile to the flank, and temporary cables were run back to the signal office at the Villa Rosarie. Much to their surprise, the German attack did not resume on the following day, and they managed to get the existing lines restored while work on the new communications began. The repairs were difficult and laborious owing to the persistent shelling and the higher water level following August's wet weather.

Even with sappers from three cable sections – BF, BE and AU Imperial Cable – and two area signal detachments from the Fourth Army, it became impossible to satisfactorily maintain a trench network of 40 miles containing 1 200 miles of cable. The corps headquarters moved to De Panne at the beginning of September and then back to Bray-Dunes.

The Lys area, December 1917 to November 1918
After some frontage readjustments in December, the XV Corps settled down to hold the sector in front of the River Lys, from Houplines to Laventie. In January 1918, the corps headquarters was shifted from Hinges to La Motte-au-Bois opposite Nieppe Forest. A decision was made to disband one cable section in each corps, to reduce the strength of the corps Air Line Section to 42 all ranks with one heavy and two light lorries. The surplus personnel would form an additional air line for each corps. BG Section was accordingly

converted into the nucleus of the new 91 Air Line Section, to which Lieutenant Dobson was appointed. At the same time, Q Wireless Section became an integral portion of the signal company, and Imperial personnel were rapidly replaced with South Africans.

Russia's defection made it certain that the Allies would be thrown on the defensive in the spring, and, as the Lys area covered Hazebrouck and the direct route to Calais, it was probable that the sector would become a main front of attack. Ample and secure communications were therefore the first priority, and a complete scheme was prepared on a scale of magnitude and thoroughness that surpassed any previous performance. Work could not commence before 25 January 1918, because the whole of the low-lying Lys Valley was waterlogged due to heavy rains. When work began, often over 1 500 men were employed simultaneously. The corps's section of the trenches was completed by the beginning of March.

BF Section was employed on another section of the scheme in and around Armentières. It accordingly spent two months securely laying many miles of cable. The new 91 Air Line Section worked on the necessary additions to the open-wire routes extending from the corps headquarters. When the storm finally broke on 9 April 1918, practically all the laid cable had been joined up and was working, and three-quarters of the original scheme had been completed.

By the morning of 10 April, the Germans had forded the river to Estaires. The town was shelled intensely all day, and BE Section's billet was blown up. Nevertheless, the corps exchange was kept going until late that night by Lieutenant Hill with 51 Air Line and a party of operators from headquarters. In the days that followed, the XV Corps was steadily driven back by the enemy's push for Hazebrouck. The 29th and 31st divisions, and the 4th Guards Brigade, were successively thrown in, but their desperate fighting only succeeded in slowing the German advance, until the entry into line of the 1st Australian Division on the night of 12 April, when the enemy was finally stopped on the edge of Nieppe Forest. Thereafter, the central battle shifted gradually northwards, to around Kemmel and Messines, while on the XV Corps's front the battle died down to localised combats. The effort to keep up communications during these days tested everyone to the limit.

When the Germans were finally held up at Kemmel on 28 April, work could commence on the defences at Hazebrouck. During the next few months, successive lines of trenches and belts of wire came into existence, seaming

APPENDIX II: SOUTH AFRICAN SIGNAL COMPANY

the country as far back as Saint-Omer. In early May, the signal company started work on a buried-cable system. When the advance began, a network of trenches extended across the whole XV Corps's area for a depth of 13 000 yards and a breadth of 7 000, embodying 30 miles of deep trench and nearly 1 200 miles of pair cable.

The Germans' decision to evacuate the Lys Salient at the end of August 1918 saw all ranks occupied in the rapid restoration of communications through the devastated area. After the successful attack of the Belgian Army and Second British Army at the end of September, in which the XV Corps cooperated on the right flank, headquarters moved to Saint-Jans-Cappel on 4 October. On 21 October, it moved to Mouvaux, following the rapid retreat of the enemy to the Scheldt River. On this occasion, 91 Air Line and BE Cable sections completed two lines across the Lys to the new headquarters, a distance of nearly 20 miles, in one day.

The signal portion of the preparations to force the passage of the Scheldt occupied the time up to 10 November, but as the enemy retired during the night, and the armistice was proclaimed the following day, they proved unnecessary. The XV Corps was not selected to accompany the advance to the Rhine, and so it fell to BE Section on 12 November to lay the last and farthest forward cable in France – from the Scheldt, crossing at Le Pecq to an observation point on the eastern side.

(All information extracted from John Buchan, *The History of the South African Forces in France*, Edinburgh: Thomas Nelson and Sons, 1920.)

APPENDIX III

South African Medical Corps

When the South African Overseas Expeditionary Force was organised on the termination of the campaign in German South-West Africa, Colonel P.G. Stock was appointed senior medical officer of the South African Medical Corps, and charged with mobilising a field ambulance and a general hospital. No. 1 South African Field Ambulance, under the command of Lieutenant-Colonel G.H. Usmar, assembled at Potchefstroom with the 1st South African Infantry Brigade, while No. 1 South African General Hospital gathered at Wynberg, its personnel composed largely of volunteers from the staffs of No. 1 General Hospital, Wynberg, and No. 2 General Hospital, Maitland. No hospital equipment was available in South Africa, but on arrival in England, the Advisory Committee on Voluntary Aid gave £15 000 to purchase equipment and a further £1 500 to augment the equipment eventually taken by the field ambulance.

Both units accompanied the 1st South African Infantry Brigade to England, the general hospital embarking on HMT *Balmoral Castle* at Cape Town on 25 September 1915 and the field ambulance on HMT *Kenilworth Castle* on 10 October. On arrival, the field ambulance proceeded to the Royal Army Military Corps Depot at Tweseldown, near Aldershot, where it began training under its own officers. It was present at Bordon when the queen reviewed the troops on 2 December. On 29 December the unit was route marched to Farnham, there entraining for Devonport, where it embarked on HMT *Corsican* for Egypt, reaching Alexandria on 13 January 1916.

In the meantime, the personnel of the general hospital were temporarily detailed to strengthen the staffs of various hospitals in England. On 20 December the unit was reassembled at Bournemouth, where it took over the Mont Dore Military Hospital, equipped for 520 patients. In February 1916 the control of the Grata Quies Auxiliary Hospital was transferred to the Mont Dore, which became a central hospital, and on 1 April, 17 additional auxiliary hospitals in the districts of Poole, Wimbourne, Swanage,

Sherbourne and Yeovil were affiliated, increasing the number of beds controlled to over 1 200.

The first patients from overseas had been admitted on 8 January 1916. Although there were a number of severe cases of 'trench foot' from Gallipoli, few wounded were received before the unit left on 3 July for Aldershot, where it would prepare before joining the British Expeditionary Force in France.

On its arrival at Aldershot, No. 1 South African General Hospital was given its final touches and about 400 shipping tons of stores and equipment were drawn. On 12 July 1916 the unit entrained for Southampton, from where it would sail to France. Their ship berthed at Le Havre at about 10:30 on 13 July. As she was urgently required elsewhere, the unloading commenced at once. The next day, the hospital left for Abbeville, arriving on 15 July, where it would be established next to No. 2 Stationary Hospital, an Imperial unit that had been there for some time.

Ploughed fields on the slopes of the hills overlooking the Somme valley had been allocated to the hospital; Abbeville itself lay about a mile away in the valley, but the railway station and triage were on the far side of the town and must have been nearly five kilometres from the hospital. Some marquees had already been erected, but the layout of the hospital was greatly handicapped by the cramped area of ground then available. Later on, by the frequent striking and re-pitching of tents, the hospital gradually took on a more symmetrical and workable shape.

By this time, the First Battle of the Somme had begun and hospital accommodation was urgently required for the large number of casualties. In the absence of any kind of buildings, a store tent was converted into an operating tent, and an improvised sterilising shelter was erected. Within 48 hours of arrival, patients were admitted and every available surgeon was hard at work. The initial difficulties were many: buildings and engineering services were almost impossible to obtain, and it was not until the end of November that the operating block was completed. But before long, additional tents were pitched, and the kitchens and stores were organised.

Until early August the hospital was without its own nursing sisters and these services were performed by members of Queen Alexandra's Imperial Military Nursing Service, the Canadian Military Nursing Service and English Voluntary Aid Detachments. On 5 August, however, Matron Creagh and 21 members of the South African Military Nursing Service arrived from England. The nurses' camp had to be pitched in the wooded grounds of a castle some distance away, but they were billeted in the town until their camp was completed.

During the autumn of 1916, the hospital received a large number of wounded direct from the Somme battlefields. Among the earliest admissions in July 1916 were South Africans wounded at Delville Wood, General Lukin being one of the first officer patients. The most severely wounded journeyed by specially fitted hospital barges, which floated down the Somme from the casualty clearing stations around Corbie to Abbeville, from where the patients were taken by motor ambulances to the hospital. Towards the end of 1916, these barges ceased running, as the winter rains rendered the passage down the Somme too dangerous.

The main road leading to the hospital proved treacherous, for part of the way was formed by sleepers, which were always a source of trouble: the underlying chalk, which quickly powdered to a fine dust during dry weather, turned into a greasy mud when the rains set in. As soon as materials and labour became available, the sleeper track was extended, and a large triage was constructed on which the ambulance wagons could turn. It was not until many months later that it became possible to build a macadamised road connecting the hospital with the Amiens road.

Progress was gradually made in the erection of temporary buildings, and by the end of 1916 there was hutted accommodation for 120 patients. During that winter, the majority of beds were under canvas. However, stoves and wooden flooring were installed, and with doors closed and the sides of the tents fastened down, the tented wards were quite comfortable.

Between 23 July and 31 December 1916, hospital admissions totalled 6 436, of whom 3 032 were listed as 'battle casualties' and 3 404 as 'sick'. During the same period, 5 719 patients were discharged. Of these, 673 returned to duty, 548 were transferred to convalescent depots, 3 306 were evacuated to the UK and 1 192 were transferred to hospitals at other bases in France. The hospital carried out 588 major operations and in all there were 236 deaths (or, calculated on the number of admissions, 3.68 per cent died). This comparatively high mortality is explained by the fact that practically every case admitted to the hospital was seriously wounded and that it was the nearest general hospital to the Somme front – many moribund patients were taken off ambulance trains on account of their being too ill to travel to more distant bases.

The appearance of the hospital grounds improved from year to year. Grass lawns and flowerbeds were planted, and vegetable gardening was carried out on a progressively larger scale. From the early days of the unit in France, a field adjoining the hospital was made available for playing football, hockey, cricket and other games. Badminton and tennis courts were constructed in the officers' and nursing sisters' quarters, and a tennis court was made on ground adjoining the recreation field for the use of other ranks of the unit. In early 1917 hutted quarters for the nursing staff and messes were added, as well as buildings for part of the quartermaster's stores.

In June 1917 the unit provided a surgical team for duty at a casualty clearing station, which performed continuously in the forward areas until December of that year. After that, a surgical team performed duty in the front areas on eight occasions. In addition, from time to time nursing sisters were detailed for duty on ambulance trains and as anaesthetists at casualty clearing stations.

Instructions were received from general headquarters that the hospital was to be enlarged from 520 beds to a normal capacity of 1 120 beds, with a 'crisis expansion' to 1 500 beds. A good thing too, for during the latter part of 1917, as many as 1 700 patients had to be accommodated at any one time.

Total admissions for the year 1917 were 19 109, of which 7 613 were battle casualties and 11 496 were sick. During the same period there were 18 277 discharges. Of these 2 638 returned to duty, 4 253 were transferred to convalescent depots, 8 749 were evacuated to the UK and 2 637 were transferred to hospitals at other bases in France. Over 1 200 major operations were performed and there were 181 recorded deaths.

An administration block and a new kitchen were built, and in October 1917 it was decided to erect as many huts as possible. A hut housing the men of the company who were over 40 years of age was built, followed by a second hut and comfortable quarters for all personnel. In January 1918, six 'Adrian' hospital huts were erected, but these were not completed until the end of March. Later, three double 'Nissen' hospital huts were added, but the last was not quite finished when the armistice was signed.

A metalled road leading to the Amiens road was laid through the hospital, and looped within, so that traffic could be more easily managed. In the summer of 1918, this road was tarred, which proved a great help in keeping down the dust. A railway siding serving the three large hospitals in this area was also established.

A church was erected within the precincts of the hospital, dedicated in the name of St Winifred to the memory of late nurse Winifred Munro of the South African Military Nursing Service.

During the German offensive of 1918, the hospital experienced its most intense period. The medical staff were depleted to replace casualties in the No. 1 South African Field Ambulance and other units in the forward areas, while all male reinforcements were sent to the field ambulance. Practically all female nursing staff from this district were withdrawn, on account of the enemy advance and frequent bombing at night by hostile aeroplanes. As a result, the number of medical officers in charge of wards was reduced to eight from the usual 22; male personnel fell to 188 from 212; and female nursing staff to eight from 88. With this depleted staff it would have seemed almost impossible to look after a normal number of patients, but many more than normal had to be dealt with during the last week of March: 1 820 were admitted and 2 365 were discharged.

The huts that had recently been erected for personnel had to be evacuated to make room for patients, of whom as many as 90 slightly wounded were packed into one hut on stretchers. The men were crowded into the remaining three huts, and the overflow slept on the football field. Owing to the threat of air attacks, it became necessary to dig protective trenches for patients, sisters, officers and other ranks, and also to erect sandbagged revetments around the wards. Though no definite attack was made by hostile aircraft on the hospital, bombs fell uncomfortably near on several occasions.

The enemy's approach and the frequency of bombing raids made the retention of fractured femur cases in the hospital inadvisable and as many as possible were evacuated to the UK. Not long after the last consignment had been despatched, the Allied offensive began, and the heavy influx of fractured femur cases made it necessary to use improvised apparatus. During June and July 1918, sick admissions to the hospital were many, owing to an influenza epidemic. From then on admissions steadily increased, of both sick and wounded, due to the offensive that began in the latter part of July and continued until the signing of the armistice in November. Between 1 January and 30 November 1918, admissions totalled 20 089.

South African Military Hospital, Richmond

When the decision to send South African troops to England became known, a number of prominent South Africans in London formed a committee, the South African Comforts Committee, under the chairmanship of Lord Gladstone to start a fund for the establishment of a hospital and for the general comfort of the South African troops. When the South African Medical Corps contingent arrived in England, a proposal was under consideration to erect huts to accommodate some 300 patients, as a South African wing to the Royal Victoria Hospital at Netley. On further investigation, however, it was found that the site would not have been suitable during the winter. After much deliberation, a site in the beautiful Richmond Park was selected.

Construction began in early March, and on 16 June 1916 the hospital was formally opened by its patroness, HRH Princess Christian. On its opening, the South African Medical Corps Depot was transferred to Richmond and some personnel of No. 1 South African General Hospital were redistributed. Major Thornton, the general hospital's adjutant and registrar, succeeded Lieutenant-Colonel Stock in command at Richmond, and Captain Basil Brooke was appointed adjutant and registrar in Thornton's stead.

Towards the end of 1916, Gladstone's committee offered the privilege of naming a bed in the hospital to any person or institution making a gift of £25, and of naming a ward for a donation of £600. The appeal resulted in 99 beds and eight wards being thus named – approximately 265 of the beds were gifts from schools in South Africa. The organisation of this endeavour was initiated and carried out by Maskew Miller of Cape Town. The main corridors and rooms in the hospital were named after well-known streets or places in South Africa, with all the principal towns in the Union being represented. This meant that familiar place names greeted the South African patients.

In February 1917, an extension to accommodate 500 patients was opened. It had hardly been in use, however, when more beds were needed. This was achieved by converting the quarters originally built for orderlies into wards, and by renting a neighbouring house as an annex, so that in April 1917 the total accommodation for patients had increased to 620 beds.

On 1 July 1918, the Richmond Military Hospital and the South African Hospital were amalgamated to form the South African Military Hospital. The enlarged hospital provided 1 098 beds, but even this was not sufficient, and 250 emergency beds were added by billeting patients in the neighbourhood. In addition, four auxiliary hospitals were attached, bringing the total number of beds to 1 321 (or 1 571, including billets).

The medical staff consisted of 13 officers of the South African Medical Corps and 11 civilian practitioners, who for various reasons were not eligible for commissions in the corps. The nursing staff under Matron Jackson of Queen Alexandra's Imperial Military Nursing Service consisted of two assistant matrons, 23 nursing sisters, 55 staff nurses and 88 probationers, the larger proportion of whom were South African. The subordinate personnel consisted, with a few exceptions, of NCOs and men who, having been invalided owing to wounds or sickness in the field, did duty at the hospital while regaining their health and strength. The hospital also served as the depot for the South African Medical Corps's subordinate personnel. Eighteen drafts, comprising 423 men, were sent to France as reinforcements for the No. 1 South African General Hospital and the No. 1 South African Field Ambulance.

From its inception until 31 October 1918, 274 officers and 9 412 men of other ranks were admitted to the hospital – this does not include those patients admitted to the Richmond Military Hospital before the date of amalgamation. Of the 9 686 patients, 2 628 belonged to Imperial units, which included a good many South Africans.

The South African Comforts Committee spared neither trouble nor money to provide for the comfort and welfare of the patients. At first the work of visitation and entertainment was organised by Lady Lionel Phillips, but was later taken over by the fund's Red Cross subcommittee. For those who could enjoy them, every possible variety of amusement was provided, including a riverside club near the hospital, for the benefit of those patients sufficiently convalescent to enjoy the garden and picturesque river views.

In the early days of the hospital, arrangements for bedside occupational work were made by lady visitors. The making of regimental crests and other work of a similar nature helped patients to pass many a weary hour in bed when they were still too weak to be doing more serious vocational work.

Shortly after the hospital was opened, the problem of dealing with the permanently disabled men of the contingent had to be faced. After negotiations with the War Office, it was arranged that a Vocational Training School would be established. The school, which was finally opened in February 1917, generated an interest among the bedridden patients in their own future, so that when well enough they might go to the classrooms and undertake extensive training courses. The South African Military Hospital was the first primary hospital in the UK in which permanently disabled men, while being restored to the best possible physical condition, were trained for a civil career to enable them on discharge from the army to become self-supporting members of the community. The cost, which was £2 335, was borne by the South African Hospital and Comforts Fund, and the Governor-General's Fund.

(All information extracted from John Buchan, *The History of the South African Forces in France*, Edinburgh: Thomas Nelson and Sons, 1920.)

APPENDIX IV

Railways and miscellaneous trades companies

In 1916 the railways, roads, canals and docks in the British zone in France were all brought under the control of Transportation, under the command of Sir Eric Geddes. The War Office appealed to the dominions for railway operating sections, or companies, each consisting of three officers and 266 men. In South Africa the position was such that the railways could, at the time, only spare sufficient men to form one company, but it was arranged to form a second from those not actually in the railway service but who had railway experience, or were in other ways fitted for the particular work required of them.

The first company assembled at Potchefstroom in November 1916, under Captain H.L. Pybus, and the second at Robert's Heights, Pretoria, under Captain W.McI. Robinson. Fifty locomotive drivers and a similar number of firemen and guards formed the backbone of each company, the balance being composed of traffic controllers, blockmen and signalmen, with the necessary mechanics and clerical staff to enable each company to operate as a separate and complete unit. Lieutenant-Colonel F.R. Collins, a mechanical superintendent in the South African Railways, was put in charge and left for England in December 1916. The companies followed later under the command of Captain Robinson, and arrived at Bordon, Hampshire, in March 1917, where the depot was formed.

Both companies arrived in France at the end of March 1917 and were detailed for railway work, which was then in its initial stage. The first company was renumbered No. 7 South African Light Railway Operating Company, and the second, No. 8 South African Light Railway Operating Company. The former was sent to Romarin, on the Belgian border; the latter proceeded to Savy, in the Arras district. Twenty-five drivers and a similar number of firemen from each company were transferred to the broad-gauge railway section, and remained on that work throughout the war.

No. 7 Company stayed at Romarin until Messines village and the ridge were taken in June 1917, during which time the Ploegsteert Light Railway

System was built. The company was responsible for all traffic using this system, the bulk being ammunition destined for the various batteries. No. 8 Company took over the light railway work from Marœuil to the north and north-east of Arras, from where lines were extended after the Vimy Ridge operations.

In June 1917 both companies proceeded to Audruicq preparatory to taking up broad-gauge work, and were designated No. 92 and No. 93 companies. During most of this period, Lieutenant-Colonel Collins was attached to Transportation headquarters, and in May 1917 was appointed assistant director of light railways for the Fifth Army, which was then operating in the Bapaume sector. When the Fifth Army was transferred to Belgium to take part in the Third Battle of Ypres, light railways, in addition to serving batteries and Royal Engineers, were now required to prepare to follow up any advance. For this purpose, the services of the South African companies were loaned to Collins, and took their place with five Imperial operating companies in the Fifth Army area. They shared in the operations until November 1917, when the offensive ceased.

During this time, No. 92 Company was employed on the system north-east of Ypres, where 11 of its members were awarded military medals for individual acts of gallantry and devotion to duty. No. 93 Company worked from Elverdinghe and Boesinghe to Langemarck, and among other duties was responsible for placing field-gun ammunition in front of the field guns on the eastern slopes of the Pilckem Ridge and in the Steenbecque Valley before the September and October 1917 attacks, which meant the front was advanced to the edge of the Houthulst Forest. Seven of its members received military medals during this time.

In January 1918 the Fifth Army took over a 45-mile sector to the south of the British front, and, in anticipation of an enemy offensive, railway construction on a considerable scale was undertaken under Lieutenant-Colonel F. Newell. Later, Collins took over the northern area and the South African companies were ordered south from Belgium.

No. 93 Company arrived in early March and was sent to Noyon, where it remained until the 23rd. Forced to retire by the enemy advance, the company proceeded by route march to Flexicourt, west of Amiens, where it was employed on the construction of defence works in company with many other transportation units, whose usual employment had been suspended for similar reasons. Later, they were employed on railway construction necessitated by

APPENDIX IV: RAILWAYS AND MISCELLANEOUS TRADES COMPANIES

the altered conditions. In July 1918, company headquarters was established at Ligny, east of Saint-Pol-sur-Ternoise, and the operation of the main trunk lines to Arras was undertaken. The German retreat caused a forward move, and the company, from November, operated over the section from Douai to Mons, with its headquarters at Somain.

No. 92 Company, after concentrating in Belgium in March for its projected move south, which was subsequently cancelled owing to the enemy's advance, went to Crombeke. From there it assisted in railway construction and other duties, until in September, when, with Berguette as headquarters, the operation of the newly constructed line towards Merville and later towards Armentières was undertaken. In November the company moved forward to Lille, and with its headquarters at Tourcoing, worked the section from Tourcoing to Tournai.

In 1917 the South African Union government consented to the formation of a Miscellaneous Trades Company for service in France. This company began to assemble at Potchefstroom in June, and, as recruiting was brisk, it was able to embark fully formed from Cape Town on 25 July, under the command of Captain C.E. Mason.

Arriving at Bordon on 28 August, the company was given a short course of training at the Royal Engineers Depot there, and sent to France on 14 October. Here the company was renumbered the 84th Miscellaneous Trades Company, Royal Engineers (South African), and sent to the director general of Transportation, Chief Mechanical Engineer Department, Locomotive Workshops, situated at Saint-Étienne-du-Rouvray, near Rouen, where five companies of the Royal Engineers, under the command of Lieutenant-Colonel Cole, were already stationed.

These were the largest locomotive workshops attached to the British Army in France and, by reason of its large proportion of skilled personnel, the 84th Company was able to take a considerable share in their activities. Captain Mason was appointed erecting works' manager, and the NCOs of the company in many instances were entrusted with positions of responsibility. On Mason's recall to South Africa, Captain N.S. Weatherley was put in command of the company. When the armistice was signed in November 1918, Lieutenant-Colonel Cole ordered a special parade of the company to express to all ranks his appreciation of their services, which he characterised in the most complimentary terms.

Cape Auxiliary Horse Transport companies

In February 1917 the Union government was asked by the War Office to raise eight companies of Cape Coloured drivers for service in France. The personnel were to include 67 officers, 23 warrant officers, 92 NCOs, and 3 482 artificers and drivers.

Towards the end of February, Lieutenant-Colonel J.D. Anderson (an officer who had considerable experience in transport work) was asked to take command, and to arrange for the recruitment and organisation of the eight companies. Kimberley was selected as the most convenient centre for mobilisation, and De Beers offered two of its compounds, which had hutted accommodation for approximately 2 000 men and all necessary amenities.

Lieutenant-Colonel Wynne was appointed camp commandant, with Captain MacKeurton as paymaster and Captain Cooper as officer in charge of the records. By 12 March recruiting began.

The results were at first disappointing, as recruiting for the Cape Coloured battalions for service in German East Africa was at this time being undertaken, and recruitment committees for this purpose were at work in all the principal centres in South Africa. In addition, there were many questions, such as the appointment of Coloured NCOs, increased rates of pay, the rejection of all Coloured drivers other than Cape Coloured drivers, and recognition by the Governor General's Fund, all of which had to be settled before the Coloured recruitment committees would lend their assistance. There was also a lack of Cape Auxiliary Horse Transport officers to conduct a special recruitment campaign.

However, these difficulties were soon overcome, and recruiting gained momentum. Johannesburg, where Captains Barlow and Rogers and Lieutenant Graham Moore inaugurated a vigorous recruitment campaign, produced 500 recruits in a short time, as did Cape Town, where Lieutenants Gillam and Sawyer, Second-Lieutenant Tracey, Staff Sergeant-Major Simmons and Company Sergeant-Major Creagh met with considerable success, and Knysna, with Second-Lieutenant Anderson and Company Quartermaster Sergeant Stertler as recruiting officers.

In the beginning, there was a substantial amount of clerical work to be done, owing to the need to reject a large number of drivers who were attested but subsequently found unsuitable. Every officer, warrant officer and NCO, however, assisted the records officer to such an extent that by the middle of April, 1 500 men were ready to leave for overseas. Unfortunately, shipping

APPENDIX IV: RAILWAYS AND MISCELLANEOUS TRADES COMPANIES

could only be found for 867, and these sailed on the SS *Euripides* on 20 April. They were shortly followed by drafts under the command of Majors Jenner and Barnard, and a reinforcement draft under Lieutenant Smith.

On the first detachment's arrival in France on 23 May 1917, the director of transportation decided to reorganise the contingent to replace Army Service Corps personnel. To this end, the men were divided into the following Army Service Corps companies:

- No. 22 Auxiliary Horse Transport Company, stationed at Dunkirk and Calais
- No. 5 Auxiliary Horse Transport Company, stationed at Boulogne-sur-Mer
- No. 2 Auxiliary Horse Transport Company, stationed at Le Havre
- No. 8 Auxiliary Horse Transport Company, stationed at Rouen
- No. 10 Auxiliary Horse Transport Company, stationed at Rouen
- No. 11 Auxiliary Horse Transport Company, stationed at Rouen

Arrangements were also made for a base depot to be established at Le Havre.

The reorganisation began at once, and as other drafts arrived they were sent to the base depot for three weeks, where they were equipped and went through a course of training before being distributed to the various Army Service Corps companies. By 31 August the Cape Auxiliary Horse Transport detachments had released all the white personnel of six companies of the Army Service Corps, with the exception of five officers and a certain number of warrant officers and NCOs, whose services, it was proposed, it would permanently retain. However, after a few months in France the reorganised companies were all commanded by officers of the detachment.

Though the men did excellent work at the base posts, Colonel Anderson felt that there were strong arguments in favour of them being moved to divisional trains or Army Auxiliary Horse Transport companies actually working in the army areas. The arguments in favour of the move from a South African point of view were unanswerable. The environments at the base posts were not good, and the work of the men chiefly lay in the less salubrious parts of the towns, where liquor sellers and those who associated with them resided. It is greatly to the credit of the men that their general conduct was exemplary in spite of the adverse conditions under which many of them worked.

The views of the military authorities in France did not, however, coincide with those of Colonel Anderson. All the commandants of the bases at which the companies were employed recommended that they should remain where they were, and wrote highly of the men's behaviour, bearing and discipline. It was a great disappointment to all that the companies were not at once employed in the army areas. Nevertheless, a promise was given that, if reinforcements proved sufficient, an experiment would be made in employing them nearer to the scenes of fighting. Eventually the 1st, 3rd and 5th Army Auxiliary Horse companies were taken over and the experiment proved a complete success. The work of these companies involved conveying ammunition and supplies to the firing lines, and transporting metal for the new roads that had to be constructed as the armies advanced.

Of the companies employed on the lines of communication, numbers 2, 5, 8 and 22 worked at the docks, conveying munitions and supplies from the docks to the different distributing centres. The work was hard, the hours long and the weather inclement. Companies 10 and 11 were designated 'forest companies', and were employed almost entirely in hauling logs from felling sites to dumping centres. In a report on the work in the forests in France, Lord Lovat, the director of forests, wrote that, without prejudice to other units, he wished to remark on the work done by the horse transport companies manned by South African (Cape Coloured) personnel, who had shown throughout both practical knowledge of the work and patriotic devotion to duty.

During their stay in France, the health of the officers, NCOs and men was much better than could reasonably have been expected. Casualties were estimated at 0.5 per cent per month.

(All information extracted from John Buchan, *The History of the South African Forces in France*, Edinburgh: Thomas Nelson and Sons, 1920.)

APPENDIX V

Victoria Crosses won by South Africans during the Great War

(The following Victoria Cross citations were all published in supplements to the *London Gazette* during the war.)

Lieutenant (Acting Captain) Andrew Weatherby Beauchamp-Proctor, No. 84 Squadron, Royal Air Force
'Between August 8, 1918, and October 8, 1918, this officer proved himself victor in twenty-six decisive combats, destroying twelve enemy kite balloons, ten enemy aircraft, and driving down four other enemy aircraft completely out of control.

Between October 1, 1918, and October 5, 1918, he destroyed two enemy scouts, burned three enemy kite balloons, and drove down one enemy scout completely out of control.

On October 1, 1918, in a general engagement with about twenty-eight machines, he crashed one Fokker biplane near Fontaine and a second near Ramicourt; on 2nd October he burnt a hostile balloon near Selvigny; on 3rd October he drove down completely out of control an enemy scout near Mont-d'Origny, and burned a hostile balloon; on 5th October, the third hostile balloon near Bohain.

On October 8, 1918, while flying home at a low altitude after destroying an enemy two-seater near Maretz, he was painfully wounded in the arm by machine-gun fire; but, continuing, he landed safely at his aerodrome, and after making his report was admitted to hospital.

In all, he has proved himself conqueror over fifty-four foes, destroying twenty-two enemy machines, sixteen enemy kite balloons, and driving down sixteen enemy aircraft completely out of control.

Captain Beauchamp-Proctor's work in attacking enemy troops on the ground and in reconnaissance during the withdrawal following on the battle of St. Quentin, from March 21, 1918, and during the victorious advance of our armies commencing on 8th August, has been almost unsurpassed in its brilliancy, and as such has made an impression on those serving in his squadron and those around him that will not be easily forgotten.

Captain Beauchamp-Proctor was awarded the Military Cross on June 22, 1918; the Distinguished Flying Cross on July 2, 1918; a bar to the Military Cross on September 16, 1918; and the Distinguished Service Order on November 2, 1918.'

Captain William Anderson Bloomfield,
Scouts Corps, South African Mounted Brigade
'At Mlali, East Africa, on August 24, 1916. For most conspicuous bravery. Finding that, after being heavily attacked in an advanced and isolated position, the enemy were working round his flanks. Captain Bloomfield evacuated his wounded and subsequently withdrew his command to a new position, he himself being among the last to retire. On arrival at the new position he found that one of the wounded – No. 2475, Corporal D.M.P. Bowker – had been left behind. Owing to very heavy fire he experienced difficulties in having the wounded corporal brought in. Rescue meant passing over some four hundred yards of open ground, swept by heavy fire, in full view of the enemy. This task Captain Bloomfield determined to face himself, and unmindful of personal danger, he succeeded in reaching Corporal Bowker and carrying him back, subjected throughout the double journey to heavy machine-gun and rifle fire. This act showed the highest degree of valour and endurance.'

Sergeant Frederick Charles Booth,
South African Forces, attached Rhodesia Native Regiment
'At Johannesbruck, near Songea, East Africa, on February 12, 1917. For most conspicuous bravery during an attack, in thick bush, on the enemy position. Under very heavy rifle fire, Sergeant Booth went forward alone and brought in a man who was dangerously wounded. Later, he rallied native troops who were badly disorganized, and brought them to the firing fine. This N.C.O. has, on many previous occasions, displayed the greatest bravery, coolness, and resource in action, and has set a splendid example of pluck, endurance, and determination.'

Private William Frederick Faulds, 1st Regiment, South African Infantry
'At Delville Wood, France, on July 18, 1916. For most conspicuous bravery and devotion to duty. A bombing party under Lieutenant Craig attempted

to rush across forty yards of ground which lay between the British and enemy trenches. Coming under very heavy rifle and machine-gun fire, the officer and the majority of the party were killed or wounded. Unable to move, Lieutenant Craig lay midway between the two lines of trenches, the ground being quite open. In full daylight Private Faulds, accompanied by two other men, climbed the parapet, ran out, picked up the officer and carried him back, one man being severely wounded in so doing.

Two days later Private Faulds again showed most conspicuous bravery in going out alone to bring in a wounded man and carrying him nearly half a mile to a dressing-station, subsequently rejoining his platoon. The artillery fire was at the time so intense that stretcher bearers and others considered that any attempt to bring in the wounded man meant certain death. This risk Private Faulds faced unflinchingly, and his bravery was crowned with success.'

Lieutenant Robert Vaughan Gorle,
A Battery, 50th Brigade, Royal Field Artillery

'For most conspicuous bravery, initiative, and devotion to duty during the attack at Ledeghem on October 1, 1918, when in command of an eighteen-pounder gun working in close conjunction with infantry. He brought his gun into action in the most exposed positions on four separate occasions, and disposed of enemy machine guns by firing over open sights under direct machine-gun fire at five hundred to six hundred yards range.

Later, seeing that the infantry were being driven back by intense hostile fire, he without hesitation galloped his gun in front of the leading infantry, and on two occasions knocked out enemy machine guns which were causing the trouble. His disregard of personal safety and dash were a magnificent example to the wavering line, which rallied and retook the northern end of the village.'

Major (Acting Lieutenant-Colonel) Harry Greenwood,
9th Battalion, King's Own Yorkshire Light Infantry

'For most conspicuous bravery, devotion to duty, and fine leadership on October 23–24, 1918. When the advance of his battalion on the 23rd October was checked, and many casualties caused by an enemy machine-gun post, Lieutenant-Colonel Greenwood, single-handed, rushed the post and killed the crew. At the entrance to the village of Ovillers, accompanied by two battalion runners, he again rushed a machine-gun post and killed the occupants.

On reaching the objective west of Duke's Wood, his command was almost surrounded by hostile machine-gun posts, and the enemy at once attacked his isolated force. The attack was repulsed, and, led by Lieutenant-Colonel Greenwood, his troops swept forward and captured the last objective with one hundred and fifty prisoners, eight machine guns, and one field gun.

During the attack on the 'Green Line' south of Poix du Nord, on 24th October, he again displayed the greatest gallantry in rushing a machine-gun post, and he showed conspicuously good leadership in the handling of his command in the face of heavy fire. He inspired his men in the highest degree, with the result that the objective was captured, and in spite of heavy casualties the line was held.

During the advance on Grand Gay Farm Road, on the afternoon of 24th October, the skilful and bold handling of his battalion was productive of most important results, not only in securing the flank of his brigade but also in safeguarding the flank of the Division. His valour and leading during two days of fighting were beyond all praise.'

Captain Percy Howard Hansen,
Adjutant, 6th (Service) Battalion, Lincolnshire Regiment
'For most conspicuous bravery on August 9, 1915, at Yilghin Burnu, Gallipoli Peninsula. After the second capture of the 'Green Knoll' his battalion was forced to retire, leaving some wounded behind, owing to the intense heat from the scrub which had been set on fire. When the retirement was effected, Captain Hansen, with three or four volunteers, on his own initiative, dashed forward several times some three hundred to four hundred yards over open ground into the scrub, under a terrific fire, and succeeded in rescuing from inevitable death by burning no less than six wounded men.'

Lieutenant (Acting Captain) Reginald Frederick Johnson Hayward,
Wiltshire Regiment
'Near Fremicourt, France, on March 21–22, 1918. For most conspicuous bravery in action. This officer, while in command of a company, displayed almost superhuman powers of endurance and consistent courage of the rarest nature. In spite of the fact that he was buried, wounded in the head, and rendered deaf on the first day of operations, and had his arm shattered two days later, he refused to leave his men (even though he received a third serious injury to his head), until he collapsed from sheer physical exhaustion.

Throughout the whole of this period the enemy were attacking his company front without cessation, but Captain Hayward continued to move across the open from one trench to another with absolute disregard of his own personal safety, concentrating entirely on reorganizing his defences and encouraging his men. It was almost entirely due to the magnificent example of ceaseless energy of this officer that many most determined attacks upon his portion of the trench system failed entirely.'

Lance-Corporal William Henry Hewitt,
2nd Regiment, South African Infantry
'At east of Ypres on September 20, 1917. For most conspicuous bravery during operations. Lance-Corporal Hewitt attacked a 'pill-box' with his section and tried to rush the doorway. The garrison, however, proved very stubborn, and in the attempt this non-commissioned officer received a severe wound. Nevertheless, he proceeded to the loophole of the 'pill-box' where, in his attempts to put a bomb into it, he was again wounded in the arm. Undeterred, however, he eventually managed to get a bomb inside, which caused the occupants to dislodge, and they were successfully and speedily dealt with by the remainder of the section.'

Second-Lieutenant (Acting Captain) Arthur Moore Lascelles,
3rd (attached 14th) Battalion, Durham Light Infantry
'At Masnieres, France, on December 3, 1917. For most conspicuous bravery, initiative, and devotion to duty when in command of his company in a very exposed position. After a very heavy bombardment, during which Captain Lascelles was wounded, the enemy attacked in strong force but was driven off, success being due in a great degree to the fine example set by this officer, who, refusing to allow his wound to be dressed, continued to encourage his men and organize the defence.

Shortly afterwards the enemy again attacked and captured the trench, taking several of his men prisoners. Captain Lascelles at once jumped on the parapet, and followed by the remainder of his company, twelve men only, rushed across under very heavy machine-gun fire and drove over sixty of the enemy back, thereby saving a most critical situation.

He was untiring in reorganizing the position, but shortly afterwards the enemy again attacked and captured the trench and Captain Lascelles, who escaped later. The remarkable determination and gallantry of this officer in the course of operations, during which he received two further wounds, afforded an inspiring example to all.'

Captain Oswald Austin Reid, 2nd Battalion, Liverpool Regiment, attached 6th Battalion, Loyal North Lancashire Regiment

'At Dialah River, Mesopotamia, on March 8–10, 1917. For most conspicuous bravery in the face of desperate circumstances. By his dauntless courage and gallant leadership he was able to consolidate a small post with the advanced troops, on the opposite side of a river to the main body, after his lines of communication had been cut by the sinking of the pontoons.

He maintained this position for thirty hours against constant attacks by bombs, machine-gun and shell fire, with the full knowledge that repeated attempts at relief had failed, and that his ammunition was all but exhausted. It was greatly due to his tenacity that the passage of the river was effected on the following night. During the operations he was wounded.'

Major (Acting Lieutenant-Colonel) John Sherwood-Kelly, Norfolk Regiment, Commanding 1st Battalion, Royal Inniskilling Fusiliers

'At Marcoing, France, on November 20, 1917. For most conspicuous bravery and fearless leading, when a party of men of another unit detailed to cover the passage of the canal by his battalion were held up on the near side of the canal by heavy rifle fire directed on the bridge. Lieutenant-Colonel Sherwood-Kelly at once ordered covering fire, personally led the leading company of his battalion across the canal, and, after crossing, reconnoitred under heavy rifle and machine-gun fire the high ground held by the enemy.

The left flank of his battalion, advancing to the assault of this objective, was held up by a thick belt of wire, whereupon he crossed to that flank and with a Lewis-gun team forced his way under heavy fire through obstacles, got the gun into position on the far side, and covered the advance of his battalion through the wire, thereby enabling them to capture the position.

Later, he personally led a charge against some pits from which a heavy fire was being directed on his men, captured the pits, together with five machine guns and forty-six prisoners, and killed a large number of the enemy.

The great gallantry displayed by this officer throughout the day inspired the greatest confidence in his men, and it was mainly due to his example and devotion to duty that his battalion was enabled to capture and hold their objective.'

Captain (Acting Lieutenant-Colonel) Richard Annesley West, late North Irish Horse (Cavalry Special Reserve) and Tank Corps

'At Courcelles and Vaulx-Vraucourt, France, on August 21, 1918, and September 2, 1918. For most conspicuous bravery, leadership, and self-sacrifice. During an attack, the infantry having lost their bearings in the dense fog, this officer at once collected and reorganized any men he could find and led them to their objective in face of heavy machine-gun fire. Throughout the whole action he displayed the most utter disregard of danger, and the capture of the objective was in a great part due to his initiative and gallantry.

On a subsequent occasion it was intended that a battalion of light tanks, under the command of this officer, should exploit the initial infantry and heavy tank attack. He therefore went forward in order to keep in touch with the progress of the battle, and arrived at the front line when the enemy were in process of delivering a local counter-attack. The infantry battalion had suffered heavy officer casualties and its flanks were exposed. Realising that there was a danger of the battalion giving way, he at once rode out in front of them under extremely heavy machine-gun and rifle fire and rallied the men.

In spite of the fact that the enemy were close upon him, he took charge of the situation and detailed non-commissioned officers to replace officer casualties. He then rode up and down in front of them in face of certain death, encouraging the men and calling to them, 'Stick it, men! Show them fight! And for God's sake put up a good fight!' He fell riddled by machine-gun bullets.

The magnificent bravery of this very gallant officer at the critical moment inspired the infantry to redoubled efforts, and the hostile attack was defeated.'

APPENDIX VI

Roll of Honour of the South African Infantry Brigade:

Operations on the Somme, July 1916

Includes 64th Field Company, Royal Engineers (attached to the Brigade) and 28th Brigade Machine Gun Company. The roll gives the rank, name, regiment, cause of death and cemetery.

3 July 1916
Private A.T. MARSHALL	3rd SAI	Accidentally killed
Péronne Road Cemetery, Maricourt		
Private S. MASON	3rd SAI	Accidentally killed

5 July 1916
Sergeant William GORDON	4th SAI	Killed in action
Péronne Road Cemetery, Maricourt		
Private Robert SCOTT	3rd SAI	Died of wounds
Dive Copse British Cemetery		

6 July 1916
Corporal W. BATES	4th SAI	Killed in action
Péronne Road Cemetery, Maricourt		
Private G. BERLIN	3rd SAI	Died of wounds
Lance-Corporal William Alexander LUNDIE	3rd SAI	Killed in action
Lance-Corporal A. MARTIN	4th SAI	Died of wounds
Lance-Corporal Richard Barry MURPHY	3rd SAI	Killed in action
Private S. PAWLEY	3rd SAI	Killed in action
Private H. TRYTHALL	1st SAI	Killed in action
Private Albert WALDEK	1st SAI	Died of wounds

7 July 1916
Private R. BOYD	3rd SAI	Died of wounds
Corbie Communal Cemetery Extension		
Lieutenant William Nimms BROWN	1st SAI	Killed in action
Thiepval Memorial		

APPENDIX VI: ROLL OF HONOUR

Lance-Corporal Stephen Herd DICK	1st SAI	Killed in action
Lieutenant H.G. OUGHTERSON	4th SAI	Killed in action
Péronne Road Cemetery, Maricourt		
Corporal W.E. RICE	4th SAI	Died of wounds
Private Herbert Christopher SMITH	1st SAI	Killed in action
Thiepval Memorial		
Private Hector H. SOUDANT	4th SAI	Killed in action

8 July 1916

Private Anthony Roland ARNOLD	2nd SAI	Killed in action
Péronne Road Cemetery, Maricourt		
Private John Silcock BROWN	2nd SAI	Killed in action
Thiepval Memorial		
Private George COOK	2nd SAI	Died of wounds
Private William Thomas EDWARDS	3rd SAI	Killed in action
Private Charles Alred HARGRAVES	3rd SAI	Killed in action
Signaller Frank MARTIN	2nd SAI	Killed in action
Private James MOWAT	2nd SAI	Killed in action
Private Hector MUNRO	2nd SAI	Died of wounds
Private Cyril NETTLETON	2nd SAI	Killed in action
Private Rochfort Lindley PHIPSON	2nd SAI	Killed in action
Lance Sergeant Frank POPHAM	2nd SAI	Died of wounds
Private Maurice ROBERTSON	2nd SAI	Died of wounds
Private John SACKVILLE	3rd SAI	Killed in action
Private Edward Vincent STUART	2nd SAI	Killed in action
Private John Carver TATTERSALL	3rd SAI	Killed in action
Private William WILLOUGHBY	2nd SAI	Killed in action
Warlencourt British Cemetery		

9 July 1916

Private R.Y. AIR	4th SAI	Killed in action
Péronne Road Cemetery, Maricourt		
Private Ami Wallis BECK	2nd SAI	Killed in action
Thiepval Memorial		
Private Guy BENINGFIELD	2nd SAI	Killed in action
London Cemetery and Extension, Longueval		
Private George Benjamin BRYAN	2nd SAI	Killed in action
Thiepval Memorial		
Private Alexander CHISHOLM (Chummie)	2nd SAI	Killed in action
Private Ernest Horatio COLQUITT	2nd SAI	Killed in action
Private A. CRAIG	2nd SAI	Killed in action
Bernafay Wood British Cemetery		
Private John Kelly DOYLE	2nd SAI	Killed in action
Thiepval Memorial		
Corporal Wilfred George ETHERIDGE	2nd SAI	Killed in action

Private Arthur D. GEOGHEGAN	2nd SAI	Killed in action
Ovillers Military Cemetery		
Private Samuel GLUCKMAN	3rd SAI	Killed in action
Thiepval Memorial		
Private Ernest Utley GRANGER	2nd SAI	Killed in action
Lance-Corporal Albert Bert JONES	2nd SAI	Killed in action
Private Charles Frederick MASON	2nd SAI	Killed in action
Private Ernest Sherwood MATHER	2nd SAI	Killed in action
Private Vernon Robert Edwin McWILLIAMS	2nd SAI	Killed in action
Private Harry Nelson PEERS	2nd SAI	Killed in action
Corporal John Samuel PRESSLY, M.M.	2nd SAI	Killed in action
Private Albert Ernest REID	2nd SAI	Killed in action
London Cemetery and Extension, Longueval		
Lance-Corporal Arthur ROE	2nd SAI	Killed in action
Ovillers Military Cemetery		
Private George William Barber SCOTT	2nd SAI	Killed in action
London Cemetery and Extension, Longueval		
Lance-Corporal Cyril Oscar WHITELAW	2nd SAI	Died of wounds
Péronne Road Cemetery, Maricourt		
Private V.R.E. WILLIAMS	2nd SAI	Killed in action

10 July 1916

Private Harold Crosbie ALGER	2nd SAI	Killed in action
Thiepval Memorial		
Private Neil BLAIR	4th SAI	Killed in action
Private Thomas BOYLE	28th Bg, MG Coy	Killed in action
Dantzig Alley British Cemetery		
Private William DODDS	4th SAI	Killed in action
Thiepval Memorial		
Private Samuel Annett FOSTER	4th SAI	Killed in action
Sergeant Hugh Francis GORDON	4th SAI	Killed in action
Private Joseph HEARNE	4th SAI	Missing in action
Corporal Mervyn Evans HOCKEY	4th SAI	Missing in action
Private Andre Bernard HOOLAHAN	1st SAI	Killed in action
Sergeant Edwin HUNTLEY	2nd SAI	Missing in action
Private Douglas Ivan KING	4th SAI	Killed in action
Private Murdock MATHESON	4th SAI	Missing in action
Private Thomas McKINLAY	4th SAI	Killed in action
Private Arthur Lorimer MORGAN	4th SAI	Killed in action
Private Stewart MUNN	4th SAI	Killed in action
Lance-Corporal James Miller ORR	4th SAI	Killed in action
Private William Goodwill PUCKRIN	2nd SAI	Died of wounds
Corbie Communal Cemetery Extension		
Lance-Corporal David PUGH	4th SAI	Killed in action
Thiepval Memorial		
Private David ROBERTSON	4th SAI	Killed in action
Corporal James Alfred SCOTT	4th SAI	Missing in action

APPENDIX VI: ROLL OF HONOUR

Private Claude Alfred Cannon SMITH	2nd SAI	Died of wounds
Dive Copse British Cemetery		
Corporal George SMITH	4th SAI	Killed in action
Thiepval Memorial		
Private Harry SOLLIS	4th SAI	Killed in action
Private James Howard SURMON	1st SAI	Died of wounds
Corbie Communal Cemetery Extension		
Private Frank Arthur SYKES	4th SAI	Killed in action
Thiepval Memorial		
Private Edward THOMPSON	4th SAI	Missing in action
Private William VAN DER POLL	1st SAI	Killed in action
Private David Alexander WILSON	4th SAI	Killed in action

11 July 1916

Private R. ALFRED	4th SAI	Killed in action
Quarry Cemetery, Montauban-en-Picardie		
Private James Gibb ALLAN	4th SAI	Killed in action
Thiepval Memorial		
Corporal Charles Revel BREDELL	4th SAI	Killed in action
Péronne Road Cemetery, Maricourt		
Private Kenneth CHRISTIE	4th SAI	Killed in action
Captain Chaplain George Thornhill COOK	3rd SAI	Killed in action
Thiepval Memorial		
Lance-Corporal John Vernon DAVISON	4th SAI	Killed in action
Private Daniel FERGUSON	4th SAI	Killed in action
Private Patrick Thomas FREEMAN	4th SAI	Died of wounds
Private V. HEEGER	4th SAI	Killed in action
Dantzig Alley British Cemetery, Mametz		
Lieut. Col Frank Aubrey JONES, CMG, DSO	4th SAI	Killed in action
Péronne Road Cemetery, Maricourt		
Private William George LARGE	4th SAI	Missing in action
Dantzig Alley British Cemetery, Mametz		
Lieut. Claude Ludovic Hickman MULCAHY	2nd SAI	Died of wounds
Corbie Communal Cemetery Extension		
Private W. PATTINSON	4th SAI	Died of wounds
Dive Copse British Cemetery		
Captain S.A. RUSSELL	4th SAI	Died of wounds
La Neuville British Cemetery, Corbie		
Private L.D. McL. SINCLAIR	4th SAI	Killed in action
Péronne Road Cemetery, Maricourt		
Private J.H. SMITH	2nd SAI	Killed in action
Lance-Corporal William James WALKER	4th SAI	Killed in action
Thiepval Memorial		

12 July 1916

Private J. FORD	2nd SAI	Killed in action
Péronne Road Cemetery, Maricourt		

Private L.V. HAAK | 3rd SAI | Killed in action
Private Clarence Percy IMPEY | 4th SAI | Killed in action
Thiepval Memorial
Sergeant P.J. KENNEDY | 2nd SAI | Killed in action
Péronne Road Cemetery, Maricourt
Lance-Corporal Herbert MARKS | 4th SAI | Died of wounds
Thiepval Memorial
Private D.P. McCLURE | 4th SAI | Died of wounds
Corbie Communal Cemetery Extension

13 July 1916

Sergeant W.S. ALLEN | 2nd SAI | Died of wounds
La Neuville British Cemetery, Corbie
Lance-Corporal P.A. COWAN | 2nd SAI | Killed in action
Dive Copse British Cemetery
Second-Lieutenant John Samuel FRY | 4th SAI | Killed in action
Thiepval Memorial
Private James Sneddon FYFE | 3rd SA | Killed in action
Private C.B. GATT | 4th SAI | Died of wounds
La Neuville British Cemetery, Corbie
Private A. HENDRICKS | 3rd SAI | Killed in action
Péronne Road Cemetery, Maricourt
Lance-Corporal Henry Clifford HULLEY | 2nd SAI | Died of wounds
La Neuville British Cemetery, Corbie
Private Francis Howard KNIGHT | 2nd SAI | Died of wounds
Private H.R. MANN | 2nd SAI | Died of wounds
Péronne Road Cemetery, Maricourt
Private George Douglas MOSSES | 4th SAI | Killed in action
Thiepval Memorial
Private D.J. REDWOOD | 2nd SAI | Died of wounds
Péronne Road Cemetery, Maricourt
Lance-Corporal W.E. SHACKLETON | 2nd SAI | Died of wounds
Dive Copse British Cemetery
Private H.G. SMITH | 2nd SAI | Killed in action
Péronne Road Cemetery, Maricourt
Private Harold Cecil STRATFORD | 3rd SAI | Missing in action
Thiepval Memorial

14 July 1916

Private Ernest BARKER | 4th SAI | Killed in action
Thiepval Memorial
Private William Eric CARLSSON | 1st SAI | Killed in action
Corporal Harry Reginald CHEESEMAN | 2nd SAI | Killed in action
Private Frederick Richard DEWING | 2nd SAI | Died of wounds
Abbeville Communal Cemetery
Private Leslie Llewellyn DREYER | 1st SAI | Killed in action
Thiepval Memorial

APPENDIX VI: ROLL OF HONOUR

Private Vernon Jeffery EDKINS	2nd SAI	Died of wounds
Corbie Communal Cemetery Extension		
Private George Gray EDWARDS	3rd SAI	Killed in action
Serre Road Cemetery No. 2		
Private William FERGUSON	1st SAI	Killed in action
Thiepval Memorial		
Private Alfred Charles FISHER	1st SAI	Missing in action
Corporal Thomas Henry FOXCROFT	1st SAI	Killed in action
Private George Frederick GREENWOOD	1st SAI	Killed in action
Private Frederick William HERBERT	4th SAI	Killed in action
Quarry Cemetery, Montauban-en-Picardie		
Private Robert McLean IRVINE	2nd SAI	Died of wounds
Corbie Communal Cemetery Extension		
Private James Yeatman NASH	1st SAI	Killed in action
Delville Wood Cemetery		
Private James Hubert QUINN	1st SAI	Killed in action
Thiepval Memorial		
Lance-Corporal Walter Thomas RAINBOW	2nd SAI	Killed in action
Private Cecil Steward ROSS	1st SAI	Killed in action
Private C.W. SCHAFER	1st SAI	Died of wounds
Corbie Communal Cemetery Extension		
Corporal A.C. SMITH	1st Field Ambulance, SAMC	Killed in action
Dantzig Alley British Cemetery, Mametz		
Private Henry TURNER	1st SAI	Killed in action
Thiepval Memorial		
Sergeant Francis WATTERS	1st SAI	Killed in action
Private Robert Joseph WHITTER	1st SAI	Killed in action
Sergeant Arthur Henry WILKINSON	2nd SAI	Killed in action

15 July 1916

Private John BELLEW	3rd SAI	Killed in action
Thiepval Memorial		
Private George John BENTLEY	2nd SAI	Killed in action
Private W.J. BERRY	3rd SAI	Killed in action
Private Johannes Petrus Lodewyk BESTER	2nd SAI	Missing in action
Private Algene Ward BRADFIELD	4th SAI	Killed in action
Quarry Cemetery, Montauban-en-Picardie		
Private Louis Gowthorpe BRAITHWAITE	3rd SAI	Killed in action
Thiepval Memorial		
Private Charles Harley BROOKS	3rd SAI	Killed in action
Private Cecil Pierce BROWN	4th SAI	Killed in action
Delville Wood Cemetery		
2nd Lieut. Thorkell Nathan BRU-DE-WOLD	2nd SAI	Killed in action
Thiepval Memorial		
Private John BURLEIGH	4th SAI	Killed in action
London Cemetery and Extension, Longueval		

Private Frederick Claud BUTCHER	3rd SAI	Killed in action
Delville Wood Cemetery		
Private John McGilvray CAIRNS	4th SAI	Killed in action
Thiepval Memorial		
Regimental Sergeant-Major John CAMERON	4th SAI	Killed in action
Lance-Corporal Chalmers CARMICHAEL	2nd SAI	Killed in action
Private Norman COLLING	1st SAI	Killed in action
Delville Wood Cemetery		
Private Albert Charles COLLINS	3rd SAI	Killed in action
Thiepval Memorial		
Lance-Corporal Alfred George COOK	3rd SAI	Killed in action
Private J.W.C. COOK	3rd SAI	Killed in action
Delville Wood Cemetery		
Corporal Charles Baldwin COOPER	2nd SAI	Died of wounds
Thiepval Memorial		
Captain Harold Evely Frederick CREED	2nd SAI	Killed in action
Private Joseph CULLEN	4th SAI	Killed in action
Private Charles DAVIS	28th Bg MG Coy	Died of wounds
Private Henry Mallinson DEELEY	2nd SAI	Killed in action
Delville Wood Cemetery		
Private Percy Edward DENNANT	2nd SAI	Killed in action
Thiepval Memorial		
Private Thomas DINGWALL	4th SAI	Killed in action
Private Samuel DUCKHAM	28th Bg MG Coy	Killed in action
Sapper Joseph James EDDY	64th Field Coy, RE	Killed in action
Private Harold EDWARDS	2nd SAI	Killed in action
Private T. ELMS	1st SAI	Died of wounds
Daours Communal Cemetery Extension		
Signaller George Henderson FENNELL	2nd SAI	Killed in action
Thiepval Memorial		
Private Frederick Maurice GATELY	2nd SAI	Killed in action
Private Cyril Phillip GERAGHTY	2nd SAI	Killed in action
Private John GLASSON	3rd SAI	Missing in action
Private John James GRAVELL	2nd SAI	Died of wounds
La Neuville British Cemetery, Corbie		
Captain William Johnston GRAY, LSM	2nd SAI	Killed in action
Sucrerie Military Cemetery, Colincamps		
Private Peter HAIG	2nd SAI	Killed in action
Thiepval Memorial		
Second-Lieutenant Alfred Charles HANKS	3rd SAI	Killed in action
Sapper T. HARDEN	64th Coy, RE	Killed in action
Private Leslie HAWTHORNE	3rd SAI	Killed in action
Private William Miles HENRICK	3rd SAI	Killed in action
Private Edward James HEWITT	4th SAI	Killed in action

APPENDIX VI: ROLL OF HONOUR

Lance-Corporal Harold HORN	4th SAI	Killed in action
Private E. HUDSON	2nd SAI	Killed in action
Delville Wood Cemetery		
Private George HUNTER	3rd SAI	Killed in action
Thiepval Memorial		
Private Aubrey Neville HUTCHINSON	2nd SAI	Killed in action
Private William IMPEY	3rd SAI	Killed in action
Lance-Corporal Arthur Nathaniel JACOBS	2nd SAI	Killed in action
Corporal Clement JENKINSON	2nd SAI	Killed in action
Private Erick JOHNS	4th SAI	Killed in action
Private Archibald Stanley KIRBY	3rd SAI	Killed in action
Lance-Corporal George Charles KNOX	4th SAI	Missing in action
Private Leonard KURZ	2nd SAI	Killed in action
Private William Vernon LAMBIE	4th SAI	Killed in action
Serre Road Cemetery No.2		
Lance-Corporal William LOGAN	4th SAI	Killed in action
Thiepval Memorial		
Private Alan Vyvyan MAGER	2nd SAI	Killed in action
Corporal Adam Neil MALCOLM	4th SAI	Killed in action
Corporal Walter John MATTHEWS	4th SAI	Killed in action
Private George MAY	3rd SAI	Killed in action
Private John William MAYS	4th SAI	Missing in action
Private Arthur Basil McCABE	4th SAI	Died of wounds
Corbie Communal Cemetery Extension		
Private Cyril Fidelis McCALLUM	4th SAI	Missing in action
Thiepval Memorial		
Private Charles Henry McCARTHY	3rd SAI	Killed in action
Company SM David James McCLELLAND	2nd SAI	Killed in action
Private Robert McDONALD	4th SAI	Killed in action
Sg William Simpson McDONALD, M.M.	3rd SAI	Missing in action
Private James Baxter McKINNON	4th SAI	Killed in action
Private Edward Hamilton McLEAN	3rd SAI	Killed in action
Private John Gammersep McLEAN	3rd SAI	Killed in action
Private George Walter MERRINGTON	4th SAI	Killed in action
Second-Lieutenant Robert Gibb MILLER	2nd SAI	Killed in action
Private Walter Charles MILLS	4th SAI	Killed in action
Sergeant William Alexander MUNRO	3rd SAI	Killed in action
Private James Richard PATTERSON	2nd SAI	Missing in action
Private Arthur Royle PAYNE	2nd SAI	Killed in action
Serre Road Cemetery No. 2		
Private James D. PILBROW	4th SAI	Killed in action
Thiepval Memorial		
Private James William POCOCK	3rd SAI	Killed in action
Private Robinson Henry READETT	3rd SAI	Missing in action
Private Lionel REDPATH	3rd SAI	Killed in action
Sergeant Charles Albert RESTALL	2nd SAI	Killed in action
London Cemetery and Extension, Longueval		

Company SM Robert Francis RYDER	2nd SAI	Killed in action
Thiepval Memorial		
L/Corporal Douglas Rutherford SANDERS	3rd SAI	Killed in action
Sergeant Herbert SHAW	3rd SAI	Killed in action
Private Francis Js Anderson SINGLEHURST	3rd SAI	Killed in action
London Cemetery and Extension, Longueval		
Private Andrew SKILLEN	4th SAI	Killed in action
Thiepval Memorial		
Lance-Corporal Laban THODAY	3rd SAI	Killed in action
Sucrerie Military Cemetery, Colincamps		
Sergeant George Henry THOMSON	2nd SAI	Killed in action
Thiepval Memorial		
Lieut. Robert Brown THORBURN, M.I.D.	4th SAI	Killed in action
Delville Wood Cemetery		
Private Alexander TOD	3rd SAI	Killed in action
London Cemetery and Extension, Longueval		
Private John VAN DER WALT	3rd SAI	Killed in action
Thiepval Memorial		
Private W.T.R. WALES	3rd SAI	Killed in action
Delville Wood Cemetery		
Private Dudley Stanton WEBSTER	2nd SAI	Missing in action
Thiepval Memorial		
Private Leslie Garnett WEBSTER	4th SAI	Killed in action
Sapper Joseph WILLIAMS	64th Coy, RE	Killed in action
Private John Buckley WOOD	2nd SAI	Killed in action
Sergeant William James WRIGHT	2nd SAI	Killed in action
Private Lawrence WYBROW	2nd SAI	Missing in action

16 July 1916

Private John Hedley ADAMS	3rd SAI	Killed in action
Thiepval Memorial		
Private Frank ALLSOP	1st SAI	Killed in action
Corporal Robert APPLETON	1st SAI	Killed in action
Delville Wood Cemetery		
Lance-Corporal Lyman Raphael BAKER	1st SAI	Killed in action
Thiepval Memorial		
Private Orlando Leonard BEAN	4th SAI	Missing in action
Lance-Corporal Fitzwilliam Charles BELL	4th SAI	Killed in action
Private A.G. BEVERLEY	4th SAI	Killed in action
Delville Wood Cemetery		
Private Aubrey William BINDON	4th SAI	Killed in action
Thiepval Memorial		
Sergeant John Rider BLEASBY	1st SAI	Killed in action
Delville Wood Cemetery		
L/Corporal Ernest Frederick BROCKWELL	2nd SAI	Killed in action
Second-Lieutenant Arthur Ernest BROWN	1st SAI	Killed in action
Thiepval Memorial		

APPENDIX VI: ROLL OF HONOUR

Private Henry BROWN	1st SAI	Killed in action
Company SM James Wilfred BRYANT	3rd SAI	Killed in action
Private Joseph William BRYANT	3rd SAI	Killed in action
Private Roy Cuthbert BURTON	3rd SAI	Killed in action
Private Vivian Roland BURTON	3rd SAI	Killed in action
Private G. CALLAGHAN	1st SAI	Killed in action
Delville Wood Cemetery		
Lance-Corporal Arthur Dowley CARLISLE	1st SAI	Killed in action
Thiepval Memorial		
Private James CARSON	4th SAI	Killed in action
Private Richard Charles CARTER	1st SAI	Killed in action
Corporal Alfred John CLEWS	1st SAI	Killed in action
Private Cyril Claude Victor CLIFT	2nd SAI	Missing in action
Lance-Corporal Augustus Victor COOMBE	4th SAI	Killed in action
Delville Wood Cemetery		
Private William Edward COOPER	4th SAI	Killed in action
Thiepval Memorial		
Private Augustus COWIE	2nd SAI	Killed in action
Thiepval Memorial		
L/Corporal Llewellyn George DAVIDSON	4th SAI	Killed in action
Quarry Cemetery, Montauban-en-Picardie		
Private Percy Frederick DAVIS	4th SAI	Killed in action
Delville Wood Cemetery		
Corporal F. DENT	3rd SAI	Died of wounds
La Neuville British Cemetery, Corbie		
Lance-Corporal Percy King DIXON	3rd SAI	Killed in action
Thiepval Memorial		
Lance-Corporal Herbert DODD	4th SAI	Killed in action
Delville Wood Cemetery		
Corporal Neville DOYLE	1st SAI	Killed in action
Thiepval Memorial		
Private Leslie Howard DRURY	3rd SAI	Killed in action
London Cemetery and Extension, Longueval		
Lance-Corporal Charles Carlisle FICHAT	3rd SAI	Killed in action
Corbie Communal Cemetery Extension		
Private Arthur FILBY	4th SAI	Missing in action
Thiepval Memorial		
Private Thomas Nuttall FLITCROFT	3rd SAI	Killed in action
Private Aubrey James FOCKENS	4th SAI	Killed in action
Sergeant John FRENCH	4th SAI	Killed in action
Private N.P. FRONEMAN	4th SAI	Killed in action
Delville Wood Cemetery		
Private Dudley Beresford Hoole FYNN	3rd SAI	Killed in action
London Cemetery and Extension, Longueval		
Lance-Corporal Norman McNab GAISFORD	4th SAI	Killed in action
Thiepval Memorial		

Lance-Corporal Francis GLAZEBROOK	1st SAI	Killed in action
Delville Wood Cemetery		
Private John Harry GOODING	4th SAI	Killed in action
Thiepval Memorial		
Private Bertie Vincent GOUGH	2nd SAI	Killed in action
Private John GRANT	4th SAI	Missing in action
Private William GRIGG	4th SAI	Killed in action
Private Alfred HAGELL	1st SAI	Killed in action
Captain Ernst Albert Linsingen HAHN	1st SAI	Killed in action
Private G.V. HAMMOND	4th SAI	Died of wounds
Favreuil British Cemetery		
Private V. HARE	4th SAI	Killed in action
Delville Wood Cemetery		
Private Ashley Ronald HARRIS	3rd SAI	Died of wounds
Thiepval Memorial		
Private Joseph HARRIS	64th Field Coy, RE	Killed in action
Private J.S. HODGE	4th SAI	Killed in action
Delville Wood Cemetery		
Private William Rule HOLLISTER	2nd SAI	Missing in action
Thiepval Memorial		
Private James HOPE	28th Bg MG Coy	Killed in action
Private Charles Sutton HOWELL	3rd SAI	Killed in action
Lance Sergeant Joseph Leigh HOWELL	1st SAI	Killed in action
Delville Wood Cemetery		
Corporal Thomas HUNTER	4th SAI	Killed in action
Thiepval Memorial		
Private Frank Horace INDGE	3rd SAI	Killed in action
Private Alexander Duncan INNES	4th SAI	Killed in action
Lance-Corporal G.R. ISRAEL	3rd SAI	Killed in action
Delville Wood Cemetery		
Private Benjamin Lombard KEET	4th SAI	Killed in action
Serre Road Cemetery No. 2		
Private George William KENSLEY	4th SAI	Killed in action
Thiepval Memorial		
Private Arnold Gerard John KUYS	1st SAI	Missing in action
Sergeant Victor Edward LEDBURY	1st SAI	Killed in action
Sergeant Curwen Margam LEWIS	3rd SAI	Killed in action
Private Dirk Jacobus LOMBARD	4th SAI	Missing in action
Corporal William S. LORIMER	28th Bg MG Coy	Killed in action
Sergeant R. LUPTON	3rd SAI	Killed in action
Delville Wood Cemetery		
Private John Charles Grant MACKINTOSH	4th SAI	Died of wounds
Thiepval Memorial		
Captain Donald Ronald MACLACHAN	3rd SAI	Killed in action

APPENDIX VI: ROLL OF HONOUR

Sergeant Robert McCLURE	3rd SAI	Killed in action
Private Murdoch McDONALD	4th SAI	Killed in action
Private Archibald McSporran Blue McKAY	4th SAI	Killed in action
Private A. McLACHLAN	4th SAI	Died as POW
Niederzwehren Cemetery, Kassel, Germany		
Private Keith Athol McLAGHLAN	3rd SAI	Killed in action
Thiepval Memorial		
Private James McLEAN	28th Bg MG Coy	Killed in action
Private Fergus David McLEROTH	3rd SAI	Killed in action
Delville Wood Cemetery		
Captain George John MILLER	1st SAI	Killed in action
Thiepval Memorial		
Private William MILLER	4th SAI	Killed in action
Dive Copse British Cemetery		
2nd Lieutenant Matthew Rankin MONTEITH	64th Field Coy, RE	Killed in action
Serre Road Cemetery No. 2		
Private Alexander Archibald MORTON	4th SAI	Missing in action
Thiepval Memorial		
Private Harvey MOSS	4th SAI	Died of wounds
Private Duncan MUNRO	1st SAI	Died of wounds
La Neuville British Cemetery, Corbie		
Private Charles Frederick William NEWELL	1st SAI	Killed in action
Thiepval Memorial		
Private Ellis Alban NEWTON	3rd SAI	Killed in action
Delville Wood Cemetery		
Private Frederick NEWTON	2nd SAI	Missing in action
Thiepval Memorial		
Private Percy NEWTON	2nd SAI	Died of wounds
Corbie Communal Cemetery Extension		
Private Stephen James O'CONNOR	1st SAI	Died of wounds
La Neuville British Cemetery, Corbie		
Private Nicholas OGDEN	28th Bg MG Coy	Killed in action
Thiepval Memorial		
Private Herbert Douglas OPENSHAW	2nd SAI	Killed in action
Lieutenant Cecil Braithwaite PARSONS	1st SAI	Killed in action
Private Theodore E. PATTERSON	1st SAI	Killed in action
Delville Wood Cemetery		
Private J.H. PERKINS	3rd SAI	Killed in action
Private Harry Glass PETRIE	3rd SAI	Killed in action
Thiepval Memorial		
Private Francis Edward POLE	4th SAI	Killed in action
Private Campbell POLLOCK	2nd SAI	Killed in action
Private Neil Morrison POLLOCK	3rd SAI	Killed in action
Private John Sherlock RAYNER	3rd SAI	Killed in action
Private David REID	3rd SAI	Killed in action

Private John William ROBINSON	28th Bg,	Died of wounds
Corbie Communal Cemetery Extension	MG Coy	
Private John Lawrie Malcolm RODGER	4th SAI	Killed in action
Thiepval Memorial		
Private Peter RODGERS	3rd SAI	Killed in action
Private Frederick John ROFFEY	2nd SAI	Killed in action
Private Sidney Charles ROGERSON	3rd SAI	Killed in action
Delville Wood Cemetery		
Private Hugh Noble ROSS	4th SAI	Killed in action
Thiepval Memorial		
Private Walter Edmund ROWE	3rd SAI	Killed in action
Sergeant Arthur Gardner SCHOOLING	1st SAI	Killed in action
Private Fleming William SMITH	2nd SAI	Killed in action
Sergeant William Cass STERICKER	3rd SAI	Killed in action
Private David Donald STRACHAN	2nd SAI	Missing in action
Private Rowland Henry TARBOTON	2nd SAI	Killed in action
Private William Hawthorn TENNANT	4th SAI	Killed in action
Delville Wood Cemetery		
Private Robert George TRACE	3rd SAI	Killed in action
Thiepval Memorial		
Private Edward Turner WOODBURN	3rd SAI	Killed in action
Private John William WOODYER	28th Bg	Killed in action
	MG Coy	
Private Gordon Garfield YOUNG	4th SAI	Killed in action

17 July 1916

Private James Douglas AFFLICK	3rd SAI	Killed in action
Thiepval Memorial		
Private Victor ANDERSON	1st SAI	Killed in action
Delville Wood Cemetery		
Cpl Alfred Ernest Benjamin ARMSTRONG	2nd SAI	Killed in action
Thiepval Memorial		
Private Sydney Norman BAISLEY	1st SAI	Killed in action
Private Joseph BEETAR	2nd SAI	Killed in action
Private David BOTHA	1st SAI	Killed in action
Private Frank BOTHA	4th SAI	Killed in action
Péronne Road Cemetery, Maricourt		
Lance-Corporal Walter BRIDSON	4th SAI	Missing in action
Thiepval Memorial		
Private Joshua Isaac BUCKINGHAM	4th SAI	Killed in action
Private Sam BUTLER	1st SAI	Died of wounds
La Neuville British Cemetery, Corbie		
Private Wilfred Franklin CAPPER	1st SAI	Killed in action
Thiepval Memorial		
Private Harold Birks CASTLE	1st SAI	Killed in action
Private William Edward CLEWS	1st SAI	Died of wounds
Carnoy Military Cemetery		

APPENDIX VI: ROLL OF HONOUR

Private Prior Hudson CLIFT	4th SAI	Killed in action
Thiepval Memorial		
Private Albert Edward COHEN	2nd SAI	Killed in action
Private Harold David COLLY	2nd SAI	Missing in action
Private Pierce Ryan COMBRINCK	4th SAI	Died of wounds
Dive Copse British Cemetery		
Private Thomas Perry CONWAY	1st SAI	Killed in action
Thiepval Memorial		
Sergeant George Henry DAVEY	3rd SAI	Killed in action
Private Thomas Oliver DAVIS	2nd SAI	Killed in action
Lance-Corporal John DE VOS	2nd SAI	Died of wounds
Private Joseph Benjamin DILLON	1st SAI	Killed in action
Private James DRUMMOND	4th SAI	Died of wounds
Private Joseph Albert DUNN	3rd SAI	Killed in action
Lance-Corporal Frederick Walter FEAST	1st SAI	Killed in action
Private Johan Jakob FOURIE	1st SAI	Died of wounds
La Neuville British Cemetery, Corbie		
Private Joseph Thomas James FRANCKLOW	1st SAI	Killed in action
Thiepval Memorial		
Corporal Horace William GARTON	4th SAI	Killed in action
Private William Greig GRAHAM	2nd SAI	Killed in action
Private Robert C. GRAY	4th SAI	Killed in action
Ovillers Military Cemetery		
Lance-Corporal E.W.H. GREENWAY	4th SAI	Died of wounds
Dive Copse British Cemetery		
2nd Lieutenant Allan Christie HAARHOFF	1st SAI	Killed in action
Thiepval Memorial		
Private William HARRISON	2nd SAI	Missing in action
Private George Bertram Lake HIRTZEL	3rd SAI	Killed in action
Corporal John David Noble HUMPHREYS	4th SAI	Killed in action
Corporal John Edgcumbe JAMES	3rd SAI	Killed in action
Lance-Corporal Philip Arthur JAMES	3rd SAI	Killed in action
Private Cyril Roland Alfred JENKINS	1st SAI	Killed in action
Sergeant William JOHNSON	3rd SAI	Killed in action
Private Vivian Albert JONES	1st SAI	Killed in action
Private Ernest William KEATING	1st SAI	Died of wounds
Corbie Communal Cemetery Extension		
Private Colin Gerald KIDSON	2nd SAI	Killed in action
Thiepval Memorial		
Private William John KIRKHAM	1st SAI	Killed in action
Delville Wood Cemetery		
Private Wessel George KLEINHANS	4th SAI	Killed in action
Thiepval Memorial		
Private Albert LETLEY	2nd SAI	Missing in action
Private Walter Bruce LITTLE	2nd SAI	Killed in action
Delville Wood Cemetery		
Private Reginald Chadwick LLOYD	1st SAI	Killed in action

THE SOMME CHRONICLES

Private Ronald LOCK	4th SAI	Missing in action
Thiepval Memorial		
Private James MACGREGOR	4th SAI	Killed in action
Private Hugh MAGEE	4th SAI	Killed in action
Private Leslie Morley MANDY	2nd SAI	Killed in action
Delville Wood Cemetery		
Private Frank McHENRY	4th SAI	Killed in action
Thiepval Memorial		
Sergeant John McINTOSH	4th SAI	Died of wounds
Corbie Communal Cemetery Extension		
Corporal J.H. McKNIGHT	1st SAI	Killed in action
Thiepval Memorial		
Lance-Corporal Alexander Coomber McLEAN	4th SAI	Killed in action
Private Charles McPHEE	4th SAI	Killed in action
Private Bertram Westley MEDLIN	3rd SAI	Died of wounds
Corbie Communal Cemetery Extension		
Private Lionel MILES	2nd SAI	Killed in action
Thiepval Memorial		
Private John MORGAN	3rd SAI	Killed in action
Ovillers Military Cemetery		
Private Charles Bernard MOZLEY	4th SAI	Killed in action
Thiepval Memorial		
Private Arnold Alexander NELSON	2nd SAI	Missing in action
Private James NOBLE	4th SAI	Killed in action
Lance-Corporal Thomas POLLOCK	3rd SAI	Killed in action
Private Henry Charles PRODEHL	1st SAI	Killed in action
Private Harold RENSHAW	2nd SAI	Killed in action
Private Henry John ROBERTS	4th SAI	Killed in action
Private Richard Frederick ROBERTS	1st SAI	Died of wounds
Bronfay Farm Cemetery, Bray-sur-Somme		
Private Frederick RUDDLE	3rd SAI	Killed in action
Thiepval Memorial		
Private Norman SCOTT	4th SAI	Died of wounds
St Sever Cemetery, Rouen		
Private George Richmond SCRUBY	2nd SAI	Killed in action
Thiepval Memorial		
RSM Edgar Samuel SHERWOOD	3rd SAI	Killed in action
Private Milan SIKIMICH	2nd SAI	Killed in action
L/Sergeant Charles Roberts SIMMONDS	3rd SAI	Killed in action
Private Walter Duncan SINCLAIR	4th SAI	Missing in action
Private John Martin SLATTERY	2nd SAI	Killed in action
Private Frank Allan SMITH	1st SAI	Died of wounds
Corbie Communal Cemetery Extension		
Private Jack SNEEZUM	3rd SAI	Killed in action
Thiepval Memorial		
Private Henry John SNOWDEN	3rd SAI	Killed in action
Private Norman Rhodes STURGEON	3rd SAI	Killed in action

APPENDIX VI: ROLL OF HONOUR

Corporal Peter STURROCK	1st SAI	Died of wounds
Corbie Communal Cemetery Extension		
Private Isaac Henry TAIT	4th SAI	Missing in action
Thiepval Memorial		
Private Bertie Cecil Smith TIMMS	4th SAI	Missing in action
Private Arthur Francis TOOKE	2nd SAI	Missing in action
Private Raymond James TRUSCOTT	3rd SAI	Killed in action
Private William Henry TUBBS	3rd SAI	Killed in action
Delville Wood Cemetery		
Second-Lieutenant Aylmer Templer WALES	2nd SAI	Died of wounds
Dive Copse British Cemetery		
Sergeant Harry WELCH	4th SAI	Died of wounds
Private John Low YULE	4th SAI	Killed in action
Thiepval Memorial		

18 July 1916

Private Francis ALLEN	2nd SAI	Killed in action
Delville Wood Cemetery		
Private James ALSOP	3rd SAI	Killed in action
Thiepval Memorial		
Private Robert ANDERSON	3rd SAI	Missing in action
Private William Ernest BAILEY	1st SAI	Missing in action
Private Herbert Alfred BAMBURY	4th SAI	Killed in action
Private Walter Arthur Henry BANSEMER	2nd SAI	Killed in action
Private J. BARRETT	2nd SAI	Died of wounds
Dive Copse British Cemetery		
Private H.W. BARTLEY	2nd SAI	Killed in action
Delville Wood Cemetery		
Second-Lieutenant Alfred Richard BARTON	3rd SAI	Killed in action
Thiepval Memorial		
Private Eric Wilhelm BEETON	4th SAI	Killed in action
Delville Wood Cemetery		
Corporal William BELSHAW	3rd SAI	Killed in action
Thiepval Memorial		
Lance-Corporal Walter Arthur BENNETT	2nd SAI	Killed in action
Private Gilbert Edward BENTLEY	1st SAI	Missing in action
Private William R.S. BICHENO	1st SAI	Missing in action
Private Thomas Cecil BIRD	2nd SAI	Died of wounds
Corbie Communal Cemetery Extension		
Private Stephen Andrew BOTHMA	1st SAI	Missing in action
Thiepval Memorial		
Private Laurence Wallace BREAKEY	1st SAI	Killed in action
Private Ernest John BRODIE	1st SAI	Missing in action
Private Aaron William John BROOKSTEIN	1st SAI	Missing in action
Private Cedric Athol BUCKLE	2nd SAI	Killed in action
Major Edward Travers BURGES	1st SAI	Killed in action
Private Douglas Ashley BURMAN	3rd SAI	Killed in action

Private John BURNSIDE	3rd SAI	Killed in action
Lance Sergeant Claude Fitzgerald BURTON	1st SAI	Missing in action
Private Percy Wilfield CARPENTER	4th SAI	Killed in action
Private A.G. CARTER	1st SAI	Killed in action
Delville Wood Cemetery		
Lance-Corporal William CHANEY	1st SAI	Missing in action
Thiepval Memorial		
Private G.W. CHEEK	2nd SAI	Killed in action
Delville Wood Cemetery		
Private Thomas Arthur CHICHESTER	2nd SAI	Killed in action
Thiepval Memorial		
Private Bertie CLACK	2nd SAI	Missing in action
Private William Henry CLARENCE	1st SAI	Missing in action
Private Timothy James CLEARY	2nd SAI	Missing in action
Lance-Corporal C.W. CLEGG	4th SAI	Killed in action
Delville Wood Cemetery		
Private N.P. CLIFTON	3rd SAI	Killed in action
Private Joseph CLINE	4th SAI	Killed in action
Thiepval Memorial		
Private E.A. COAD	3rd SAI	Killed in action
Delville Wood Cemetery		
Private A.E.J. COMERFORD	4th SAI	Died of wounds
Boulogne Eastern Cemetery		
Corporal Edwin George COOMBE	2nd SAI	Missing in action
Thiepval Memorial		
Private Alfred Edward COUZENS	4th SAI	Missing in action
Private James CUSACK	1st SAI	Missing in action
Private Collins DALE	2nd SAI	Missing in action
Corporal Thomas Archibald Hugh DALL	4th SAI	Killed in action
Private Angelo Joseph DANIA	1st SAI	Missing in action
Private William George DAVIDS	1st SAI	Missing in action
Private Frank DAVIS	3rd SAI	Killed in action
Private Harry DAVIS	1st SAI	Missing in action
Private Rodney William DAVIS	1st SAI	Missing in action
Private Thomas DAVIS	1st SAI	Killed in action
Delville Wood Cemetery		
Sergeant James DEATCHER	28th Bg MG Coy	Killed in action
Thiepval Memorial		
Private James L. DIGNAM	1st SAI	Killed in action
Private H.O. DINGLEY	2nd SAI	Killed in action
Serre Road Cemetery No. 1		
Private Robert Conn DONNELL	3rd SAI	Died of wounds
Dive Copse British Cemetery		
Private T.A. DOWNEY	1st SAI	Killed in action
Delville Wood Cemetery		
Private Douglas Dennis DOYLE	1st SAI	Killed in action
Thiepval Memorial		

APPENDIX VI: ROLL OF HONOUR

Private Michael John DUNNEEN	1st SAI	Killed in action
Private L. DUSTING	1st SAI	Killed in action
Delville Wood Cemetery		
Private Frederick Lewis Archibald EATON	2nd SAI	Killed in action
Guillemont Road Cemetery		
Private Harold EDWARDS	2nd SAI	Killed in action
Thiepval Memorial		
Private Frederick EHKE	1st SAI	Killed in action
Lieutenant Harold George ELLIOT	3rd SAI	Missing in action
Private Edward Francis ELLIOTT	1st SAI	Killed in action
Sucrerie Military Cemetery, Colincamps		
Private Henry ELLIOTT	3rd SAI	Killed in action
Delville Wood Cemetery		
Lance-Corporal Douglas ESTILL	3rd SAI	Killed in action
Private Theophilus Jones EVANS	2nd SAI	Missing in action
Thiepval Memorial		
Private Charles EVISON	4th SAI	Missing in action
Private Charles EWAN	1st SAI	Died of wounds
Dive Copse British Cemetery		
Private Frederick E. EYDEN	1st SAI	Killed in action
Delville Wood Cemetery		
Private Ernest FAURE	1st SAI	Missing in action
Thiepval Memorial		
Lance Sergeant Christopher James FINDLAY	1st SAI	Killed in action
Lieutenant Wilfred Hopley FLEMMER	2nd SAI	Died of wounds
Corbie Communal Cemetery Extension		
Private Archibald McAllister FLETCHER	3rd SAI	Killed in action
Thiepval Memorial		
Private Frank FOADEN	2nd SAI	Missing in action
Private John FRASER	1st SAI	Missing in action
Private Stanley Morris FULLER	2nd SAI	Missing in action
Private C.A. FURMIDGE	1st SAI	Killed in action
Delville Wood Cemetery		
Private Ralph Collie Smith GILLON	2nd SAI	Missing in action
Thiepval Memorial		
Private Edward Bertram GOING	1st SAI	Killed in action
Private W.H. GOODACRE	1st SAI	Killed in action
Delville Wood Cemetery		
Private Harry Arthur GREEN	2nd SAI	Missing in action
Thiepval Memorial		
Private Edward Wormald GREGORY	1st SAI	Killed in action
Private W.A. GROENEWALD	4th SAI	Killed in action
Delville Wood Cemetery		
Private Frank GURNEY	1st SAI	Missing in action
Thiepval Memorial		
Lance-Corporal Eden Lashley HALL	1st SAI	Missing in action
Private Joseph Welsey HAMILTON	2nd SAI	Missing in action

THE SOMME CHRONICLES

Lance-Corporal Harold John HAMMOND	2nd SAI	Killed in action
Private Charles Augustus HARRIS	1st SAI	Killed in action
Private Guy Alexander HARRISON	1st SAI	Missing in action
Sergeant William HAWKINS	1st SAI	Missing in action
Private Cecil Edward HEATHCOTE	1st SAI	Killed in action
Private William Henry Routledge HEWETT	1st SAI	Killed in action
Sergeant Edward Joseph HINTON	1st SAI	Missing in action
Private Eric Wilson HOPPER	1st SAI	Killed in action
Serre Road Cemetery No. 2		
Captain Wallace Frank HOPTROFF	2nd SAI	Killed in action
Private Walter Basil HORSLEY	2nd SAI	Missing in action
Thiepval Memorial		
Sergeant Patrick Robertson HUME	1st SAI	Missing in action
Private John Wilmot HUTTON	1st SAI	Killed in action
Delville Wood Cemetery		
Private Lawrence Godfrey IMMELMAN	1st SAI	Missing in action
Thiepval Memorial		
Private Bertram Joseph INTRONA	2nd SAI	Missing in action
Private Leslie William ISEMONGER	1st SAI	Killed in action
Delville Wood Cemetery		
Private Herbert JACKSON	2nd SAI	Missing in action
Thiepval Memorial		
Private Thomas Edward JACKSON	3rd SAI	Killed in action
Lance Sergeant James Thomas JAMES	2nd SAI	Killed in action
Private Frederick Joseph JANSEN	1st SAI	Missing in action
Private Arthur JOHNSON	1st SAI	Missing in action
Private Frederick John JOHNSON	3rd SAI	Killed in action
Private John KABER	1st SAI	Missing in action
Private Charles Duncan KALLIS	1st SAI	Missing in action
Private Arthur Rosseau KANNEMEYER	2nd SAI	Killed in action
Private Edward George KENSIT	1st SAI	Killed in action
Private Albert Edward KEYS	1st SAI	Killed in action
Private George Alfred KING	1st SAI	Missing in action
Private Alfred John KIRKMAN	2nd SAI	Missing in action
Private Joseph KRIGE	1st SAI	Missing in action
Sergeant Louis Charles LAERMAN	1st SAI	Died of wounds
Corbie Communal Cemetery Extension		
Private Fred Henry William LANG	1st SAI	Killed in action
Thiepval Memorial		
Private Ben Hudson LANSDOWN	2nd SAI	Killed in action
Private Ernest Edward LARSON	1st SAI	Killed in action
Private Jacobus Johannes LAUBSCHER	1st SAI	Killed in action
Private Oliver Clarence LAVENDER	1st SAI	Missing in action
Signaller George Alan LEAK	1st SAI	Killed in action
Private George Hosking LEDDRA	4th SAI	Killed in action
Private William Ivor LLOYD	3rd SAI	Died of wounds
La Neuville British Cemetery, Corbie		

APPENDIX VI: ROLL OF HONOUR

Private Peter John MACDONALD	2nd SAI	Killed in action
Thiepval Memorial		
Lance-Corporal Ronald MACDONALD	4th SAI	Killed in action
Private Thomas James MACKIE	4th SAI	Missing in action
Private Alexander MACNAUGHTON	4th SAI	Killed in action
Private Charles MADDEN	1st SAI	Killed in action
Delville Wood Cemetery		
Private J.J. MAHERRY	3rd SAI	Killed in action
Private James Henry MALIN	2nd SAI	Killed in action
Thiepval Memorial		
Private Arthur Charles Maynard MALLET	3rd SAI	Killed in action
Corporal Frederick Gordon MALLETT	2nd SAI	Killed in action
Serre Road Cemetery No. 2		
CQMS John Horace St Clair MALLEY	2nd SAI	Killed in action
Thiepval Memorial		
Private Arthur George MARLES	1st SAI	Killed in action
Private Herbert Charles MARSH	3rd SAI	Killed in action
Dive Copse British Cemetery		
Private Robert MARSHALL	2nd SAI	Killed in action
Thiepval Memorial		
Private Ivor Llewellyn MARTIN	1st SAI	Missing in action
Private William MARTIN	3rd SAI	Killed in action
Sergeant John Robert MATHESON	1st SAI	Missing in action
Private Allen James McDONALD	2nd SAI	Killed in action
Delville Wood Cemetery		
Private Duncan Munro McDONALD	1st SAI	Killed in action
Thiepval Memorial		
Private James Corbitt McGREGOR	1st SAI	Missing in action
Private William McGREGOR	1st SAI	Missing in action
Private William Arthur McKENZIE	1st SAI	Missing in action
Private Douglas Rorke McLEAN	2nd SAI	Killed in action
Sergeant Henry Duncan McNAB	2nd SAI	Killed in action
Private Joseph MILLER	2nd SAI	Killed in action
Dive Copse British Cemetery		
Private Robert Frederick MILLER	2nd SAI	Missing in action
Thiepval Memorial		
Private Frederick James MILLS	1st SAI	Killed in action
Private Frank MOCKE	1st SAI	Killed in action
Private Harry James MOMSEN	1st SAI	Missing in action
Private William John MORGAN	1st SAI	Killed in action
Private Robert Walter MORRISON	1st SAI	Died of wounds
Corbie Communal Cemetery Extension		
Private Reginald NAYLOR	3rd SAI	Killed in action
Delville Wood Cemetery		
Private Lionel Collingwood NEDHAM	4th SAI	Killed in action
Thiepval Memorial		
Private William NEEDHAM	1st SAI	Killed in action

Private Charles Victor NESBITT | 4th SAI | Killed in action
Corporal George Henry NEWELL | 1st SAI | Missing in action
Private Alfred NICHOLSON | 4th SAI | Killed in action
Quarry Cemetery, Montauban-en-Picardie
Private Arthur John NOWELL | 1st SAI | Missing in action
Thiepval Memorial
Private Clarence Frederick Reid O'CONNOR | 2nd SAI | Missing in action
Private Charles Cecil O'NEILL | 2nd SAI | Missing in action
Private James Edward OWEN | 3rd SAI | Killed in action
L/Corporal Edwin Evens Cragg PADDON | 1st SAI | Missing in action
Private George Hall PALPHRAMAND | 1st SAI | Killed in action
Private Ralph Hall PALPHRAMAND | 1st SAI | Missing in action
Private David Henry PARSONS | 3rd SAI | Killed in action
Private Charles Henri PATRICK | 3rd SAI | Killed in action
Second-Lieutenant David Balfour PATRICK | 28th Bg MG Coy | Killed in action
Private Victor Reginald PATTISON | 1st SAI | Killed in action
Private John PAUL | 4th SAI | Killed in action
London Cemetery and Extension, Longueval
Private Arthur PEARCE | 1st SAI | Killed in action
Delville Wood Cemetery
Lance-Corporal David Charles PEARCE | 2nd SAI | Missing in action
Thiepval Memorial
Private Ernest William PHELAN | 2nd SAI | Missing in action
Private Peter Begg PHILP | 4th SAI | Killed in action
Private John PLAYSTED | 1st SAI | Killed in action
Sergeant Gerald Daniel POTGIETER | 1st SAI | Killed in action
RSM Elgar Edward PREBBLE, DCM | 2nd SAI | Missing in action
Private H. PULFORD | 2nd SAI | Killed in action
Delville Wood Cemetery
Corporal William Ogilvie PURVES | 2nd SAI | Died of wounds
La Neuville British Cemetery, Corbie
Private Guy Clifford PUSEY | 2nd SAI | Killed in action
Thiepval Memorial
Private John Wilson QUAIL | 2nd SAI | Missing in action
Private William Lucas RANDALL | 4th SAI | Killed in action
Private Harold Cuthbert RAPHAEL | 1st SAI | Killed in action
Serre Road Cemetery No. 1
Private Thomas Frederick John REID | 2nd SAI | Killed in action
Thiepval Memorial
Private William REID | 2nd SAI | Killed in action
Private Charles Hammond RICHARDSON | 2nd SAI | Killed in action
Private A.E. ROBERTS | 2nd SAI | Killed in action
Delville Wood Cemetery
Private Wouda Herschel ROZENZWEIG | 2nd SAI | Died of wounds
AIF Burial Ground

APPENDIX VI: ROLL OF HONOUR

Private John RYDER	1st SAI	Killed in action
Thiepval Memorial		
Private Charles John SCHOU	1st SAI	Killed in action
Private Geoffrey Lawrence SCOTT	4th SAI	Killed in action
Delville Wood Cemetery		
Private Cyril Oswald SELBY	1st SAI	Killed in action
Thiepval Memorial		
Private Arthur Gordon SELLER	1st SAI	Killed in action
Private Stanley Charles SEMARK	1st SAI	Missing in action
Private Wilfred Percival SHILTON	3rd SAI	Killed in action
Private Joseph SINCLAIR	4th SAI	Killed in action
Private Thomas Robert SLATEM	1st SAI	Missing in action
Private A.E. SMITH	1st SAI	Died of wounds
Corbie Communal Cemetery Extension		
Private Ernest John Oscar SMITH	1st SAI	Killed in action
Thiepval Memorial		
Corporal Frank James SMITH	2nd SAI	Missing in action
Private Jacob Jacobus SMITH	2nd SAI	Missing in action
Private Walter Cecil SMITH	1st SAI	Killed in action
Private George William Albert SOAL	3rd SAI	Died of wounds
Wimereux Communal Cemetery		
Lance-Corporal Sydney Inch SOBEY	4th SAI	Killed in action
Thiepval Memorial		
Private Charles David SODERLAND	1st SAI	Killed in action
Private Albert Joseph SPARKES	1st SAI	Missing in action
Private Clifton SPENCER	3rd SAI	Killed in action
Private Shedwell STEPHENS	4th SAI	Killed in action
Private Charles STEWART	4th SAI	Killed in action
Private Duncan STEWART	4th SAI	Killed in action
Private James Cathcart STEWART	4th SAI	Killed in action
Private Christian Martin Frank STOFFBERG	1st SAI	Missing in action
Private Adrian STRUTT	1st SAI	Killed in action
AIF Burial Ground		
Private Charles Henry STUART	1st SAI	Killed in action
Delville Wood Cemetery		
Private Charles SULLIVAN	1st SAI	Killed in action
Thiepval Memorial		
Private George SWANEPOEL	1st SAI	Killed in action
Private Percival Francis SWEMMER	4th SAI	Died of wounds
Dive Copse British Cemetery		
Private John James TALJAARD	3rd SAI	Killed in action
Delville Wood Cemetery		
Second-Lieutenant Erol Victor TATHAM	2nd SAI	Killed in action
Thiepval Memorial		
Private W.C.R. THEOBALD	2nd SAI	Killed in action
Delville Wood Cemetery		

Private John Deans THOMPSON	3rd SAI	Killed in action
Thiepval Memorial		
Private Douglas John THOMSON	2nd SAI	Killed in action
Private Henry Charles Graham THOMSON	1st SAI	Killed in action
Private George Edward THORPE	2nd SAI	Missing in action
Private Ernest George TRENT	1st SAI	Killed in action
Private Edward Edney TUCKER	3rd SAI	Killed in action
Private Lionel James TUCKETT	2nd SAI	Killed in action
Private Harold TURRELL	2nd SAI	Killed in action
Serre Road Cemetery No. 1		
Private Joseph Harold TWEEDIE	3rd SAI	Killed in action
Thiepval Memorial		
Private Kenneth Reginald TWEEDIE	2nd SAI	Killed in action
Lance-Corporal C. VAN BLERK	1st SAI	Killed in action
Delville Wood Cemetery		
Private John Henry VAN DER SPUY	1st SAI	Killed in action
Thiepval Memorial		
Private Johannes Nicholas VAN TONDER	2nd SAI	Missing in action
Private J.B. WALKER	1st SAI	Killed in action
Delville Wood Cemetery		
Private Edward WALLACE	1st SAI	Missing in action
Thiepval Memorial		
Private Frank WALTON	2nd SAI	Missing in action
Sergeant Philip WARD	1st SAI	Missing in action
Private John WARDROP	4th SAI	Killed in action
Private Henry Templar WARREN	2nd SAI	Killed in action
Private Edward WATKINS	2nd SAI	Killed in action
Private James WATSON	3rd SAI	Killed in action
Private Cyril George WELDON	1st SAI	Killed in action
Private Harry WILES	1st SAI	Killed in action
Private Richard WILLIAMS	2nd SAI	Missing in action
Private Walter WILLIAMS	1st SAI	Missing in action
Private William WILLS	28th Bg MG Coy	Killed in action
Company Sergeant-Major W.E. WILLSON	1st SAI	Killed in action
Delville Wood Cemetery		
Lance-Corporal Alexander Mallock WILSON	2nd SAI	Killed in action
Thiepval Memorial		
Private Thomas Henry WISE	1st SAI	Killed in action
Lance-Corporal Ernest WOOD	3rd SAI	Killed in action
Delville Wood Cemetery		
Private Albert Henry WOOLCOT	4th SAI	Killed in action
Thiepval Memorial		
Private G. WRIGHT	3rd SAI	Died of wounds
Kensal Green Cemetery, London		
Private Harold Barber WRIGHT	1st SAI	Died of wounds
La Neuville British Cemetery, Corbie		

APPENDIX VI: ROLL OF HONOUR

Signaller William Cain YOUNG | 2nd SAI | Missing in action
Thiepval Memorial

19 July 1916

Private Vernon Liddell ADAMS | 3rd SAI | Killed in action
Thiepval Memorial
L/Corporal Percival (Percy) Joseph ALLEN | 1st SAI | Killed in action
Private Richard Harold BELL | 2nd SAI | Died of wounds
Corporal George Sydney BIGGS | 3rd SAI | Missing in action
Lance-Corporal William Garcia BIRCH | 4th SAI | Died of wounds
Étaples Military Cemetery
Lance-Corporal Clavell Monkhouse BLOUNT | 2nd SAI | Killed in action
Thiepval Memorial
Lance-Corporal Edwin Samuel BOWLEY | 4th SAI | Killed in action
Caterpillar Valley Cemetery, Longueval
Private Harold Angus BROWN | 3rd SAI | Killed in action
Thiepval Memorial
Private Percival Austen BROWN | 4th SAI | Missing in action
Private Howard Godfrey CAPEL | 3rd SAI | Killed in action
Captain Herbert Edward CLIFFORD | 2nd SAI | Died of wounds
St Sever Cemetery, Rouen
Private John James CORLETT | 2nd SAI | Killed in action
Thiepval Memorial
Private Scott Chisholme DAVIDSON | 3rd SAI | Killed in action
Private Peter Clifford Gilbert DE REUCK | 2nd SAI | Missing in action
Private William Richard DOR | 2nd SAI | Killed in action
Private John Jackson EWBANK | 4th SAI | Missing in action
Private William Edward FENTON | 4th SAI | Missing in action
Private Bernadus Lambertes FERREIRA | 2nd SAI | Missing in action
Private Wilfrid Henry FLACK | 2nd SAI | Killed in action
Major Harry Herbert Allan GEE | 2nd SAI | Died of wounds
Delville Wood Cemetery
Private Ronald Cecil GLEAVES | 3rd SAI | Killed in action
Thiepval Memorial
Lance-Corporal Ralph Eric HARRIS | 3rd SAI | Killed in action
Private John HARWOOD | 3rd SAI | Killed in action
Private James HUSBAND | 3rd SAI | Killed in action
Sg. William James Miller HUSBAND, MSM | 2nd SAI | Died of wounds
Dive Copse British Cemetery
Private John IRELAND | 1st SAI | Killed in action
Private Frank Trenbath JANION | 2nd SAI | Killed in action
Thiepval Memorial
Private Robert Evans JONES | 2nd SAI | Died of wounds
Péronne Road Cemetery, Maricourt
Lance-Corporal Harold Gordon KIRBY | 4th SAI | Killed in action
Thiepval Memorial
Private Charles LAKE | 2nd SAI | Killed in action

201

Private Thomas Huxley LANGSTON	4th SAI	Killed in action
Private Abe LEWIS	3rd SAI	Killed in action
Private Edwin Dennis LEWIS	2nd SAI	Killed in action
Private Menyn Coote LOVEROCK Delville Wood Cemetery	3rd SAI	Killed in action
Signaller Jas Andrew MAYNES Thiepval Memorial	4th SAI	Died of wounds
Private Donald Watson McDONALD	4th SAI	Killed in action
Private James Gradon MIDDLEMISS	4th SAI	Killed in action
Private Morris Hyman MYERS	2nd SAI	Killed in action
Lance-Corporal Joseph Bonan O'SHEA Quarry Cemetery, Montauban	64th Field Coy, RE	Killed in action
Private John Allan PARKER Thiepval Memorial	2nd SAI	Killed in action
Private George POOLE	2nd SAI	Killed in action
Private Edward Warrwick RAFTER Delville Wood Cemetery	2nd SAI	Killed in action
Corporal Stanley Francis RAPHAEL La Neuville British Cemetery, Corbie	1st SAI	Died of wounds
Sergeant Frank Victor Wallace REID Thiepval Memorial	3rd SAI	Killed in action
Private James ROYAN	4th SAI	Killed in action
Private Alfred George SERVICE	4th SAI	Missing in action
CQMS Archibald Gray SHORT Warlencourt British Cemetery	4th SAI	Killed in action
Lance-Corporal Robert Rossouw SHORT Thiepval Memorial	4th SAI	Killed in action
Private William Henry SIEBERT	3rd SAI	Killed in action
Lance-Corporal William SINCLAIR	2nd SAI	Killed in action
Sergeant Albert SLACK	28th Bg MG Coy	Died of wounds
Lance-Corporal Leslie Stuart SLADE	4th SAI	Killed in action
Corporal James John SMITH	28th Bg MG Coy	Killed in action
Coy Sg. Major Livingston Hastie SNEDDON Delville Wood Cemetery	4th SAI	Killed in action
Private Stanley THOMAS Corbie Communal Cemetery Extension	1st SAI	Died of wounds
Private William TWEEDIE Thiepval Memorial	4th SAI	Killed in action
Private Francis VEITCH	4th SAI	Missing in action
Private Jack WALCOTT	4th SAI	Killed in action
Lance-Corporal John Henry WALLACE	4th SAI	Missing in action
Private William WATKINS London Cemetery and Extension, Longueval	4th SAI	Killed in action
Private Geoffrey WENSLEY Thiepval Memorial	4th SAI	Killed in action

APPENDIX VI: ROLL OF HONOUR

Private Charles Harold Frere WENTWORTH	3rd SAI	Killed in action
Private Frederick Henry Herman WILLIAMS	2nd SAI	Killed in action
Private Frank WILLSHIRE	3rd SAI	Killed in action
Sucrerie Military Cemetery, Colincamps		
Private G.A. WILSON	64th Coy, RE	Died of wounds
La Neuville British Cemetery, Corbie		

20 July 1916

Private William Norman ANDERSON	4th SAI	Died of wounds
Favreuil British Cemetery		as POW
Private James Caesar BAIRD	3rd SAI	Killed in action
Delville Wood Cemetery		
Lieutenant Charles Stewart BELL	4th SAI	Killed in action
Sucrerie Military Cemetery, Colincamps		
Lieutenant Charles Edward BRITTEN	3rd SAI	Died of wounds
Abbeville Communal Cemetery		
Lieutenant Arthur Hugh BROWN	4th SAI	Killed in action
Delville Wood Cemetery		
Private Herbert CAMPBELL	2nd SAI	Killed in action
Thiepval Memorial		
Private William Stephen CLIFTON	2nd SAI	Killed in action
Private James Alexander COLVIN	1st SAI	Died of wounds
La Neuville British Cemetery, Corbie		
2nd Lieutenant Joseph George CONNOCK	2nd SAI	Killed in action
Delville Wood Cemetery		
Private Christian Frederick COOK	1st SAI	Died of wounds
Corbie Communal Cemetery Extension		
Sergeant Hugh Leonard COXFORD	3rd SAI	Died of wounds
Étaples Military Cemetery		
Second-Lieutenant Charles Henry DICK	3rd SAI	Killed in action
Thiepval Memorial		
Private Ardale Valentine Ernest EDWARDS	4th SAI	Died of wounds
Corbie Communal Cemetery Extension		
Private Lewis William HAWES	3rd SAI	Killed in action
Thiepval Memorial		
Lieutenant Walter James HILL	2nd SAI	Killed in action
2nd Lieut. John Manson HOLLINGWORTH	1st SAI	Killed in action
Delville Wood Cemetery		
Private Jack Sedgwick HOOK	2nd SAI	Killed in action
Thiepval Memorial		
Private Arthur Leopold HUBER	2nd SAI	Missing in action
Major John William JACKSON	3rd SAI	Killed in action
Private A.R. JEFFERIES	4th SAI	Died of wounds
La Neuville British Cemetery, Corbie		
Private John Edward JOHNSON	3rd SAI	Missing in action
Thiepval Memorial		

Captain Percy John JOWETT | 1st SAI | Killed in action
Serre Road Cemetery No. 2
Private Henry Joseph Page KALIS | 1st SAI | Killed in action
Corbie Communal Cemetery Extension
Drummer F. KANE | 3rd SAI | Killed in action
Delville Wood Cemetery
Private George Henry KEOGH | 3rd SAI | Died of wounds
Corbie Communal Cemetery Extension
Private Robert William LEES | 2nd SAI | Killed in action
La Neuville British Cemetery, Corbie
2nd Lieut. Charles T. Kenneth LETCHFORD | 2nd SAI | Killed in action
Delville Wood Cemetery
Private Henry Harebottle McCUAIG | 3rd SAI | Killed in action
Thiepval Memorial
Private Thomas PARKES | 1st SAI | Died of wounds
Private William Robert Colquhoun PEARSON | 3rd SAI | Killed in action
Lance-Corporal Charles Reeves PITTS | 3rd SAI | Died of wounds
Second-Lieutenant Donald ROSS | 4th SAI | Killed in action
Second-Lieutenant Francis Henry SOMERSET | 3rd SAI | Died of wounds
Delville Wood Cemetery
Second-Lieutenant Russell Pears TATHAM | 2nd SAI | Killed in action
Thiepval Memorial
Pioneer Albert Henry WAIN | 64th Coy, RE | Killed in action
Private Robert Ball WILLIAMS | 4th SAI | Killed in action
Sucrerie Military Cemetery, Colincamps

21 July 1916

Second-Lieutenant Hugh Wilfred GOVE | 3rd SAI | Missing in action
Thiepval Memorial
Private Francis Hatfield GRAY | 3rd SAI | Died of wounds
La Neuville British Cemetery, Corbie
Private Mathew Herbert JACKSON | 1st SAI | Died of wounds
Private Reuben Francis McCoy KEMP | 3rd SAI | Died of wounds
Favreuil British Cemetery | | as POW
Lance-Corporal Eric Montague KIDSON | 3rd SAI | Died of wounds
Étaples Military Cemetery
Private James Aloysius KINLAY | 4th SAI | Died of wounds
Wimereux Communal Cemetery
Private Ernest Donald McKAY | 4th SAI | Killed in action
Sucrerie Military Cemetery, Colincamps
Lance-Corporal William Astbury McNEIL | 3rd SAI | Died of wounds
La Neuville British Cemetery, Corbie
Driver James McPHERSON | 64th Coy, RE | Died of wounds
Corbie Communal Cemetery Extension
Private Cecil Norman MOLLER | 1st SAI | Died of wounds
La Neuville British Cemetery, Corbie

APPENDIX VI: ROLL OF HONOUR

Lance-Corporal Ernest William SPENCER	3rd SAI	Died of wounds
Abbeville Communal Cemetery		
Private Horace Clayton TOWERS	4th SAI	Missing in action
Thiepval Memorial		
Private Robert WALLACE	4th SAI	Killed in action

22 July 1916

Private Bernard Frederick ANDERSON	1st SAI	Died of wounds
Abbeville Communal Cemetery		
Private John Philip DU PLESSIS	2nd SAI	Died of wounds
Kensal Green Cemetery, London		
Private Wilfrid HETHERINGTON	1st SAI	Died of wounds
Abbeville Communal Cemetery		
Sapper W. NORMAN	64th Coy, RE	Died of wounds
Étaples Military Cemetery		

23 July 1916

Private Frederick Wall JACOBSEN	1st SAI	Died of wounds
La Neuville British Cemetery, Corbie		
Private George Henry ROSSER	1st SAI	Died of wounds
Richmond Cemetery, UK		
Private Uriah TETLOW	2nd SAI	Died of wounds
Abbeville Communal Cemetery		

24 July 1916

Private Leslie Thomas PARKER	1st SAI	Died of wounds
Boulogne Eastern Cemetery		
Private Alexander George WATT	4th SAI	Died of wounds
Peterhead Old Churchyard, Aberdeenshire		

25 July 1916

Private Kenneth S. GIBBON	3rd SAI	Died of wounds
Wandsworth Cemetery, London		
Lieutenant Percy Richardson ROSEBY	2nd SAI	Died of wounds
Corbie Communal Cemetery Extension		
Private Robert Alexander STEVENS	2nd SAI	Died of wounds
Abbeville Communal Cemetery		

26 July 1916

Private Abel Edward CUTLER	4th SAI	Died of wounds
West Wycombe Churchyard, UK		
Private James Watson SUTHERLAND	1st SAI	Died of wounds
Abbeville Communal Cemetery		

27 July 1916

Private Henry George William DONDOVICH	3rd SAI	Died of wounds
St Sever Cemetery, Rouen		
Private Thomas Porteous GOW	4th SAI	Died of wounds
Abbeville Communal Cemetery		
Private Richard Frank HARRIS	1st SAI	Died of wounds
La Neuville British Cemetery, Corbie		
Private William Thomas JARRETT	3rd SAI	Died of wounds
St Sever Cemetery, Rouen		
Private Walter Campbell THOM	4th SAI	Died of wounds

28 July 1916

Private Richard Henry ELLIS	4th SAI	Died of wounds
Abbeville Communal Cemetery		
L/Corporal George Peters HAGGIS	4th SAI	Died of wounds
St Sever Cemetery, Rouen		

29 July 1916

Private Arthur Webster SLY	2nd SAI	Died of wounds
Nunhead Cemetery, London		

30 July 1916

Private William Beaconsfield HICKMAN	2nd SAI	Died as POW
Le Cateau Military Cemetery		
Private Walter Oswald KEW	3rd SAI	Died of wounds
La Neuville British Cemetery, Corbie		

31 July 1916

Lance-Corporal C. BAKER	4th SAI	Died of wounds
St Sever Cemetery, Rouen		
Private William Lloyd HOLLINGBERRY MM	3rd SAI	Died of wounds
Abbeville Communal Cemetery		
Private H.J. JOHNSTON	4th SAI	Died of wounds
St Sever Cemetery, Rouen		

Men whose exact date of death is unknown and were declared on 1 August 1916 'Missing in action, death presumed'

Driver Llewellyn Leonard ADENDORFF	3rd SAI	Missing in action
Thiepval Memorial		
Private Neville ARONSON	3rd SAI	Missing in action
Corporal Alfred BARKER	3rd SAI	Missing in action
Private Gilbert BARTLETT	3rd SAI	Missing in action
Corporal Robert James BLACK	3rd SAI	Missing in action
Private George William BUNN	3rd SAI	Missing in action
Private William Chapman CARNEGIE	3rd SAI	Missing in action
Private William CLARK	3rd SAI	Missing in action

APPENDIX VI: ROLL OF HONOUR

Private Lionel CROSSLEY	3rd SAI	Missing in action
Private George DEMIN	3rd SAI	Missing in action
Private John DILLON	3rd SAI	Missing in action
Private Henry DINAN	3rd SAI	Missing in action
Private Robert DOUGLAS	3rd SAI	Missing in action
Private Walter Hastie DUTTON	3rd SAI	Missing in action
Private Robert FIVAZ	3rd SAI	Missing in action
Private Norman Edward FRANKISH	3rd SAI	Missing in action
Private Clement James FRASER	3rd SAI	Missing in action
Private Donald FRASER	3rd SAI	Missing in action
Private John Fraser HAIG	3rd SAI	Missing in action
Private Reginald Charles HARPER	3rd SAI	Missing in action
Sergeant Francis Danby HESTER	3rd SAI	Missing in action
Private Alexander HOOD	3rd SAI	Missing in action
Private Frederick George HOOKHAM	3rd SAI	Missing in action
Thiepval Memorial		
Private Henry James HORNE	3rd SAI	Missing in action
Private William Adrian ISOM	3rd SAI	Missing in action
Private Even JAMES	3rd SAI	Missing in action
Private Albertus Fredrick JEAREY	3rd SAI	Missing in action
Private Willie JENNINGS	3rd SAI	Missing in action
Private Henry JOHNSON	3rd SAI	Missing in action
Private Herbert John KERSWILL	3rd SAI	Missing in action
Private Hugh KEYS	3rd SAI	Missing in action
Private Arthur Ernest LAHEE	3rd SAI	Missing in action
Private Joseph LUPTON	3rd SAI	Missing in action
Private John Herman MAADE	3rd SAI	Missing in action
Private William MATHER	3rd SAI	Missing in action
Private Edward McAULEY	3rd SAI	Missing in action
London Cemetery and Extension, Longueval		
Private Walter McBROOM	3rd SAI	Missing in action
Thiepval Memorial		
Lance-Corporal James McCULLOCH	3rd SAI	Missing in action
Private John Andrew MILLS	3rd SAI	Missing in action
Private C. NEWBERRY	3rd SAI	Missing in action
Delville Wood Cemetery		
Lance-Corporal William Rowland PRINCE	3rd SAI	Missing in action
Thiepval Memorial		
Private Andrew Edward QUIRK	3rd SAI	Missing in action
Private Willem Diederick RAUTENBACH	3rd SAI	Missing in action
Lance-Corporal Thomas Jaffray READ	3rd SAI	Missing in action
Private Bernard Kenneth REYNOLDS	3rd SAI	Missing in action
Private John ROBB	3rd SAI	Missing in action
Private Arthur Alfred SALMOND	3rd SAI	Missing in action
Private John Edward SANSBURY	3rd SAI	Missing in action
Private Tom SCHOFIELD	3rd SAI	Missing in action
Driver William SMITH	3rd SAI	Missing in action

Driver Frank STAGG	3rd SAI	Missing in action
Private John Johannes Jacobus STEYN	3rd SAI	Missing in action
Serre Road Cemetery No. 2		
Private George William STONE	3rd SAI	Missing in action
Thiepval Memorial		
Private Percy Jones STREETON	3rd SAI	Missing in action
Private James Moir THOM	3rd SAI	Missing in action
Corporal Mark TRAVILL	3rd SAI	Missing in action
Private David Stuart VAN HOLST	3rd SAI	Missing in action
Lance-Corporal Harold Shaw WALKER	3rd SAI	Missing in action
Private Henry William WALKER	3rd SAI	Missing in action
Private John Herbert WHATMORE	3rd SAI	Missing in action
Private Alexander WHEATLEY	3rd SAI	Missing in action
Private Richard WILLETT	3rd SAI	Missing in action
Private John WRIGHT	3rd SAI	Missing in action

Men who died of wounds received in the operations on the Somme in July 1916

Private Philip PITMAN	4th SAI	1 August 1916
Richmond Cemetery, UK		
Private Robert Alexander SAYLE	3rd SAI	1 August 1916
Niederzwehren Cemetery, Germany		as POW
Private Michael Daniel FRIEDENTHAL	3rd SAI	2 August 1916
Le Cateau Military Cemetery		as POW
Private John O'CONNOR	3rd SAI	2 August 1916
Porte-de-Paris Cemetery, Cambrai		as POW
Private W.H. GORDON	3rd SAI	4 August 1916
Lyne Churchyard, UK		
Private Theophilus Herman GRIFFIN	2nd SAI	4 August 1916
Thiepval Memorial		
Private Arthur George MACLACHAN	4th SAI	4 August 1916
Private Ivan Merle McCUSKER	3rd SAI	5 August 1916
Wandsworth Cemetery, London		
Private Edward William SMITH	4th SAI	8 August 1916
St Sever Cemetery, Rouen		
Private Mark Lawrence DAVEY	4th SAI	9 August 1916
Étaples Military Cemetery		
Private William Lange THOMAS	3rd SAI	13 August 1916
Kensal (All Souls) Cemetery, London		

APPENDIX VII

A note on the role of black South Africans

For many years, white races have drafted Africans for wars on southern African soil. As far back as 1854, the Boers deployed the Bakgatla in the Rustenburg district in their campaign against Baga-Mokopane. In 1865/6 they used Africans against the Basotho of Moshoeshoe and in 1879 they drafted two Baphalane regiments in support of their campaign against Sekhukhune in the northern Transvaal. During the Anglo-Boer War of 1899–1902, the Boers employed Africans as labourers, while the British used them as spies and blockhouse sentries. In 1906, the British deployed the Natal Native Horse regiment against Chief Bambatha in what became known as the Bambatha Rebellion.[1]

When the Great War broke out in 1914, the Union of South Africa's own defence force was two years old, but still a part of the British Empire. It could, therefore, not remain neutral. In a show of loyalty to Britain, the South African Native National Congress, the predecessor of the African National Congress, passed a resolution of loyalty to the Empire at its annual conference in Bloemfontein. It is estimated that as many as 83 000 African and 2 000 Coloured men ended up serving in the war.[2]

The country's internal politics at the time prescribed that only whites would be armed. Therefore, Africans and Coloureds would be recruited as unarmed railway labourers or transport workers. The Cape's large Coloured community, however, wished to send men to fight, and so after the campaign in German South-West Africa the South African government offered to raise an infantry battalion of Coloured soldiers for overseas service. The British government agreed to class the men as Imperial troops, equating their service conditions with those of the black British West Indies Regiment.

On 25 October 1915, the Recruiting Committee called for volunteers throughout South Africa. Lieutenant-Colonel George A. Morris was appointed commander of the unit, with Major C.N. Hoy his second in command. Nineteen white warrant officers and senior ranks were recruited to fill key appointments. The battalion sailed from Cape Town on 9 February 1916 aboard HMS *Armadale Castle*, and once in East Africa, became part of Major-General J.M. Stewart's 1st East Africa Division.

This Cape Corps saw action in East Africa, Egypt, Palestine and Northern Rhodesia, while the Africans served as civilian batmen (personal servants of commissioned officers) and labourers in the South African Labour Corps, assisting General Louis Botha in South-West Africa and General Jan Smuts in East Africa.

Due to the admirable work done by the South African Labour Corps in Africa, a South African Native Labour Contingent (SANLC) was recruited for service in Europe. Of the first convoy, two ships landed safely in France, but the third, the SS *Mendi*, was sunk off the Isle of Wight on 21 February 1917 after a collision with the SS *Darro* in thick fog. The *Mendi* sank within about 25 minutes of the collision, and 616 out of the 823 South Africans of the 5th Battalion SANLC on board lost their lives. While some of the men died on impact, most drowned in the icy waters of the English Channel. The disaster is regarded as one of South Africa's worst war tragedies.[3] Most of the dead are remembered at the Hollybrook Memorial, in Southampton, England, while the Mendi Memorial in Avalon Cemetery, Soweto, also commemorates the disaster.

Between 1916 and 1918, almost 21 000 black South African volunteers served with the SANLC in France, where they formed part of a labour force that consisted of French, British, Chinese, Japanese, Indian, Egyptian and Canadian labourers, as well as German prisoners of war. During their stay in France they were housed in closed compounds, not unlike the camps used to hold the prisoners.

By the time the unit was disbanded in early 1918, the men of the SANLC had laid and repaired roads and railway lines, and unloaded supply ships and loaded trains in the French harbours of Le Havre, Rouen and Dieppe. Most of the 333 African men who died on active duty are buried at the British military cemetery at Arques-la-Bataille.[4]

Prime Minister Botha paid tribute to the African soldiers in France in an address to Parliament on 10 March 1917:

> If we have ever lived in times when the Native people of South Africa have shown great and true loyalty, it is in times like the present ... I have all my life dealt with the Natives, but at no other time have they displayed greater

APPENDIX VII: THE ROLE OF BLACK SOUTH AFRICANS

loyalty than they have done in the difficult, dark days through which we are now passing... These people [the Natives] said: 'This war is raging and we want to help', and in so doing they have shown their loyalty to their flag, their King, and country, and what they have done will resound to their everlasting credit.[5]

Following the armistice in 1918, the African troops of the SANLC were returned to South Africa and disbanded. Unfairly, and despite their sacrifices, none were awarded medals or ribbons, while those blacks from the High Commission Territories who had served in the same units were, as well as the blacks who had served in South-West Africa with the South African Artillery and the South African Mounted Rifles.[6]

Notes

INTRODUCTION

1   Martin Gilbert, *Somme: The Heroism and Horror of War*, London: John Murray, 2006, p. xvii.
2   Ibid., p. 24.

CHAPTER I: THE BIRTH OF THE SOUTH AFRICAN BRIGADE

1   From http://africanhistory.about.com/od/glossarya2/g/Afrikaner-Rebellion.htm.
2   H.L. Silberbauer, 'Reminiscences of the First World War from the memoirs of the late Lt Col H L Silberbauer', *Military History Journal* 10 (5), June 1997.
3   Ibid.
4   Ibid.
5   Ibid.
6   Letter from Captain Trevitt to a Mrs Wood of Trentham, UK, published in the *Long Eaton Advertiser*, 16 July 1915.
7   Max Arthur, *Forgotten Voices of the Great War*, London: Ebury Press, 2002, pp. 16–17.
8   Ibid., pp. 14–15.
9   Sir Charles Preston Crewe fought in the Ninth Frontier War between 1878 and 1879, and the Basutoland War between 1880 and 1881. He held the office of member of the legislative assembly (MLA) (Cape of Good Hope) between 1899 and 1910. He gained the rank of brigadier-general in the service of the South African Defence Force. He was invested as a Companion, Order of the Bath and was decorated with the award of the Royal Naval Volunteer Reserve Officers' Decoration. He fought in the Boer War between 1900 and 1902. He held the office of colonial secretary of the Cape of Good Hope between 1904 and 1907, and the office of secretary for agriculture (Cape of Good Hope) between 1907 and 1908. He was invested as a Knight Commander, Order of St Michael and St George. He held the office of MLA (Union of South Africa) between 1910 and 1919, for East London. He fought in the First World War, in East Africa. He was chief owner of the East London *Daily Despatch* and the Queenstown *Daily Representative*.

10 Written on the flyleaf of a copy of the book. Ian Uys, 'The South Africans at Delville Wood', *Military History Journal* 7 (2), December 1986.
11 Dawson served in India and Malaya from 1893 to 1897 and in Robert's Horse during the Boer War. He became inspector of the Orange River Colony Police in 1908 and commanded the 4th South African Mounted Rifles in the South-West Africa campaign. Tanner joined the Natal Carbineers in 1893, and served in the Boer War and in the Bambatha Zulu Rebellion in 1906, and in the South-West Africa campaign as a major in the Union Defence Force. Thackeray was an interesting character. He left for America in 1886, where he spent four years as a cowboy before joining the East Surrey Regiment in 1890. Two years later he became a corporal in the 11th Hussars, serving in India in the Chitral Campaign. He then came to South Africa where he served in the Matabeleland campaign and the Boer War (with the Southern Rhodesian Volunteers and Kitchener's Fighting Scouts). After the war he joined the South African Constabulary and then the Union Defence Force, serving in the South-West Africa campaign as chief staff officer. Jones served with the Welsh Regiment in the Boer War and as brigade-major to the 1st Infantry Brigade in South-West Africa.
12 Ian Uys, *Delville Wood*, Germiston: I. Uys Publishers, 1983, p. 10.
13 Ibid.
14 Anton Ludwig August von Mackensen (b. 6 December 1849; d. 8 November 1945), born August Mackensen, became one of the German Empire's most prominent military leaders. After the armistice, Mackensen was interned for a year. He retired from the German Army in 1920 and was made a Prussian state councillor in 1933 by Hermann Göring. From http://en.wikipedia.org/wiki/August_von_Mackensen.
15 John Buchan, *The History of the South African Forces in France*, Edinburgh: Thomas Nelson & Sons, 1920, pp. 23–25.
16 Ibid.
17 General Sir William Eliot Peyton, KCB, KCVO, CB, DSO, was born on 7 May 1866. He joined the 7th Dragoon Guards in 1885, becoming a major in 1899, major-general in 1914, lieutenant-general in 1921 and general in 1927. He commanded the 15th Hussars from 1903 to 1907. He served in the Sudan and in South Africa, and commanded the Meerut Cavalry Brigade from 1908 to 1912. At Gallipoli he commanded the 2nd Mounted Brigade, and the 40th Division in France and Flanders, from June 1918 to March 1919. He was military secretary to the secretary of state for war (1922–26) and commander in chief, Scottish Command, from 1926 to 1930, when he retired.
18 Buchan, *The History of the South African Forces in France*, pp. 32–35.
19 Uys, *Delville Wood*, p. 15.
20 Ibid., p. 16.

21 A year later the Grand Senussi, who had been living in the Siwa Oasis, made an attempt to shift his quarters. Major-General Watson, who then commanded the Western Frontier Force, sent a column of armoured cars, which on 3 February 1917 broke up his camp, drove him into the outer deserts and destroyed for good any little military prestige that remained to him.
22 Ian Uys, *Rollcall: The Delville Wood Story*, Johannesburg: I. Uys Publishers, 1991, pp. 12–13.
23 Buchan, *The History of the South African Forces in France*, pp. 41–42.

CHAPTER 2: BERNAFAY AND TRÔNES WOODS
1 Silberbauer, 'Reminiscences of the First World War from the memoirs of the late Lt Col H L Silberbauer'.
2 Ibid.
3 Ibid.
4 General Sir Walter Norris Congreve, VC, KCB, MVO, DL (b. 20 November 1862; d. 28 February 1927) was a British Army captain in the Rifle Brigade (Prince Consort's Own) during the Second Anglo-Boer War when he was awarded his Victoria Cross. On 15 December 1899 at the Battle of Colenso, Captain Congreve and several others saved two guns of the 14th and 66th Batteries, Royal Field Artillery, when the detachments serving the guns had all become casualties or been driven from their guns.
5 Peter Digby, *Pyramids and Poppies: The 1st SA Infantry Brigade in Libya, France and Flanders 1915–1919*, Benoni: Ashanti Publishing, 1993, p. 112; and J. Ewing, *The History of the 9th (Scottish) Division 1914–1919*, London: John Murray, 1921, p. 96.
6 Buchan, *The History of the South African Forces in France*, p. 45.
7 The Battle of Verdun was fought from 21 February to 18 December 1916 between the German and French armies on the Western Front, on the hills north of Verdun-sur-Meuse in north-eastern France.
8 Buchan, *The History of the South African Forces in France*, p. 45.
9 Ibid., p. 46.
10 Uys, *Rollcall: The Delville Wood Story*, pp. 14–15.
11 The north-central area of the Somme was the terrain of a series of battles during World War I, which took place between 1 July and 18 November 1916 on either side of the river.
12 Uys, *Rollcall: The Delville Wood Story*, p. 17.
13 Silberbauer, 'Reminiscences of the First World War from the memoirs of the late Lt Col H L Silberbauer'.
14 Buchan, *The History of the South African Forces in France*, pp. 47–48.
15 Ibid., p. 50.

16 'Extracts from *Combat In and Over Delville Wood*: Memoirs of Arthur Henry Betteridge', http://www.delvillewood.com/betteridge.htm.
17 Buchan, *The History of the South African Forces in France*, pp. 51–52; see also R. Cornwell, 'The South Africans at Delville Wood', *Militaria* 7 (2), 1977, pp. 21–22.
18 John Masefield, *The Old Front Line*, New York: Macmillan, 1917, pp. 25–26.
19 In *The Story of Delville Wood Told in Letters from the Front* (Cape Town: Cape Times Ltd, 1918), his name is given as Leonard Louis Arrons. According to the Delville Wood Roll of Honour, however, his name is Louis Leonard Aarons.
20 Cape Times, *The Story of Delville Wood Told in Letters from the Front*, Cape Town: Cape Times Ltd, 1918, p. 19.
21 'Extracts from the diary of Walter Giddy', recorded by Walter Giddy on 9 July 1916, http://www.delvillewood.com/giddy.htm. Giddy was born at Barkly East in 1895, the third son of Henry Richard Giddy and Catherine Octavia Dicks/Giddy, and attended Dale College in King William's Town. He volunteered for overseas military service in 1915 and served in the 2nd South African Infantry Regiment. He survived the Battle of Delville Wood, but was killed in action by shrapnel on 12 April 1917 near Fampoux in France. He is commemorated by a special memorial in the Point-du-Jour Military Cemetery, Athies.
22 Buchan, *The History of the South African Forces in France*, pp. 52–53.
23 Cape Times, *The Story of Delville Wood Told in Letters from the Front*, p. 19.
24 'Extracts from the diary of Walter Giddy', http://www.delvillewood.com/giddy.htm.
25 Ibid.
26 'Extracts from *Combat In and Over Delville Wood*: Memoirs of Arthur Henry Betteridge', http://www.delvillewood.com/betteridge.htm.
27 Ibid.
28 Buchan, *The History of the South African Forces in France*, pp. 53–55.
29 Ibid., pp. 55–56.
30 Silberbauer, 'Reminiscences of the First World War from the memoirs of the late Lt Col H L Silberbauer'.
31 Ibid.
32 Buchan, *The History of the South African Forces in France*, p. 57.
33 Ibid., pp. 57–58.
34 Ewing, *The History of the 9th (Scottish) Division 1914–1919*, p. 102.

CHAPTER 3: LONGUEVAL
1 Buchan, *The History of the South African Forces in France*, pp. 57–58.
2 Uys, 'The South Africans at Delville Wood'.

3   'Extracts from the diary of Walter Giddy', http://www.delvillewood.com/giddy.htm.
4   'Extracts from *Combat In and Over Delville Wood*: Memoirs of Arthur Henry Betteridge', http://www.delvillewood.com/betteridge.htm.
5   Uys, *Rollcall: The Delville Wood Story*, p. 36.
6   Ibid., p. 37.
7   E. Solomon, *Potchefstroom to Delville Wood (with the 3rd South African Infantry). Together with Some Experiences as a Prisoner of War in Germany*, Johannesburg: Football & Sports Publishers, n.d., p. 61; Buchan, *The History of the South African Forces in France*, pp. 58–59; and Uys, *Delville Wood*, pp. 54–55.
8   Buchan, *The History of the South African Forces in France*, p. 59; and John Giles, *The Somme Then and Now*, Folkestone: Bailey Brothers & Swinfen, 1977, pp. 69–70.
9   Buchan, *The History of the South African Forces in France*, p. 60.
10 Ibid., pp. 60–61.
11 Giles, *The Somme Then and Now*, pp. 70–71; Buchan, *The History of the South African Forces in France*, pp. 61–62; and Uys, *Delville Wood*, pp. 54–56.
12 Buchan, *The History of the South African Forces in France*, p. 63.
13 Buchan, *The History of the South African Forces in France*, pp. 63–65; Digby, *Pyramids and Poppies: The 1st SA Infantry Brigade in Libya, France and Flanders 1915–1919*, pp. 123–124; and Uys, *Delville Wood*, pp. 99–100.
14 Buchan, *The History of the South African Forces in France*, pp. 76–77.

CHAPTER 4: DELVILLE WOOD

1   Solomon, *Potchefstroom to Delville Wood (with the 3rd South African Infantry). Together with Some Experiences as a Prisoner of War in Germany*, p. 61.
2   Uys, *Rollcall: The Delville Wood Story*, p. 45.
3   Ibid.
4   Ibid.
5   Uys, '*The South Africans at Delville Wood*'.
6   Buchan, *The History of the South African Forces in France*, p. 65.
7   G.G.J. Lawrence, 'Echoes of War', *Militaria* 8 (4), 1978, p. 46; and Solomon, *Potchefstroom to Delville Wood (with the 3rd South African Infantry): Together with Some Experiences as a Prisoner of War in Germany*, p. 63.
8   Uys, *Delville Wood*, p. 74.
9   Cape Times, *The Story of Delville Wood Told in Letters from the Front*, p. 26.
10 Buchan, *The History of the South African Forces in France*, pp. 65–66.
11 William Frederick Faulds (b. 1895; d. 1950) of Cradock, Eastern Cape, was awarded 11 medals during his military career. He was awarded the Military

Cross for his endeavours during his unit's retreat to Marrières Wood in March 1918. He went on to serve in the Second World War. A new conference and function facility, the Capt W F Faulds VC MC Centre, was officially opened at the South African National Museum of Military History in Saxonwold, Johannesburg, on 29 November 1995.

12 Buchan, *The History of the South African Forces in France*, p. 66.
13 Cape Times, *The Story of Delville Wood Told in Letters from the Front*, p. 23.
14 Cape Times, *The Story of Delville Wood Told in Letters from the Front*, p. 35. Private Ryan enlisted on 17 August 1915 and served in the Egyptian campaign before going to France. Following the events on 16 July, he suffered from shell-shock and was treated at a military hospital in Fulham.
15 Buchan, *The History of the South African Forces in France*, pp. 66–67.
16 Cape Times, *The Story of Delville Wood Told in Letters from the Front*, p. 44.
17 Ibid., p. 41.
18 'Extracts from *Combat In and Over Delville Wood*: Memoirs of Arthur Henry Betteridge', http://www.delvillewood.com/betteridge.htm.
19 Buchan, *The History of the South African Forces in France*, p. 67.
20 Haldane was in charge of the armoured train ambushed by the Boers near Chieveley, Natal, when he was captured along with Churchill (then a war correspondent) and other troops during the Second Anglo-Boer War.
21 'Extracts from *Combat In and Over Delville Wood*: Memoirs of Arthur Henry Betteridge', http://www.delvillewood.com/betteridge.htm.
22 Buchan, *The History of the South African Forces in France*, p. 68.
23 'Extracts from *Combat In and Over Delville Wood*: Memoirs of Arthur Henry Betteridge', http://www.delvillewood.com/betteridge.htm.
24 Buchan, *The History of the South African Forces in France*, pp. 68–70.
25 'Extracts from *Combat In and Over Delville Wood*: Memoirs of Arthur Henry Betteridge', http://www.delvillewood.com/betteridge.htm.
26 Uys, 'The South Africans at Delville Wood'.
27 Buchan, *The History of the South African Forces in France*, pp. 75–76.
28 Cape Times, *The Story of Delville Wood Told in Letters from the Front*, p. 52.
29 Uys, 'The South Africans at Delville Wood'.
30 Phillips was awarded the Military Cross for his actions. He was wounded at the Butte de Warlencourt and died on 16 October 1916. See Uys, 'The South Africans at Delville Wood'; and Buchan, *The History of the South African Forces in France*, pp. 70–71.
31 Buchan, *The History of the South African Forces in France*, p. 71.
32 Uys, 'The South Africans at Delville Wood'.
33 J.A. Lawson, *Memories of Delville Wood*, Cape Town: Maskew Miller, 1918, p. 13.

34 Buchan, *The History of the South African Forces in France*, p. 72.
35 Digby, *Pyramids and Poppies: The 1st SA Infantry Brigade in Libya, France and Flanders 1915–1919*, pp. 131–132.
36 Buchan, *The History of the South African Forces in France*, p. 77.
37 Uys, 'The South Africans at Delville Wood'.
38 Ibid.
39 Wepener is presumably referring to the regimental sergeant-major (RSM) of the 3rd South African Infantry Regiment. The RSM of the 3rds, however, was W.K. Lawson, who survived both the battle and the war. The RSM of the 4ths, J. Cameron, was killed on 15 July, and it is probably he to whom Wepener is referring.
40 Uys, *Rollcall: The Delville Wood Story*, pp. 102–103.
41 Uys, 'The South Africans at Delville Wood'.
42 Uys, *Rollcall: The Delville Wood Story*, p. 106.
43 Uys, 'The South Africans at Delville Wood'.
44 Uys, *Rollcall: The Delville Wood Story*, p. 107.
45 Ibid., pp. 113–114.
46 Buchan, *The History of the South African Forces in France*, p. 72.
47 Uys, 'The South Africans at Delville Wood'.
48 Author's interview with William Thorne, Oudtshoorn, 1976. See 'First Brigade survivors pay homage to the fallen', *Die Suid-Westelike Herald*, no date (file H3044B).
49 'Extracts from the diary of Walter Giddy', available at http://www.delvillewood.com/giddy.htm.
50 Later a second-lieutenant, Lee, died of wounds on 9 April 1917, near Arras, and was buried in the St Nicolas British Cemetery.
51 'Letter from Frederick Charles Lee', available at http://www.delvillewood.com/lee.htm.
52 Major John William Jackson was killed on 20 July 1916. Captain Donald Ronald MacLachlan was killed on 16 July 1916. Both are commemorated at the Thiepval Memorial to the Missing of the Somme.
53 Named after Jack Johnson, the American heavyweight boxer, a 'Jack Johnson' was the British nickname for a heavy, black German 15-cm artillery shell.
54 'Letter from Frederick Charles Lee', available at http://www.delvillewood.com/lee.htm.
55 Cape Times, *The Story of Delville Wood Told in Letters from the Front*, p. 51.
56 Giles, *The Somme Then and Now*, p. 73.
57 Walter Giddy's diary, 22 July 1916. From 'Extracts from the diary of Walter Giddy', available at http://www.delvillewood.com/giddy.htm.
58 Uys, 'The South Africans at Delville Wood'.

59 Ibid., p. 74.
60 Bill Nasson, *Springboks on the Somme: South Africa in the Great War 1914–1918*, Johannesburg: Penguin, 2007, pp. 142–143; see also *Mercedes-Benz Southern Africa Golf Hall of Fame Special Commemorative Edition* newsletter, July 2013.
61 Buchan, *The History of the South African Forces in France*, p. 73.
62 Ibid., p.78.
63 Buchan, *The History of the South African Forces in France*, pp. 73; 78.
64 Uys, 'The South Africans at Delville Wood'.
65 First published in C.B. Purdom (ed.), *Everyman at War: Sixty Personal Narratives of the War*, London: J.M. Dent, 1930; see http://www.firstworldwar.com/diaries/delvillewood.htm.

CHAPTER 5: LIFE IN THE TRENCHES

1 Arthur, *Forgotten Voices of the Great War*, p. 83.
2 Ibid., p. 169.
3 Gilbert, *Somme: The Heroism and Horror of War*, p. 28.
4 Tolkien was ordered to France in June 1916 with the Lancashire Fusiliers. Although initially held in reserve, he helped capture the German stronghold at Ovillers. As a battalion signalling officer, he had been in and out of the trenches for three months. In late October, the Fusiliers were sent on to Ypres but, suffering from trench fever – caused by a louse bite – Tolkien was sent to a Birmingham hospital instead. He spent the rest of the war convalescing and then training fresh troops in Staffordshire and Yorkshire. In the months before the Somme, three former school friends had become the first Middle Earth fans, but two of them, Robert Gilson and Geoffrey Bache Smith, were killed on the Western Front. See www.telegraph.co.uk/history/world-war-one; news.bbc.co.uk/2/hi/uk_news/magazine; and Gilbert, *Somme: The Heroism and Horror of War*, pp. 114, 239–240.
5 J.R.R. Tolkien, *The Lord of the Rings*, London: Unwin Books, 1966, Introduction.
6 Masefield, *The Old Front Line*, pp. 23–24.
7 Letter from Lieutenant John Raws to his mother, 9 July 1916. Raws was with the 23rd Battalion, Australian Imperial Force, and killed in action at Pozières on 23 August 1916. He was 33 years old. Before the war he was a journalist with the *Melbourne Argus*. His war correspondence is held at the Australian War Memorial, Canberra (2DRL/0481).
8 Masefield, *The Old Front Line*, pp. 23–24.
9 Cape Times, *The Story of Delville Wood Told in Letters from the Front*, p. 18; and G. Genis, 'Delville Wood: Eighty years July 1916–July 1996', *Scientia Militaria, South African Journal of Military Studies* 26 (1), 1996, p. 10.

NOTES

10. G.W. Warwick, *We Band of Brothers: Reminiscences from the 1st SA Infantry Brigade in the 1914–1918 War*, Cape Town: Howard Timmins, 1962, p. 71; and Genis, 'Delville Wood: Eighty years July 1916–July 1996', p. 10.
11. Lawson, *Memories of Delville Wood*, p. 6.
12. Cape Times, *The Story of Delville Wood Told in Letters from the Front*, pp. 28–29.
13. Lawson, *Memories of Delville Wood*, p. 13.
14. Solomon, *Potchefstroom to Delville Wood (with the 3rd South African Infantry). Together with some experiences as a prisoner of war in Germany*, p. 66; and Cape Times, *The Story of Delville Wood Told in Letters from the Front*, pp. 26, 44.
15. Letter from Lieutenant John Raws to his brother, 12 August 1916.
16. John Simkin, *First World War Encyclopedia*, London: Spartacus Educational, 2012, p. 87.
17. Cape Times, *The Story of Delville Wood Told in Letters from the Front*, p. 39.
18. Warwick, *We Band of Brothers*, p. 71.
19. Silberbauer, 'Reminiscences of the First World War from the memoirs of the late Lt Col H L Silberbauer'.
20. Broughton, a member of the 1st Battalion, was wounded on 17 July 1916. From Cape Times, *The Story of Delville Wood Told in Letters from the Front*, p. 28.
21. Ibid., p. 106.
22. 'Extracts from the diary of Walter Giddy', http://www.delvillewood.com/giddy.htm.
23. Uys, 'The South Africans at Delville Wood'.
24. From 'Extracts from *Combat In and Over Delville Wood*: Memoirs of Arthur Henry Betteridge', available at http://www.delvillewood.com/betteridge.htm.
25. Lawson, *Memories of Delville Wood*, p. 12.
26. Cape Times, *The Story of Delville Wood Told in Letters from the Front*, p. 32.
27. Lawson, *Memories of Delville Wood*, p. 13.
28. Cape Times, *The Story of Delville Wood Told in Letters from the Front*, p. 49.
29. Letter dated 28 July 1916. From Cape Times, *The Story of Delville Wood Told in Letters from the Front*, p. 54.
30. Genis, 'Delville Wood: Eighty years July 1916–July 1996', p. 12.
31. Cape Times, *The Story of Delville Wood Told in Letters from the Front*, p. 53.
32. Lawson, *Memories of Delville Wood*, p. 7.
33. Arthur, *Forgotten Voices of the Great War*, pp. 45–46.
34. Ibid., p. 242.
35. Silberbauer, 'Reminiscences of the First World War from the memoirs of the late Lt Col H L Silberbauer'.
36. Russell Barratt, 'A South African in France 1916/1917', *Military History Journal* 8 (2).

37 Silberbauer, 'Reminiscences of the First World War from the memoirs of the late Lt Col H L Silberbauer'.
38 Arthur, *Forgotten Voices of the Great War*, pp. 242–243.
39 Ibid.
40 Silberbauer, 'Reminiscences of the First World War from the memoirs of the late Lt Col H L Silberbauer'.
41 Arthur, *Forgotten Voices of the Great War*, p. 85. See also Silberbauer, 'Reminiscences of the First World War from the memoirs of the late Lt Col H L Silberbauer': 'I had never believed that rats could grow as big as large cats. They were loathsome creatures and had no fear of humans.'
42 Arthur, *Forgotten Voices of the Great War*, p. 97.
43 Ibid., p. 243.
44 Barratt, 'A South African in France 1916/1917'.
45 Gilbert, *Somme: The Heroism and Horror of War*, p. 223.
46 Arthur, *Forgotten Voices of the Great War*, pp. 95, 97.
47 Silberbauer, 'Reminiscences of the First World War from the memoirs of the late Lt Col H L Silberbauer'.
48 Arthur, *Forgotten Voices of the Great War*, pp. 56–57.
49 Ibid., p. 169.
50 Letter from Lieutenant John Raws to his mother, 20 July 1916.

CHAPTER 6: THE BUTTE DE WARLENCOURT

1 Buchan, *The History of the South African Forces in France*, pp. 83–84.
2 Barratt, 'A South African in France 1916/1917', entry for 14 September 1916.
3 Buchan, *The History of the South African Forces in France*, p. 84.
4 Barratt, 'A South African in France 1916/1917'.
5 Buchan, *The History of the South African Forces in France*, pp. 84–85.
6 Barratt, 'A South African in France 1916/1917'.
7 Ibid.
8 Buchan, *The History of the South African Forces in France*, p. 85.
9 Cape Times, *The Story of Delville Wood Told in Letters from the Front*, pp. 46–47.
10 http://patrickwright.polimekanos.com/wp-content/uploads/tank_chapter-3.pdf, pp. 2–3.
11 Buchan, *The History of the South African Forces in France*, pp. 87–88.
12 Ibid., pp. 88–89.
13 http://www.westernfrontassociation.com/history-wfa/2361-did-you-know-the-butte-de-warlencourt.html.
14 Bradford was a second-lieutenant when the war began. In February 1915 he was awarded a Military Cross and in August 1916 was given command as a temporary lieutenant-colonel of the 9th Battalion, Durham Light Infantry. He

won his Victoria Cross after being ordered to take command of the 6th Battalion, Durham Light Infantry, and advanced towards the German lines as part of the 50th Division. Ten days after being given the command of the 186th Brigade as a brigadier-general (which, at the age of 25, made him the youngest general officer in the British Army), Bradford was killed by a stray German shell during the Battle of Cambrai on 30 November 1917.

15 Buchan, *The History of the South African Forces in France*, pp. 94–95.
16 Barratt, 'A South African in France 1916/1917'.
17 Buchan, *The History of the South African Forces in France*, pp. 88–89.
18 Ibid., pp. 96–97.
19 Ibid.
20 Ibid., pp. 97–98.
21 W.D. Croft, *Three Years with the 9th (Scottish) Division*, London: John Murray, 1919, p. 84.
22 Buchan, *The History of the South African Forces in France*, pp. 98–99.
23 Ibid., pp. 100–101.
24 Ibid., p. 102.
25 Gilbert, *Somme: The Heroism and Horror of War*, pp. 238; 250.

CHAPTER 7: THE BATTLE OF ARRAS

1 Barratt, 'A South African in France 1916/1917', entries for 7 and 8 November 1916.
2 Buchan, *The History of the South African Forces in France*, pp. 104–106.
3 Barratt, 'A South African in France 1916/1917', entry for 9 December 1916.
4 Buchan, *The History of the South African Forces in France*, p. 108.
5 Ibid., pp. 108–109.
6 Alfred Mahncke, 'Into the fire: A German officer's impressions of the Western Front, 1917', *Military History Journal* 7 (3), June 1987.
7 Edwin Kiester Jnr, *An Incomplete History of World War I*, London: Murdoch Books, 2007, pp. 183–187.
8 Buchan, *The History of the South African Forces in France*, pp. 108–114.
9 Mahncke, 'Into the fire: A German officer's impressions of the Western Front, 1917'.
10 Silberbauer, 'Reminiscences of the First World War from the memoirs of the late Lt Col H L Silberbauer'.
11 Buchan, *The History of the South African Forces in France*, pp. 114–116.
12 Ibid., p. 118.
13 Ibid., pp. 118–199.
14 Ibid., pp. 121–122.
15 Private R.W. Nelson deserves special mention here. He had carried stretchers

continuously from the morning of 9 April, and was already worn out when the attack began on the 12th. He worked on steadily until he collapsed late in the evening, but refused to be relieved. After a short rest, he returned to his post and carried seven cases before the morning. See Buchan, *The History of the South African Forces in France*, p. 126.
16 Buchan, *The History of the South African Forces in France*, pp. 126–127.

CHAPTER 8: THE FINAL PUSH
1 Buchan, *The History of the South African Forces in France*, pp. 128–136.
2 Ibid., pp. 142–143.
3 Ibid., p. 143.
4 The loophole was a hole in the side of the pillbox for shooting through (similar to those in the Boer War blockhouses).
5 Hewitt farmed in Natal after the war and later in Kenya. He served as a major during the Second World War. After the war he moved to Hermanus. He died in England in 1966. See Uys, *Rollcall: The Delville Wood Story*, p. 174.
6 Buchan, *The History of the South African Forces in France*, p. 144.
7 Uys, *Rollcall: The Delville Wood Story*, p. 125.
8 Buchan, *The History of the South African Forces in France*, pp. 145–147.
9 Ibid., pp. 151–153.
10 Uys, *Delville Wood*, p. 226.
11 Tudor (b. 1871; d. 1965) was a Boer War veteran who went on to take part in the Irish War of Independence (1919–21). See en.wikipedia.org/wiki/Henry_Hugh_Tudor; and Buchan, *The History of the South African Forces in France*, pp. 149–150.
12 Buchan, *The History of the South African Forces in France*, pp. 158–163.
13 Lawrence, 'Echoes of War (Part 4)', pp. 1–2.
14 Buchan, *The History of the South African Forces in France*, pp. 158–167.
15 Ibid., pp. 169–175.
16 Ibid., pp. 175–178.
17 Lawrence, 'Echoes of War (Part 4)', p. 3.
18 Buchan, *The History of the South African Forces in France*, p. 180–182.
19 Ibid., p. 184.
20 Ibid., pp. 183–184.
21 Ibid., pp. 185–187.
22 Ibid., p. 187.
23 Dawson died of enteric fever in East Africa, in October 1920. See Uys, *Rollcall: The Delville Wood Story*, p. 172.
24 Buchan, *The History of the South African Forces in France*, pp. 187–188; and Lawrence, 'Echoes of War (Part 4)', p. 5.

25 Buchan, *The History of the South African Forces in France*, pp. 188–189.
26 Lawrence, 'Echoes of War (Part 4)', p. 6.
27 Buchan, *The History of the South African Forces in France*, pp. 189; and Lawrence, 'Echoes of War (Part 4)', p. 6.
28 Buchan, *The History of the South African Forces in France*, p. 190.
29 Ibid., pp. 189–190.
30 Michelin & Cie, *The Somme Vol II*, Clermont-Ferrand: Pneu Michelin, 1919, pp. 14–23.
31 Frank Mitchell, 'When Tank Fought Tank', http://www.firstworldwar.com/diaries/whentankfoughttank.htm. See also C.B. Purdom (ed.), *Everyman at War: Sixty Personal Narratives of the War*, London: J.M. Dent, 1980.
32 Giles, *The Somme Then and Now*, pp. 130–133.
33 Lawrence, 'Echoes of War (Part 4)', p. 9.
34 Michelin & Cie, *The Somme Vol II*, pp. 46–48; and Buchan, *The History of the South African Forces in France*, pp. 224–225.
35 Buchan, *The History of the South African Forces in France*, pp. 230–255.
36 Ibid., pp. 259–260.

APPENDIX VII: THE ROLE OF BLACK SOUTH AFRICANS

1 J.S. Mohlamme, 'Soldiers without reward: Africans in South Africa's wars', *Military History Journal* 10 (1), June 1995.
2 Ibid.
3 G. Swinney, 'The sinking of the SS *Mendi*, 21 February 1917', *Military History Journal* 10 (1), June 1995.
4 Ibid.
5 S. Horwitz, 'The non-European war record in South Africa', in E. Hellman (ed.), *Handbook on Race Relations in South Africa*, Oxford: Oxford University Press, 1949, pp. 537–538.
6 K.W. Grundy, *Soldiers Without Politics: Blacks in the South African Armed Forces*, Berkeley: University of California Press, 1983, p. 56.

Bibliography

BOOKS

Alhadeff, V. *South Africa in Two World Wars*. Cape Town: Don Nelson, 1979

Arthur, Max. *Forgotten Voices of the Great War*. London: Ebury Press, 2002

Birkby, C. *The Saga of the Transvaal Scottish Regiment*. London: Hodder & Stoughton, 1950

Blake, Arthur. *Vlieghelde van Suid-Afrika*. Cape Town: Nasionale Boekhandel, 1966

Buchan, John. *The History of the South African Forces in France*. Edinburgh: Thomas Nelson and Sons, 1920

———— *The Battle of the Somme: The First Phase*. London: Thomas Nelson, 1917

Cape Times. *The Story of Delville Wood Told in Letters from the Front*. Cape Town: Cape Times Ltd, 1918

Chappell, Michael. *The Somme 1916: Crucible of a British Army*. Marlborough: Crowood, 1999

Collyer, J.J. *The Campaign in German South West Africa, 1914–1915*. Pretoria: Government Printer, 1937

Croft, W.D. *Three Years with the 9th (Scottish) Division*. London: John Murray, 1919

Digby, Peter. *Pyramids and Poppies: The 1st SA Infantry Brigade in Libya, France and Flanders 1915–1919*. Benoni: Ashanti Publishing, 1993

Ewing, J. *The History of the 9th (Scottish) Division 1914–1919*. London: John Murray, 1921

Fourie, D. 'Delville Wood' in *History of the First World War Vol 4*. London: Purnell, no date

Gilbert, Martin. *Somme: The Heroism and Horror of War*. London: John Murray, 2006

———— *The First World War: A Complete History*. Clearwater: Owl Books, 2004

Giles, John. *The Somme Then and Now*. Folkestone: Bailey Brothers & Swinfen, 1977

Grundlingh, A. *Fighting Their Own War: South African Blacks and the First World War*. Johannesburg: Ravan Press, 1987

Grundy, K.W. *Soldiers Without Politics: Blacks in the South African Armed Forces*. Berkeley: University of California Press, 1983

Hellman, E. (ed.). *Handbook on Race Relations in South Africa*. Oxford: Oxford University Press, 1949
Johnstone, R. *Ulundi to Delville Wood*. Cape Town: Maskew Miller, no date
Juta, H.C. *The History of the Transvaal Scottish*. Cape Town: Hortors, 1933
Kiester, Edwin Jnr. *An Incomplete History of World War I*. London: Murdoch Books, 2007
Lawson, J. *Memories of Delville Wood*. Cape Town: Maskew Miller, 1918
Liddle, H. Peter. *Passchendaele in Perspective: The Third Battle of Ypres*. London: Leo Cooper, 1997
Masefield, John. *The Old Front Line*. New York: Macmillan, 1917
Michelin & Cie. *The Somme Vol II*. Clermont-Ferrand: Pneu Michelin, 1919
Nasson, Bill. *Springboks on the Somme: South Africa in the Great War 1914–1918*. Johannesburg: Penguin, 2007
Prior, Robin. *The First World War*. London: Cassell, 1999
Purdom, C.B. (ed.). *Everyman at War: Sixty Personal Narratives of the War*. London: J.M. Dent, 1930
Simkin, John. *First World War Encyclopedia*. London: Spartacus Educational, 2012
Simonds, Frank H. *History of the World War*. Garden City, NY: Doubleday, 1919
Solomon, E. *Potchefstroom to Delville Wood (with the 3rd South African Infantry). Together with some experiences as a prisoner of war in Germany*. Johannesburg: Football & Sports Publishers, no date
Stewart, David & James Fitzgerald. *The Great War: Using Evidence*. Melbourne: Thomas Nelson, 1987
The Somme. Volume I: The First Battle of the Somme (1916–1917). Clermont: Michelin, 1919
Tolkien, J.R.R. *The Lord of the Rings*. London: Unwin Books, 1966
Uys, Ian. *Delville Wood*. Germiston: I. Uys Publishers, 1983
——— *Rollcall: The Delville Wood Story*. Johannesburg: I. Uys Publishers, 1991
Warwick, G.W. *We Band of Brothers: Reminiscences from the 1st SA Infantry Brigade in the 1914–1918 War*. Cape Town: Howard Timmins, 1962

MAGAZINE AND NEWSPAPER ARTICLES

Barratt, Russell. 'A South African in France 1916/1917', *Military History Journal* 8 (2)
Cockrell, Alan. '"Just Fancy Us …" The First World War letters of Lt Frederick Charles Wilton, DFC Royal Flying Corps/Royal Air Force', *Military History Journal* 14 (3), June 2008
Cornwell, R. 'The South Africans at Delville Wood', *Militaria* 7 (2), 1977
Debergh, Filip & Jaco van Wyk. 'Pretoria's Hoërskool Waterkloof commemorates … South African soldiers of the Great War in Flanders, 1915–18', *Military History Journal* 14 (2), December 2007
'First Brigade survivors pay homage to the fallen', *Die Suid-Westelike Herald*, no date

Genis, G. 'Delville Wood: Eighty years July 1916–July 1996', *Scientia Militaria, South African Journal of Military Studies* 26 (1), 1996
Hall, D.D. 'The 1917 Diary of 2/Lt R.E. Stevenson', *Military History Journal* 7 (1), June 1986
Lawrence, G.G.J. 'Echoes of War (Part 4)', *Scientia Militaria* 8 (4), 1978
Long Eaton Advertiser, 16 July 1915
Mahncke, A. 'Into the fire: A German officer's impressions of the Western Front, 1917', *Military History Journal* 7 (3), June 1987
Mohlamme, J. S. 'Soldiers without reward: Africans in South Africa's wars', *Military History Journal* 10 (1), June 1995
Monick, S. 'Horror recollected in tranquillity: The classic memoirists of the Western Front', *Military History Journal* 7 (3), June 1987
────── 'The Poet under fire: Four poets of World War I', *Military History Journal* 7 (1), June 1986
Paterson, Hamish. 'First Allied victory: The South African campaign in German South-West Africa, 1914–1915', *Military History Journal* 13 (2)
Rodway, C.G.R. 'Fred Hanpson – Infantryman', *Sedge News*, Jan/Feb 1989
Silberbauer, H.L. 'Reminiscences of the First World War from the memoirs of the late Lt Col H L Silberbauer', *Military History Journal* 10 (5), June 1997
Southern Africa Golf Hall of Fame. *Mercedes-Benz Southern Africa Golf Hall of Fame Special Commemorative Edition*, July 2013
Swinney, G. 'The sinking of the SS *Mendi*, 21 February 1917', *Military History Journal* 10 (1), June 1995
Uys, Ian. 'The Lessons of Delville Wood', *Military History Journal* 6 (1)
────── 'The South Africans at Delville Wood', *Military History Journal* 7 (2), December 1986

PERSONAL INTERVIEWS

Author's interview with the late William R. Thorne, Oudtshoorn, 1976

ELECTRONIC SOURCES

http://africanhistory.about.com
http://en.wikipedia.org
http://patrickwright.polimekanos.com
http://theauxiliaries.com
www.delvillewood.com
www.firstworldwar.com/diaries
www.nzhistory.net.nz/war/battle-of-the-somme
www.rfdiv.mil.za
www.westernfrontassociation.com
www.telegraph.co.uk

Index

1st Canadian Heavy Artillery Group 146
1st South African Field Ambulance 10–11, 44–45, 85, 115, 117, 136
1st South African Infantry Regiment (Cape of Good Hope Regiment)
    Arras, Battle of 107, 109, 113–118
    Bernafay and Trônes woods 19–20, 25–30, 32
    Butte de Warlencourt 93–94, 100–101, 103, 106
    casualties 137–138
    Delville Wood 48–51, 54, 57, 60–61, 70–72
    demobilisation 137
    Egypt, campaign in 13–17
    Gauche and Marrières woods 125, 127
    Longueval, attack on 37, 39–41, 43–44
    Lys, Battle of the 134–136
    raising of 9–10, 12
    reorganised 132, 136
    as stretcher-bearers 85
    Ypres, Third Battle of 121, 123–124
2nd South African Infantry Regiment (Natal and Orange Free State Regiment)
    Arras, Battle of 107, 109, 114–118
    Bernafay and Trônes woods 19, 22, 25, 28–30, 32
    Butte de Warlencourt 93–94, 99–101, 106
    casualties 137–138
    Delville Wood 46–47, 52, 54, 58, 64–65, 67, 71–72
    demobilisation 137
    Egypt, campaign in 14, 16
    Gauche and Marrières woods 125, 127, 130–131
    Longueval, attack on 40–43
    Lys, Battle of the 135–136
    raising of 9–10, 12
    reorganised 132, 136
    Ypres, Third Battle of 121, 123–124
III Corps 72, 96, 146
3rd Division 54, 56–57, 67
3rd South African Infantry Regiment (Transvaal and Rhodesia)
    Arras, Battle of 107, 109, 113–118
    Bernafay and Trônes woods 19, 22, 25, 28–30, 32
    Butte de Warlencourt 93–94, 100–104, 106
    casualties 85, 137–138
    Delville Wood 47–51, 56, 58–61, 63–64, 69, 71–72
    disbanded 124
    Egypt, campaign in 14–16
    Longueval, attack on 37, 40–43
    raising of 9–10, 12
    rations 81
    Ypres, Third Battle of 121, 123–124
IV Corps 72, 93, 118
4th Division 111, 113, 115, 116
4th South African Infantry Regiment (South African Scottish Regiment)
    Arras, Battle of 107, 109, 113–118
    Bernafay and Trônes woods 19, 25–26, 28–32
    Butte de Warlencourt 93–94, 100–101, 104, 106
    casualties 137–138
    Delville Wood 61–62, 67–68, 72
    demobilisation 137
    Egypt, campaign in 16
    Gauche and Marrières woods 125, 127–130
    Longueval, attack on 40–41, 43–44
    Lys, Battle of the 135–136
    raising of 9–10, 12
    rations 81

reorganised 132, 136
Ypres, Third Battle of 121, 123–124
VI Corps 106, 111
VII Corps 109, 111, 118, 136, 148
9th (Scottish) Division
　Arras, Battle of 107–109, 111, 113, 116
　Bernafay and Trônes woods 19–26, 30
　Butte de Warlencourt 93, 99, 106
　Delville Wood 52, 56
　Gauche and Marrières woods 125, 130, 132
　Longueval, attack on 38, 44
　Lys, Battle of the 134, 136
　South African brigade and 17
　Ypres, Third Battle of 121–123
XIII Corps 19, 25, 26, 32–33, 36, 147–148
XIV Corps Heavy Artillery 142, 154
14th (Light) Division 72
XV Corps Signal Company 150–157
15th (Scottish) Infantry Division 96, 99–100, 116, 144
15th Sikhs 14
XVII Corps 111, 118, 148
XVIII Corps 123
18th Division 44
21st Division 125, 130, 132
23rd Division 99
26th Brigade
　Arras, Battle of 109, 113, 115, 117
　brigades comprising 20
　Butte de Warlencourt 100, 103
　Delville Wood 61
　Gauche and Marrières woods 125, 132
　Longueval, attack on 37
　Ypres, Third Battle of 121
27th Brigade
　Arras, Battle of 113, 118
　Bernafay and Trônes woods 26, 28
　brigades comprising 20
　Butte de Warlencourt 100
　Delville Wood 49, 54
　Gauche and Marrières woods 125
　Longueval, attack on 37
　Ypres, Third Battle of 121
28th Brigade Machine Gun Company 25, 72
30th Division 22, 29, 30, 31
34th Division 109, 111
35th Division 130, 132

44th (South African) Heavy Artillery Brigade 141, 143–144
47th (1/2nd London) Division 99, 125
50th Division 99
50th (South African) Heavy Artillery Brigade 145, 146, 147–148
51st (Highland) Division 109, 111, 148
71st Siege Battery, Royal Garrison Artillery 141
72nd Siege Battery, Royal Garrison Artillery 145–146, 147
73rd Siege Battery, Royal Garrison Artillery 139–140, 143–144
74th Siege Battery, Royal Garrison Artillery 144–145, 147
75th Siege Battery, Royal Garrison Artillery 146–147
84th Miscellaneous Trades Company, Royal Engineers (South African) 167
91 Air Line Section 156
125th Siege Battery, Royal Garrison Artillery 141–143
496th (South African) Siege Battery 147

Aarons, Sergeant Louis Leonard 27–28, 29
Adams, Sergeant J.W. 84
aerial photographs 22
aeroplanes 112, 153, 162
African National Congress 209
Africans *see* black South Africans
Afrikaans-speaking personnel 9
Agagia, Battle of 15
aircraft 112, 153, 162
Aisne, Second Battle of the 117
Aitken, Second-Lieutenant A. 122
Albert (town) 23
alcohol *see* rum
Allied Powers 1, 107–108
Alston, Major C.W. 145–146
ammunition 20, 130, 132, 144
Anderson, Lieutenant-Colonel J.D. 168–169
Anglo-Boer War *see* Boer War
animals used for transport 84, 85
Anzac *see* Australian and New Zealand Army Corps
Argyll and Sutherland Highlanders 20, 37
Armadale Castle 210
armistice, 11 November 1918 137

INDEX

armoured cars *see* tanks
Army Post Office 112
Arras, Battle of 107–119, 140, 142, 145
artillery *see* South African Heavy Artillery Brigade
Ashurst, Sergeant George 90
as-Senussi, Ahmed Sharif 13
Australian and New Zealand Army Corps (Anzac) 152
Australian Camel Corps 16
Austria–Hungary 1–2

Bain, Captain J.T. 122
Balmoral Castle 158
Bam, Cyril 22, 34
Bamford, Lieutenant-Colonel H.W.M. 136
Bancroft, Lieutenant 126, 128
barges, hospital 160
Barlow, Captain 168
Barnard, Major 169
Barratt, Frederick 87, 89, 93, 94–95, 101–102, 107, 108
Bazentin-le-Petit (village) 34–35
Beauchamp-Proctor, Captain Andrew Weatherby 171–172
Begbie, Major R.P.G. 142, 143
Belgium 2, 119, 155
Bell, Second-Lieutenant C.S. 65
Bennett, Lieutenant-Colonel G.M. 144, 145, 148
Bernafay Wood 18–36
Betteridge, Private Arthur 25–26, 31–32, 38–39, 52–56, 57, 81, 84
Beverley, Captain 130–131
Beviss, Lieutenant 126–127, 128
Beyers, General Christiaan 5
Bisset, Sir Murray 6
Black Hand 2
black South Africans 168–170, 209–211
Black Watch 20, 37, 65
Blanchard, Second-Lieutenant W.J. 122
Blew, Lieutenant-Colonel T.H. 143, 144
Bliss, Lieutenant 15
blizzard of 1916 150
Bloom, Corporal Hermann 52
Bloomfield, Captain William Anderson 172
Boer War 5–6, 75, 209

booby traps 26
Booth, Sergeant Frederick Charles 172
Botha, General Louis 5–7, 10, 210–211
Bowker, Corporal D. M. P. 172
Bradford, Lieutenant-Colonel Roland 99
Brooke, Captain Basil 163
brotherhood-in-arms 137
Broughton, Private Weldon 83
Brown, Second-Lieutenant 144
Brown, Angus 69
Browne, Major 128
Browne, Captain Claude Melville 62, 66
Bryant, Captain E.C. 124
Brydon, Major Walter 139–140, 143–144
Buchan, John
   9th Division 20
   Afrikaans-speaking personnel 9
   Arras, Battle of 114
   Butte de Warlencourt 98, 105–106
   Delville Wood 48, 52, 72–73
   Gauche and Marrières woods 130
   Longueval, attack on 37, 41, 43
   on South Africans 137
   Trônes Wood 24–26, 35–36
   Ypres, Third Battle of 121
Bulgaria 1
Bunce, Captain 127
Burges, Major Edward 57
Burgess, Captain 127–128, 132
Burke, Lieutenant Ulrich 86, 87–88
Burrows, Lieutenant 115
Butte de Warlencourt 93–106, 146
Byng, General Julian 111, 123

Cambrai, Battle of 123, 141
campaign for 1917 107–108, 119
Campion, Lieutenant 140
Canadian Corps 97, 111, 123, 142, 146–148
Canadian Military Nursing Service 159
Cape Auxiliary Horse Transport companies 168–170
Cape Times 59
Carey, Private Sidney Martin 39
Carpenter, Foreman 72
carrier pigeons 112, 153
Carrington, Captain Charles 91

233

casualties
    Arras, Battle of 109, 113–118
    Bernafay and Trônes woods 19, 23, 28–32
    Butte de Warlencourt 102–103, 106
    Cape Auxiliary Horse Transport
        companies 170
    Delville Wood 54–60, 69, 71–72
    Egypt, campaign in 14–16
    First World War 1, 3
    Gauche and Marrières woods 127–128,
        130–131
    Longueval, attack on 38–39, 43
    Lys, Battle of the 135–136
    South African brigade 4, 137–138
    South African Heavy Artillery Brigade
        142–143, 145–146
    Ypres, Third Battle of 122–124
Centlivres, Chief Justice 6
chloride of lime 88
Christian, HRH Princess 163
Christian, Lieutenant-Colonel E. 99, 113–114,
    123, 127, 131
Christmas armistice 90–91
Churchill, Winston 21, 54, 76
Clerk, Major 128
Clifford, Captain H.E. 30, 48
Cochran, Major 121, 130, 131
Cole, Lieutenant-Colonel 167
Collins, Lieutenant-Colonel F.R. 165, 166
Coloured community 168–170, 209–210
communications *see* South African Signal
    Company (Royal Engineers)
Congreve, General Sir Walter 19, 26, 37, 55
Connock, Second-Lieutenant Joseph G. 65
Cooper, Captain 168
Cooper, Lieutenant 130–131
Cooper, Second-Lieutenant A.B. 122
Corps of Royal Engineers 149
Corps Signal Salvage Unit 154
Corps Signal School 154–155
Corsican 13, 158
couriers *see* runners
Covernton, Lieutenant R.H. 149, 151
Cowie, Captain G.R. 148
Coxen, Second-Lieutenant C.F. 122
Craig, Lieutenant Arthur William 50, 172–173
Creagh, Company Sergeant-Major 168

Creagh, Matron 159
Creighton, Private 94, 102
creosol 88
Crewe, Sir Charles Preston 9–10
Croft, Lieutenant-Colonel W.D. 103
Cruddas, Lieutenant N. 101, 122
Cullis, Private 94, 101
Currie, Second-Lieutenant J. 140
cyclical nature of life in trenches 77

daily routine in trenches 78–80
Dalrymple, Colonel W. 10
Darro 210
Davis, Captain F.M. 122
dawn attacks 78
Dawson, General Frederick Stuart 10, 40, 43,
    51, 60, 85, 103–105, 107, 121–122,
    128–131, 133
De Beers 168
Decauville trains 122
Delville Wood, Battle of vii, 36–37, 39–42,
    46–74, 151–152
Demuth, Private Norman 75–76
De Villiers, Jackie 6
De Wet, General Christiaan 5
Dickerson, Second-Lieutenant V.S. 124
Dingwall, Lieutenant J.A. 149
disabled men 164
diseases 19, 61, 81–82, 84, 87–89, 118, 159
disinfecting agents 88
Distinguished Service Order 140, 172
Dobson, Lieutenant 156
Donaldson, Lieutenant 101
Dorset Yeomanry 16
Dorward, Lieutenant 115
Drummond, Lieutenant Jack 96
Duke of Edinburgh's Own Volunteer Rifles
    5–6
Duke of Lancaster's Yeomanry 14–15
Dunes, Battle of the 155
Dunvegan Castle 12
Durham Light Infantry 66, 106

East Africa 3, 138, 168, 210
Eastern Front 2
Eckersley, Kitty 9
Egypt 12–17

INDEX

Elliott, Lieutenant Harold 104, 114
Ellis, Lieutenant 114
English Voluntary Aid Detachments 159
equipment carried by soldiers 23, 80
esprit de corps 137
Estill, Lieutenant 102
Estreé-Cauchy 93
Euripides 169

families of soldiers 75–76, 91
Farrell, Captain 38
Farrow, Corporal 68
fatigue *see* neurasthenia
Faulds, Lieutenant William Frederick 50, 131, 172–173
Featherstone, Second-Lieutenant Clive 39–40
femurs, fractured 162
Fergusson, Lieutenant-General Sir Charles 109, 111
Fifth Army 98, 107, 121, 126–127, 142, 144
First Army 93, 107
First World War, background to 1–4, 75
Fitzpatrick, Major P.N.G. 141
Flanders, battlefield in 76
fleas 89–90
fog *see* weather conditions
food *see* rations
Forder, Major C.J. 148
Forder, Second-Lieutenant W.G.S. 122
Fourie, Jopie 5
Fourth Army 19, 95, 99, 150
fractured femur cases 162
France 1–4, 12
Franz Ferdinand, Archduke of Austria 1–2
French, John 3
Furse, General William T. 19, 28, 40, 51, 55–56, 100
futility of battle 73–79
Fynn, Dudley 16

Gaafer Pasha 13, 15
gas attacks 24, 30, 38, 39, 68, 84, 89, 125–126, 142
gas-masks 68, 84
Gauche Wood 125–133
Geddes, Sir Eric 11, 165

Gemmell, Captain D. 122
George V, King 94
German soldiers 62–64, 72, 110
German South-West Africa campaign 3, 5–7, 10
Germany 1–4, 25, 96, 126
Giddy, Private Walter 28–29, 30–31, 38, 68–69, 82, 83
Gillam, Lieutenant 168
Gladstone, Lord 162
Godfrey, Lieutenant 115
Goodwin, Lieutenant B.W. 109, 136
Gordon, Lieutenant-Colonel J.L.R. 14
Gorle, Lieutenant Robert Vaughan 173
Gough, Sir Hubert 126
Grady, Captain E.C.D. 114, 117
Grata Quies Auxiliary Hospital 158
Gray, Captain W.J. 48
Great War, background to 1–4, 75
Green, Captain Garnet George 62, 65, 67, 126–128
Greenwood, Lieutenant-Colonel Harry 173–174
Greenwood, Private G.F. 39
Grimsdell, Robert 72
Guard, Lieutenant 63–64

Haig, General Sir Douglas 3, 4, 20, 32, 36, 96, 97–98, 107–108, 119–120
Haldane, Major-General Aylmer 54, 56
Hamilton, Ian 3
Hands, Captain P.A.M. 140, 144
Hansen, Captain Percy Howard 174
Hardwich, Lieutenant 115
Harris, Lieutenant 102
Harrison, Major H.C. 141
Harrison, Major N. 149, 150
Harrison's Pomade 89–90
Harvey, Lieutenant 136
Hayward, Captain Reginald Frederick Johnson 174–175
Heal, Lieutenant-Colonel F.H. 107, 114, 121, 127, 131
heavy artillery *see* South African Heavy Artillery Brigade
Hendry, Second-Lieutenant N.T. 122
heroes, South Africans' reputation as 137–138

Hewitt, Lance-Corporal William Henry 122, 175
Hill, Lieutenant 156
Hill, Captain E. 62
Hill, Padre Eustace 124, 131
Hindenburg Line 4, 108, 109, 141, 147, 154
History of the South African Forces in France, The 72–73, 137
Hitler, Adolf 110–111
Hogg, Lieutenant 135
Hollybrook Memorial, England 210
Hong Kong and Singapore Mountain Battery 16
Hopgood, Second-Lieutenant 135
horses *see* animals used for transport
Hotel Beau-Rivage, Cannes 11
Hoy, Major C.N. 209
Hugo, Charles 50
Hunt, Lieutenant 115
Hunt, Major Donald Rolfe 44, 52, 100
Hunter, General Sir Archibald 12

Investigator 150
Italy 1

Jack, Lieutenant J. 149
Jackson, Captain 69
Jackson, Matron 163
Japan 1
Jenkins, Major H.H. 103, 128, 136
Jenner, Lieutenant 132
Jenner, Major 169
Johnson, Lieutenant 154–155
Jones, Lieutenant-Colonel Frank Aubrey 'Fatty Roe' 10, 28, 31, 32, 82
Jowett, Captain P.J. 7

Keating's Powder 89
Keith, Regimental Sergeant-Major 130
Kenilworth Castle 149, 158
Kennedy, Second-Lieutenant 126
King's Own Scottish Borderers 20, 30, 105
kit of soldiers 23, 80

Lane, Private Clifford 89–90
Langdale, Captain 104
Lascelles, Captain Arthur Moore 175–176

latrines 88
Lawrence, Lieutenant Geoffrey G.J. 48, 122, 125–126, 128, 132, 135
Lawrie, Captain M.B. 62
Lawson, Private John 58–59, 61, 81, 84, 85
Lee, Lieutenant Frederick Charles 69–70, 115
Lees, Lieutenant 117
Leicestershire Regiment 5, 18, 22, 24, 82
Lenin, Vladimir 119
letters 112
Lewis gun 35, 43, 50–51
Libya 13
lice 89–90
Liebson, Captain Stephen 65, 127
Lilburn, Lieutenant Percy 94
lime 88
Longueval, attack on 36–45
Lord of the Rings, The 76
Lovat, Lord 170
Lucas, Lieutenant E.D. 122
Lukin, General Henry Timson
  Arras, Battle of 107
  background of 10
  Butte de Warlencourt 101
  Delville Wood 47, 49, 51, 55–56, 60–61, 62–63, 71
  Egypt 14–17
  on leave 125
  Longueval, attack on 37, 40, 42–43
  No. 1 South African General Hospital 160
  Trônes Wood 28
  Ypres, Third Battle of 124
Lys, Battle of the 133–136, 155–157

Maasdorp, Second-Lieutenant 144
machine guns 2
MacKeurton, Captain 168
MacLachlan, Captain 69
MacLeod, Lieutenant-Colonel Donald M. 32, 52, 121, 127, 128, 136
Mahncke, Alfred 109–110, 111–112
mail 112
Mallet, Private Hugh 47–48
Mallett, Lieutenant 102–103
Mametz Wood 95, 151
Mandy, Lance-Corporal Alf 21–22
Mandy, Second-Lieutenant G.J.S. 124

INDEX

Marillier, Frank 58, 67, 83–84
Maritz, Lieutenant-Colonel Manie 5
Marrières Wood 125–133
Mary, Queen 12
Masefield, John 26–27, 77, 79–80
Maskew Miller, Cape Town 163
Mason, Captain C.E. 167
Maxwell, General Frank 121, 122
McCusker, Gunner Ivan 50–51
McDonald, Captain Albert 62
McDonald, Captain A.W.H. 122
McFee, Sergeant 124
McIndoe, Private Tom 88–89
McLauchlin, Lance-Corporal Arthur 85
McLeod, Major 68–69
medical staff
   1st South African Field Ambulance 10–11, 44–45, 85, 115, 117, 136
   Decauville trains 122
   Delville Wood 62, 66
   dressing stations 102
   No. 1 General Hospital, Wynberg 158
   No. 1 South African Field Ambulance 158, 162, 164
   No. 1 South African General Hospital 11, 158–164
   No. 2 General Hospital, Maitland 158
   No. 2 Stationary Hospital 159
   stretcher-bearers 33, 44–45, 55–56, 60, 85, 115, 117
Medlicott, Lieutenant 102
Medlicott, Captain Richard 42, 63–64
Megantic 19
memorial service at Delville Wood 124
Mendi 210
Mendi Memorial, Avalon Cemetery, Soweto 210
Meredith, Dudley 11–12
Messines, Battle of 120
Michell, Lieutenant F.H. 149
Military Cross 111, 172
Miscellaneous Trades Company 167
Mitchell, Captain 128
Mitchell, Lieutenant Frank 133–134
modesty of soldiers 137
Moll, Toby 22, 34
Money, Lieutenant 114

Monro, Sir Charles 93
Mont Dore Military Hospital 158
Moore, Lieutenant Graham 168
Moorina 13
Morris, Lieutenant-Colonel George A. 209
Morrison, Lieutenant 114
motor transport *see* transportation
mud 18, 45, 86–87, 105
Mullins, Captain A.G. 146
Munro, Winifred 161
Murray-MacGregor, Major 145

naming of battlefield locations 41–42, 47
neurasthenia 82, 84
Newbery, Second-Lieutenant J. 122
Newell, Lieutenant-Colonel F. 166
New Zealander soldiers 14, 97
Nivelle Offensive 108
No. 1 General Hospital, Wynberg 158
No. 1 South African Field Ambulance 158, 162, 164
No. 1 South African General Hospital 11, 158–164
No. 2 General Hospital, Maitland 158
No. 2 Stationary Hospital 159
no-man's-land 3, 79, 90, 98
Nose 104–105
number of soldiers 1, 12, 209
nursing staff 159–160, 162, 163–164

October Revolution 119
Old Front Line, The 26–27
Oriana 19
Ormiston, Major 104, 105, 128, 130
Otto, Private Johann 70
Ottoman Empire 1
Ounsworth, Gunner Leonard 89

Packer, Fusilier Victor 75, 88
payment 8
Pearse, Captain 128
Pearse, Lieutenant 101
Pearse's Trench 101, 104
Pearson, Second-Lieutenant 61
Peggs, Private Will 85
Pegler, Captain D.H. 97
Peyton, Major-General W.E. 14, 16

237

Phillips, Lieutenant Edward J. 60, 62, 65–67
Phillips, Lady Lionel 164
Phillips, Sid 31
photographs, aerial 22
Pickburn, Major 144–145
pigeons 112, 153
'pillbox' 120, 122
Plumer, General Herbert 120
pointlessness of battle 73–79
Porteous, Lieutenant 117
post office *see* Army Post Office; Union Post Office
post-traumatic stress disorder *see* shell-shock
Pozières, Battle of 96
Princip, Gavrilo 2
prisoners 27–28, 63–64
Prussian Guards 55
psychological trauma *see* shell-shock
Pybus, Captain H.L. 165

Queen Alexandra's Imperial Military Nursing Service 159, 163
Queen's Own Cameron Highlanders 20, 37, 38, 41, 44, 52
Quentin Redoubt 125–127
Q Wireless Section 156

railways and trades companies 11, 165–170
rain *see* weather conditions
rations 53–54, 57, 66–67, 80–81, 89
rats 88–89, 95
Rawbone, Private Ronald Talson Murray 49
Rawlinson, Sir Henry 73
Raws, Private John Alexander 77–78, 81–82, 91–92
Rebellion of 1914 5, 8
recruitment of soldiers 8–9, 168
Reid, Captain Oswald Austin 114, 176
reinforcements 8
religion 112
Richards, Private R. 83
Richmond Military Hospital 163
Ridley, Major 148
Ridley, Captain E.G. 148
Robinson, Captain W.McI. 165
Roffe, Captain T. 113
Rogers, Captain 128, 168

Romania 97
Roseby, Lieutenant Percy R. 40, 47, 56
Ross, Lieutenant F.M. 149
Ross, Lieutenant J.M. 117
Ross, Captain Thomas 101, 104
Royal Flying Corps 4
Royal Garrison Artillery 10, 139
Royal Marine Artillery 10
Royal Scots 20, 30, 37, 49–50, 136
Royal Welch Fusiliers 67
rum 26, 80, 81
runners 80–81, 112, 129
Russell, Captain 31
Russia 1–4, 119, 156
Ryan, Private William Walter Daniel 51

Sampson, Private Hallam Wills 59
sanitation 88
SANLC (South African Native Labour Contingent) 210–211
Sarrail, General Maurice 97
Sawyer, Lieutenant 168
Saxonia 13
Schlieffen Plan 2
Scotian 19
Seaforth Highlanders 20, 37
Second Army 120, 147
Senussi brotherhood 13–16
Serbia 1, 12
shell-shock 61, 81–82
Sherman, Private Henry 15
Sherwood-Kelly, Lieutenant-Colonel John 176
sickness *see* diseases
signal company *see* South African Signal Company (Royal Engineers)
Silberbauer, Harold Lewis 5–7, 18–19, 22–24, 33–35, 82, 86–87, 90, 112
Simmons, Staff Sergeant-Major 168
Simpson, Private J. 52, 82
sleep, lack of 63, 66–67, 70, 82, 84, 90, 92, 105, 116
smells 39, 68, 88, 126
Smith, Lieutenant G. 114, 132, 169
Smuts, General Jan 6, 10, 113, 124, 210
Snag and Tail 100–105
snipers, German 31, 62, 66, 81–84, 115
Société Française du Cap 11

INDEX

Solomon, Lance-Corporal Ernest 46, 48–49
Somerset, Lieutenant Francis 80
Sophie, Duchess of Hohenberg 2
South African Brigade Trench Mortar Battery 25, 126
South African Comforts Committee 162, 164
South African Forces in France, The 9
South African Heavy Artillery Brigade 10, 12, 139–148
South African Light Railway Operating Company 165–167
South African Light Trench Mortar Company 60, 136
South African Medical Corps 81, 85, 158–164
South African Military Hospital 11, 162–164
South African Military Nursing Service 159–160, 161
South African Native Labour Contingent (SANLC) 210–211
South African Native National Congress 209
South African Overseas Expeditionary Force 9–10, 158
South African Signal Company (Royal Engineers) 12, 149–157
South-West Africa *see* German South-West Africa campaign
Sprenger, Captain 102
Sprenger, Lieutenant 128
Spyker, Second-Lieutenant E. 122
Stanley, Arthur C. 84
Stapleton, Lieutenant 103
steam engines *see* transportation
Stein, Captain 128
Stertler, Company Quartermaster Sergeant 168
Stewart, Major J.G. 143
Stock, Colonel P.G. 10, 158, 163
Strannock, Lieutenant W.G. 14
stretcher-bearers 33, 44–45, 55–56, 60, 85, 115, 117
Style, Lieutenant S.W.E. 66
Suez Canal 12
Sweeney, Second-Lieutenant W.P. 122
Symmes, Major H.C. 115

Tamplin, Major E.H. 144, 145
tanks 97, 112, 133–134
Tanner, General William Ernest Collins 10, 14, 41–43, 46–47, 54, 56, 73, 114, 123, 136
Tara 13
Tayfield, Sergt 102
Taylor, Lieutenant 38
tea 53–54, 62, 80–81
  see also rations
tear gas 24, 30, 39, 84
  see also gas attacks
Terry, Lieutenant 128
Thackeray, Lieutenant-Colonel Edward Talbot 10, 15, 47, 56–57, 60, 62, 65–67, 71, 113–114, 121
Third Army 95, 107, 123, 126–127, 133
Thomas, Lieutenant Owen 61, 63
Thomas, Lieutenant W.F.G. 109
Thomson, Sergeant-Major James MacAulley 65
Thorne, William vii, 67–68
Thornton, Major 163
Tintoretto 19
tobacco 80
Tolkien, J.R.R. 76, 89
Tomlinson, Captain L.W. 17, 42
Tracey, Second-Lieutenant 168
training 11–12, 18, 20–21, 149–150
transportation 98, 165–170
trenches 20–21, 48–49, 75–92
trench fever 87, 89
trench foot 87–88, 159
Trethewy, Second-Lieutenant B.D. 122
Trevitt, Captain 7
Tripp, Lieutenant-Colonel W.H.L. 146, 147
Trônes Wood 26–36
Tudor, General Henry Hugh 125, 130, 132–133
Turkey 13

Union Defence Force 5–6, 10
Union Post Office 149
United States 1
Usmar, Lieutenant-Colonel G.H. 158
Uys, Lieutenant 136
Uys, Ian 73

Vaughan, Private F.B. 8
Verdun, attack on 20

239

Vickers machine gun 43
Victoria Crosses 50, 122, 171–177
Vimy Ridge, battle for 94–95, 109–111, 146
Vivian, Captain E.V. 114, 115, 122
Vocational Training School 164
Von Armin, Friedrich Bertram Sixt 120
Von Mackensen, August 12
Von Papen, Hauptmann 110

'walking wounded' 85
Wallace, Major-General A. 13–14
Walmer Castle 18
Walsh, Captain J.D. 14
Walsh, Lieutenants F.G. 94
Walvis Bay, blockhouse in 7
Ward, Captain C.P. 127–128, 135, 146
Warner, Pelham 'Plum' 18
Warwick, Lance-Corporal George W. 82
Warwickshire Regiment 35, 91
water, supply of 16
Waterlot Farm 38, 44, 47–48
weapons 2–3, 20, 35, 43, 50–51
weather conditions 82, 86–88, 94–95, 98, 107–108, 118–121, 123, 125–126
Weatherley, Captain N.S. 167
Webber, Major 118
Welsh, Captain 117

Welsh, Staff Sergeant Tom 44–45
Wepener, Eric 64
Wepener, Horace 64
Wepener, John 64
Wepener, Private Victor 64
West, Lieutenant-Colonel Richard Annesley 177
Western Front 2
whale oil 88
Whiting, Captain 103
Williams, Second-Lieutenant D.A. 122
Williamson, Rifleman Henry 86
Wilson, Lieutenant-General Sir Henry 93
women 8–9, 91
World War I, background to 1–4, 75
Worsley, Captain S.J. 74
Wynne, Lieutenant-Colonel 168

Young, Lieutenant-Colonel 132
Young, Lieutenant Alexander 104
Ypres
   First Battle of 86
   Second Battle of 140
   Third Battle of 120–124, 141, 145, 147, 166

Zulu language 09